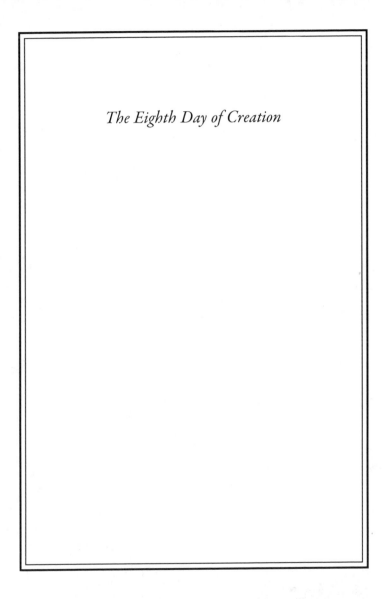

The Eighth Day of Creation

The Eighth Day of Creation

AN ANTHOLOGY
OF CHRISTIAN SCRIPTURE

*Selected, Arranged,
and Introduced by*

C. Clifton Black

WILLIAM B. EERDMANS PUBLISHING COMPANY
GRAND RAPIDS, MICHIGAN / CAMBRIDGE, U.K.

Published 2008 by

Wm. B. Eerdmans Publishing Co.

2140 Oak Industrial Drive N.E., Grand Rapids, Michigan 49505 /

P.O. Box 163, Cambridge CB3 9PU U.K.

Printed in the United States of America

14 13 12 11 10 09 08   7 6 5 4 3 2 1

Library of Congress Cataloging-in-Publication Data

The eighth day of creation: an anthology of Christian Scripture /

selected, arranged, and introduced by C. Clifton Black.

p.   cm.

Includes bibliographical references and index.

ISBN 978-0-8028-6272-3 (cloth: alk. paper)

1. Creation — Biblical teaching.   2. Bible — Quotations.

3. Bible — Criticism, interpretation, etc.

I. Black, C. Clifton (Carl Clifton), 1955-

BS680.C69E34   2008

220.5208 — dc22

2008019798

www.eerdmans.com

To Caroline
My beloved daughter,
in whom I am well pleased

Contents

Contents

The Seventh Day   303

Sabbath

Sanctuary

Death and Restoration

Rest and Peace

Foreword

Brilliant in its conceptualization and assembly, *The Eighth Day of Creation* presents us with the Bible as a work whole and complete in creative integrity, rather than merely narrative in thrust. The Bible opened to us here is not, as we are so often taught, a group of sixty-odd "books" melded into one book by virtue of a kind of shared canonization. No, the "wholeness" exposed here is that of a body whose feet may appear very different from its arms, and both of those very different from its head or trunk, yet all are of one consciousness and of one circulating vitality that feeds and informs all its parts.

This approach to sacred literature is a comfort to the soul, inviting us to do less puzzling over "meaning" and enjoy more engagement with the aesthetic and spirit of Holy Writ. As a result, Black's work is a boon to both the religious and the secular reader.

To call *The Eighth Day* a skillful anthology by an especially able anthologizer and then stop there, however, would be an unfortunate understatement, as well as a great disservice to what C. Clifton Black has accomplished. By his own admission, Black has shaped this volume for what he calls "the common reader" and what I would probably be inclined to call "Everyman" and "Everywoman." By whatever name, though, what he has shaped is as much for the inveterate appreciator of the Bible as it is for any inveterate student of it.

This presentation of Scripture is, first and foremost, for folk who, from time to time, find themselves seeking within the forest of sacred words for the sanctuary of a perfect glen or, at other times, for the vigor of steep ascent to a panoramic view or, at still other times, just for the nourishing waters of deep wisdom.

There is another gift here as well, though, that of the poet-organizer himself. This is not to say that there is poetry in these pages (save, of course, for that already found in the Bible). It is to say, instead, that Black's arrangements and his softly spoken commentary, over and over again, expose for us the elusive tensions and confluences that are the rhythms and pacing of the Bible across all its exegetical and literary divisions.

I am very sure that Dr. Black always knew what he was about as he was working. I am almost as certain that he relished every piece of the process of accomplishing it all. Otherwise, why choose for his volume, once it was done, the mystery-kissed name of *The Eighth Day?*

The teasing idea of an eighth day of creation runs like a leitmotif through centuries of Judeo-Christian thought. The day after God rested. . . . What must it have been like? Or what would it be? Or perhaps instead, what is it yet to be? No one knows the answer to that set of questions, of course. But, Black says, whatever the eighth day of our creation may be, we begin to enter it when we begin making associations within Scripture for ourselves, when we begin to intuit resonances there and discover sympathies, when we at last learn to eavesdrop on the murmuring, sweet conversation of Scripture when it is speaking to itself as well as to us.

May it be so for all of us.

PHYLLIS TICKLE

Acknowledgments

To all who encouraged an unconventional project, I am profoundly grateful:

Bill Eerdmans, fellow reveler in Rylands, who immediately recognized possibilities in something cognate and subsequently humored a finicky author;

Linda Bieze, a supportive and delightful editor;

Gayle Kerr, who considered the manuscript with a sensitive educator's eye;

Dennis Olson, who judiciously critiqued a lengthier, frantic version, while eliciting welcome nuance of my comments in Appendix 3;

Laura Sweat, a gifted biblical scholar and perceptive editor, who labored mightily in the taming of a tighter, leaner wombat;

Harriet Black, still indulging her absentminded husband with grace and good cheer;

Caroline Black, who blesses so many with joy, most especially her mother and father;

The Man on Edinburgh's Bench, to whom the reader shall be introduced presently and in whom I wonder if I entertained an angel unawares (Hebrews 13:2).

C.C.B.

Introduction

This book's framework derives from the Bible's opening words, which poetically picture one God in caring dominion over all things. This is a God who lives and creates, who orders and blesses all of creation. It may be appropriate, therefore, to say something about this volume's own origins and its structuring principle.

For a busman's holiday in Great Britain with my family, I packed a few books: a Greek New Testament (for reference at an academic conference), a prayer-book, and George Rylands's splendid anthology of Shakespearean verse, *The Ages of Man* (1939). Rylands assembled his compilation for one like myself: the common reader who loved and had long been caught up by the Bard's poetry, but who had much difficulty finding his way through the vast corpus of all those comedies, histories, tragedies, and sonnets impossible to lug around. And so, courtesy of George Rylands, my excursion to Shakespeare's homeland was punctuated by a series of glorious passages: Enobarbus's report of Cleopatra's majestic barge, King Harry's rousing of his tattered band of brothers on Saint Crispin's Day, Portia's temperate wisdom on mercy's unstrained quality, Falstaff's apprehension of the chimes at midnight.

Soon after arriving in Edinburgh, thick with jet lag, I arose before sunrise and, pipe and prayer-book in hand, sat myself down on a bench outside the bed-and-breakfast. While reading and meditating, I became aware of a well-dressed gentleman, about ten years older and of darker complexion than I, chain-smoking and pacing with conspicuous restlessness up and down the sidewalks around me. After a time, he crossed the street and seated himself next to me. We greeted each other, then sat in silence. Politely he excused himself, saying that he needed to walk some more. Minutes later he was again beside me, puffing away. "I noticed your prayer-book," he said. "I wonder if there might be in it something peaceful." Turning to random pages, I read him some Psalms. "Yes," he murmured between verses, "yes, that's very good." He then took his leave for more pacing. This ritual we repeated a couple more times before shaking hands and taking our separate paths. I never saw him again.

Later, however, I mused: If my companion had access to a wee book that offered him Scripture as Rylands had served me Shakespeare, I imagine he might have found in it such relief as he sought. Thus dawned *The Eighth Day of Creation*.

This too is a book for the common reader. It is intended to be as accessible to the shrewd jurist as to the canny carpenter. I have in mind the average person who knows little or nothing about the Bible, save some ancient phrases — swords into plowshares, the patience of Job, the valley of the shadow — that have become common property among all who converse in English. I imagine those, whether Christian or not, who would enjoy Scripture if they did not find it so intimidating in size, complexity, and the frightening things sometimes ascribed to it. For them I offer up a simple and, I hope, friendly introduction to Christian Scripture. By its nature this book is no one's *Bible* — least of all mine — though it is thoroughly *biblical* in content. For that reason I have kept prefatory comments in each chapter to a bare minimum. Following each numbered excerpt is a chapter-and-verse reference to the biblical book at its source. I hope many will make serendipitous discoveries: "So *that's* where that saying comes from."

Anthologies, whether of poetry or prose, must number in the hundreds of thousands. Yet anthologies of biblical literature — which as a corpus is every bit as disparate, exquisite, and resonant in our culture — are comparatively few. Though rarely regarded as such, Handel's *Messiah* (1741) may be the most influential of scriptural anthologies, whose general reach probably recedes with each passing year. The other most obvious exceptions are prayer-books like the one I packed for Britain: compendia authorized by some denominations, which abridge and embed portions of Scripture within the liturgical life of those Christians who use them in both corporate worship and private devotion. But what of those Christians who have traditionally been without access to prayer-books? And what of the millions of non-Christians whose art and music and literature are saturated with biblical characters and coinages, yet for whom the Christian Bible remains for the most part a closed book and who lack even the simplest coordinates for orientation and navigation? For them, and for others, this anthology may fill a gap.

Biblical anthologies are, to be sure, nothing new. They are as old as Judaism and Christianity themselves. We now know of written *florilegia,* bouquets of Hebrew Scripture, among the Dead Sea Scrolls. Small compilations of Gospels or letters by the Apostle Paul very likely circulated among fledgling Christians, congregated throughout the Mediterranean world, several centuries before anything like a recognizable New Testament took shape. Because books in antiquity were expensive, for fifteen centuries most Christians carried scriptural anthologies in their heads, formed by constant recitation and rehearsal among the church at worship. By 1455 Gutenberg's printing press made compilations — whole Bibles, digests, and prayer-books — more affordable and thus more widespread. A famous, if not infamous, abridged anthology of the Gospels (1804) was prepared by Thomas Jefferson, who pulled together many of Jesus' jeweled precepts after — to his Enlightenment way of thinking — having salvaged and washed them clean from the embarrassing dung-heap of miracle stories and accounts of Christ's resurrection.

It is often and accurately observed that the Bible is not so much a book as a collection of books. The contents span about ten centuries and give voice to as many different points of view as the authors — most of them anonymous — represented. It is as ludicrous to apologize for all these internal tensions and contradictions as for those things in Scripture that ruffle our contemporary feathers. (The reader will find here no bowdlerized, Jeffersonian Bible.) Throughout the present collection I have deliberately, at times playfully, set representative and contrastive points of view — all equally biblical — alongside one another, cheek by jowl. From the church's infancy right up to the present day, it has been an established maxim that "Scripture interprets Scripture." That is so because Scripture is in constant, internal dialogue with Scripture. The truth about God and about ourselves, to which the whole of the Bible points, is too vast and multidimensional to be puréed, dumbed down, or reduced to a single precept or doctrine. For that reason a plumber stands on the same bumpy plain as a Pope. Both discover in Scripture thoughts that alternately complement and clash with one another; both leave that encounter alternately confused and refreshed, exposed and illuminated. Reconciliation of the Bible's disparities is possible, in the view of most Christians, only by the same Holy Spirit that originally motivated Scripture's diverse authors to speak or take pen in hand. That Spirit, it is further believed, continues to be mediated by God through that body of believers known as the church. The invitation extended by this anthology to study the Bible more intensively, within that corporate and worshiping context, lies before the reader to accept or to decline. "The wind bloweth where it listeth" (John 3:8).

On the other hand — and this must be firmly emphasized — the present volume makes no pretense of offering the reader an "unmediated" introduction to Christian Scripture. The selection and arrangement of materials is entirely my own: personal, though informed, I hope, and not brazenly eccentric. Adapting the Rylands strategy, a Shakespearean anthology constructed on the framework of Jaques's dyspeptic survey of man's seven ages (*As You Like It* 2.7), I have adopted as my loose structuring principle the seven days of creation narrated in the opening chapter of Genesis. This, mind you, is nothing more than a slender clothesline — occasionally quite tenuous — on which to hang an array of texts. It should be taken only as a cohesive principle by which one anthologist has judged it well to proceed. Other compilers would approach the task very differently, more imaginatively, and with greater success than I. In any event this book's arrangement is such that it need not be read from beginning to end. I doubt many would do so. One may pick it up, thumb to a pleasant or arresting spot, read a bit, then lay it aside without detriment or harm. Nor does this collection unfold in flatness of foot from the Old Testament to the New, or from the earliest books to the latest. No attempt has been made to impose a conventional or systematic structure upon the Bible, of the sort that is the professional theologian's bread and butter: from God and creation, through humanity's fall and redemption, to the impress of Christ and Spirit upon moral conduct and the unveiling of last things. Such topics, important to be sure, would tell the common reader much more about penguins than the zoo's casual visitor needs to know. Nor is this a sectarian compilation, with either a consciously conservative or liberal axe to grind. Organizing things with so heavy a hand would betray the constituent texts themselves, most of which gather up many issues at once and resist occupying the narrowly reasoned cubbyholes into which we might be tempted to force them. Here, instead, I strive for a sensible assemblage of different passages, both familiar and strange, that take up recurring ideas and frame them in ways both argumentatively and complementarily: a condensed arrangement of variations on common themes or, to shift the metaphor, a moderated conversation among the Bible's different voices. My hope is that the reader may leave these excursions into Scripture partially satisfied and mildly irritated, with an appetite whetted for deeper reflection and continued study. And I trust the common reader's intuitive sympathy with these texts to draw her own conclusions, making intelligent associations that would never have occurred to me. When such things happen, we enter the eighth day of creation, which extends from the present until our life's end and — I believe — beyond.

Throughout I have adopted the King James Version, some of whose archaisms I have silently emended or asterisked (*) for explanation in the Glossary. Use of the King James will surely raise eyebrows among my colleagues in the scholarly guild, who know full well that discoveries of ancient manuscripts since the seventeenth century have rendered earlier translations obsolete. The modern reader put off by Jacobean English will discover other reasons to think of me less than charitably. To that decision, nevertheless, I hold fast. For all its deficiencies and the language's subsequent evolution, the English version of 1611 is a monument in the history of that tongue. The prose and poetry of the King James Version have decidedly influenced all English translations ever since, even as they have molded all subsequent English literature. For many in the present day, Christians and non-Christians alike, the King James remains *the* English version of the Bible: not because of any special inspiration at its point of origin, but owing to the grandeur of its cadence, which catches something of the majesty to which Scripture itself refers. For that we are indebted to William Tyndale (d. 1536), a scholar of singular ability and remarkable courage whose Englishing of the finest Greek and Hebrew manuscripts available to him created the template to which all English Bibles after him have adhered. Most of his labor was literally criminal under the statutes of Henry VIII's England. Tyndale's translation was accomplished under extreme duress, smuggled to friends while in hiding and on the run, with a God-intoxicated determination that eventually landed him on the stake. It is one of history's supreme ironies that, within years of his execution by royal decree, the subjects of another English sovereign drew upon Tyndale's incomparable version in perfecting their own. Those scholars in 1611 frankly acknowledged their debt: "not to make a new translation, but to make a good one better, or out of many good ones, one principal good one." Following Tyndale's lead, James I's translators accomplished their purpose so well that, as Lord Macaulay observed, "If everything else in our language should perish, [the King James Bible] would alone suffice to show the whole extent of its beauty and power" (*On John Dryden,* 1828). As with Shakespeare, so too with this version: Though its language at times puzzles, it retains the power to lift one to heights where obscurity yields to radiance. Just as Shakespeare still walks beside each "poor player,/That struts and frets his hour upon the stage,/And then is heard no more" (*Macbeth* 5.5), so too does Tyndale whisper into the ear of every Christian who continues to pray, "Our Father, which art in Heaven, Hallowed be thy name" (Matthew 6:9).

There is another reason for returning to Old King James. Because the Christian Bible is so commonplace, available in hundreds of thousands of versions from stiff to slangy, it is easy for the common reader to forget that its constituent testaments were written in ancient tongues that no one any longer speaks: classical Hebrew and *koinē* ("working-clothes") Greek. Every translation entails exegetical choices, masking many problems in ancient texts that are often obscure. When twenty-first-century readers take up a seventeenth-century translation, they encounter something simultaneously familiar and strange. That interpretive tension of intimacy and distance is salubriously humbling. Like Scripture itself, it invites while it teases.

What does the reader lose in an anthology like this? Quite a lot. Simply regarded, the Bible tells a single story: a narrative of God's creation, intervention, and reclamation of this world, and of the tensions generated and resolved amidst a tumult of divine-human interactions. Plucking extracts from that travelogue ruptures the plotline from Genesis to Revelation. Characters whose backgrounds receive at least minimal sketching — Abraham, Moses, Ruth and Boaz, David, Mary, Jesus, Peter, and Paul — are bleached of much of their color, as well as their proper chronology and relationships among one another. For that reason, I have appended, at the back of the book, a timeline that correlates these and other figures, and the books in which they appear. Still, some knowledgeable readers may so keenly feel these rips in Scripture's narrative fabric that the present volume becomes for them nearly unbearable to read. With them I sympathize. To them I can only apologize by acknowledging these deficits and suggesting that this book may not have been prepared for you.

All is not loss, however. An anthology like this offers some compensation. First, at least a *sense* of Scripture's comprehensiveness is conveyed, if not the thing itself. Second, the Bible's recurring themes and variations come more sharply into focus. (Christian worshipers regularly enjoy this benefit through prayers and preaching that follow a common lectionary, which is yet another sort of anthology.) Third — and this for Rylands was a principal justification for his *Ages of Man* — is an opportunity afforded the reader to concentrate one's mind on two primary elements: the thing said and the way in which it is said. That holds also, not only for the Bible's most famous passages, but as well for its less familiar portions.

More so than any other collection of writings I know — yes, even Shakespeare — the Bible lays bare the mysterious fullness of life: all of its love and anger, arrogance and pathos, despondency and passion, disquiet and yearnings. Christian Scripture spreads a lifelong banquet, of which this volume offers but a tray of savory canapés. Extended to the common reader — the homemaker for whom sleep comes fitfully if at all, the patient lying on a hospital bed, the executive who tosses a book into a satchel, the churchgoer wanting a different approach to Bible study, the soldier strained by tedium or fear, the student with eyes glazed before a computer screen — this anthology intends to offer delight. That, as much perhaps as anything else, is Christian Scripture's chief preoccupation: neither terror nor guilt nor secret knowledge, but endless joy — the joy of a fully human life, fully lived before the God who beyond all measure enjoys us and all of creation. If this book opens unto its readers a deeply human and holy delight, and by so doing invites one seated beside me to rest more at peace in this tormented world, it shall have achieved its modest purpose.

C. CLIFTON BLACK
19 JUNE 2007

The Eighth Day of Creation

Preface

In the beginning God created the heaven and the earth.
And the earth was without form, and void; and darkness was upon the face of the deep. And the Spirit of God moved upon the face of the waters.

And God said, "Let there be light": and there was light.
And God saw the light, that it was good: and God divided the light from the darkness.
And God called the light Day, and the darkness he called Night.
And the evening and the morning were the first day.

And God said, "Let there be a firmament in the midst of the waters, and let it divide the waters from the waters."
And God made the firmament, and divided the waters which were under the firmament from the waters which were above the firmament: and it was so.
And God called the firmament Heaven.
And the evening and the morning were the second day.

And God said, "Let the waters under the heaven be gathered together unto one place, and let the dry land appear": and it was so.

And God called the dry land Earth; and the gathering together of the waters called he Seas: and God saw that it was good.

And God said, "Let the earth bring forth grass, the herb yielding seed, and the fruit tree yielding fruit after his kind, whose seed is in itself, upon the earth": and it was so.

And the earth brought forth grass, and herb yielding seed after his kind, and the tree yielding fruit, whose seed was in itself, after his kind: and God saw that it was good.

And the evening and the morning were the third day.

And God said, "Let there be lights in the firmament of the heaven to divide the day from the night; and let them be for signs, and for seasons, and for days, and years:

And let them be for lights in the firmament of the heaven to give light upon the earth": and it was so.

And God made two great lights; the greater light to rule the day, and the lesser light to rule the night: he made the stars also.

And God set them in the firmament of the heaven to give light upon the earth,

And to rule over the day and over the night, and to divide the light from the darkness: And God saw that it was good.

And the evening and the morning were the fourth day.

And God said, "Let the waters bring forth abundantly the moving creature that hath life, and fowl that may fly above the earth in the open firmament of heaven."

And God created great whales, and every living creature that moveth, which the waters brought forth abundantly, after their kind, and every winged fowl after his kind: and God saw that it was good.

And God blessed them, saying, "Be fruitful, and multiply, and fill the waters in the seas, and let fowl multiply in the earth."
And the evening and the morning were the fifth day.

And God said, "Let the earth bring forth the living creature after his kind, cattle, and creeping thing, and beast of the earth after his kind": and it was so.
And God made the beast of the earth after his kind, and cattle after their kind, and every thing that creepeth upon the earth after his kind: and God saw that it was good.
And God said, "Let us make man in our image, after our likeness: and let them have dominion over the fish of the sea, and over the fowl of the air, and over the cattle, and over all the earth, and over every creeping thing that creepeth upon the earth."
So God created man in his own image, in the image of God created he him; male and female created he them.
And God blessed them, and God said unto them, "Be fruitful, and multiply, and replenish the earth, and subdue it: and have dominion over the fish of the sea, and over the fowl of the air, and over every living thing that moveth upon the earth."
And God said, "Behold, I have given you every herb bearing seed, which is upon the face of all the earth, and every tree, in the which is the fruit of a tree yielding seed; to you it shall be for meat.*
And to every beast of the earth, and to every fowl of the air, and to every thing that creepeth upon the earth, wherein there is life, I have given every green herb for meat": and it was so.
And God saw every thing that he had made, and, behold, it was very good.
And the evening and the morning were the sixth day.

Thus the heavens and the earth were finished, and all the host of
   them.
And on the seventh day God ended his work which he had made; and
   he rested on the seventh day from all his work which he had made.
And God blessed the seventh day, and sanctified it: because that in it
   he had rested from all his work which God created and made.

Genesis 1:1–2:3

Prelude

The Majesty and Mystery of God

The Holy Spirit

Formlessness and Void

Shadows

Plumbing Wisdom's Depths

IN THE BEGINNING: GOD. This is a fundamental claim of Christian Scripture. It acquires densities of color and texture in its confessional development. Genesis speaks of God's Spirit, hovering over turbulent waters. Centuries before Christ, some in Israel conceived of that Spirit as a companionate expression of the one God, an intermediary agent of creation. Personified as Wisdom or as Word, this figure provided creation coherence with God and within itself. Early Christians regarded Christ Jesus himself as God's Spirit incarnate, the Word infleshed. Israel and the church believed that, at creation, the Creator established their identities and final destination in God's eternal purposes.

This is a formidable cluster of beliefs, whose implications ancient Jews and Christians grappled with. God is at once close to his creatures yet transcendently beyond them. Human beings struggled to come to terms with that confession. Some reported glimpses of the Almighty. Others sought to fathom the depths of God's appropriable wisdom. Others, keenly aware of their frailty and mortality, despaired of such pursuits. Still others succumbed to idolatry, futilely attempting to shrink God's majesty to manageable size. All were confounded by the irreducible mystery of a God who would not leave them alone, for which they were alternately exasperated and grateful. For those who believe, so it remains.

1   In the beginning God created the heaven and the earth. And the earth was without form, and void; and darkness was upon the face of the deep. And the Spirit of God moved upon the face of the waters.

Genesis 1:1-2

2   In the beginning was the Word, and the Word was with God, and the Word was God. The same was in the beginning with God. All things were made by him; and without him was not any thing made that was made.

John 1:1-3

3   Doth not wisdom cry?
        And understanding put forth her voice? . . .
    The LORD possessed me in the beginning of his way,
        Before his works of old.
    I was set up from everlasting,
        From the beginning, or ever the earth was.
    When there were no depths, I was brought forth;
        When there were no fountains abounding with water.
    Before the mountains were settled,
        Before the hills was I brought forth:
    While as yet he had not made the earth, nor the fields,
        Nor the highest part of the dust of the world.
    When he prepared the heavens, I was there:
        When he set a compass upon the face of the depth:
    When he established the clouds above:

When he strengthened the fountains of the deep:
When he gave to the sea his decree,
    That the waters should not pass his commandment:
When he appointed the foundations of the earth:
    Then I was by him, as one brought up with him:
And I was daily his delight, rejoicing always before him;
    Rejoicing in the habitable part of his earth;
    And my delights were with the sons of men.

Proverbs 8:1, 22-31

4   God, who at sundry times and in divers manners spake in time past unto
     the fathers by the prophets, hath in these last days spoken unto us by his
     Son, whom he hath appointed heir of all things, by whom also he made
     the worlds; who being the brightness of his glory, and the express image
     of his person, and upholding all things by the word of his power, when he
     had by himself purged our sins, sat down on the right hand of the Maj-
     esty on high; being made so much better than the angels, as he hath by in-
     heritance obtained a more excellent name than they.

Hebrews 1:1-4

5   The LORD by wisdom hath founded the earth; by understanding
            hath he established the heavens.
     By his knowledge the depths are broken up, and the clouds
            drop down the dew.

Proverbs 3:19-20

6 For ye know the grace of our Lord Jesus Christ, that, though he was rich, yet for your sakes he became poor, that ye through his poverty might be rich.

2 Corinthians 8:9

7 Look unto me, and be ye saved,
    All the ends of the earth:
    For I am God, and there is none else.
I have sworn by myself,
    The word is gone out of my mouth in righteousness,
    And shall not return,
    That unto me every knee shall bow, every tongue shall swear.

Isaiah 45:22-23

8 Let this mind be in you, which was also in Christ Jesus:
Who, being in the form of God,
    Thought it not robbery to be equal with God:
But made himself of no reputation,
    And took upon him the form of a servant,
    And was made in the likeness of men:
And being found in fashion as a man, he humbled himself,
    And became obedient unto death, even the death of the cross.
Wherefore God also hath highly exalted him,
    And given him a name which is above every name:
That at the name of Jesus every knee should bow,
    Of things in heaven, and things in earth, and things

under the earth;
And that every tongue should confess
    That Jesus Christ is Lord, to the glory of God the Father.

Philippians 2:5-11

9 Ye are my witnesses, saith the LORD,
    And my servant whom I have chosen:
That ye may know and believe me,
    And understand that I am he:
Before me there was no God formed,
    Neither shall there be after me.
I, even I, am the LORD;
    And beside me there is no saviour.
I have declared, and have saved, and I have shewed,
    When there was no strange god among you:
    Therefore ye are my witnesses, saith the LORD, that I am God.
Yea, before the day was I am he;
    And there is none that can deliver out of my hand:
    I will work, and who shall let it?

Isaiah 43:10-13

10 And without controversy great is the mystery of godliness:
    God was manifest in the flesh,
    Justified in the Spirit,
    Seen of angels,
    Preached unto the Gentiles,

Believed on in the world,
Received up into glory.

1 Timothy 3:16

11   Give unto the LORD, O ye mighty,
      Give unto the LORD glory and strength.
   Give unto the LORD the glory due unto his name;
      Worship the LORD in the beauty of holiness.
   The voice of the LORD is upon the waters:
      The God of glory thundereth:
      The LORD is upon many waters.
   The voice of the LORD is powerful;
      The voice of the LORD is full of majesty.
   The voice of the LORD breaketh the cedars;
      Yea, the LORD breaketh the cedars of Lebanon.
   He maketh them also to skip like a calf;
      Lebanon and Sirion like a young unicorn.
   The voice of the LORD divideth the flames of fire.
   The voice of the LORD shaketh the wilderness;
      The LORD shaketh the wilderness of Kadesh.
   The voice of the LORD maketh the hinds to calve,
      And discovereth the forests:
      And in his temple doth every one speak of his glory.
   The LORD sitteth upon the flood;
      Yea, the LORD sitteth King for ever.
   The LORD will give strength unto his people;
      The LORD will bless his people with peace.

Psalm 29:1-11

12 Strengthened with all might, according to his glorious power, unto all patience and longsuffering with joyfulness; giving thanks unto the Father, which hath made us meet* to be partakers of the inheritance of the saints in light: Who hath delivered us from the power of darkness, and hath translated us into the kingdom of his dear Son: In whom we have redemption through his blood, even the forgiveness of sins:

> Who is the image of the invisible God,
>> The firstborn of every creature:
>
> For by him were all things created,
>> That are in heaven, and that are in earth,
>> Visible and invisible,
>> Whether they be thrones, or dominions,
>> Or principalities, or powers:
>
> All things were created by him, and for him:
> And he is before all things,
>> And by him all things consist.
>
> And he is the head of the body, the church:
>> Who is the beginning, the firstborn from the dead;
>> That in all things he might have the preeminence.
>
> For it pleased the Father that in him should all fulness dwell;
> And, having made peace through the blood of his cross,
>> By him to reconcile all things unto himself;
>> By him, I say, whether they be things in earth, or things
>> in heaven.

Colossians 1:11-20

13 Our help is in the name of the LORD, who made heaven and earth.

Psalm 124:8

14 Blessed be the God and Father of our Lord Jesus Christ, who hath blessed us with all spiritual blessings in heavenly places in Christ: According as he hath chosen us in him before the foundation of the world, that we should be holy and without blame before him in love: Having predestinated us unto the adoption of children by Jesus Christ to himself, according to the good pleasure of his will, to the praise of the glory of his grace, wherein he hath made us accepted in the beloved. In whom we have redemption through his blood, the forgiveness of sins, according to the riches of his grace; wherein he hath abounded toward us in all wisdom and prudence; having made known unto us the mystery of his will, according to his good pleasure which he hath purposed in himself: That in the dispensation of the fulness of times he might gather together in one all things in Christ, both which are in heaven, and which are on earth.

Ephesians 1:3-10

15 And this is his commandment, That we should believe on the name of his Son Jesus Christ, and love one another, as he gave us commandment. And he that keepeth his commandments dwelleth in him, and he in him. And hereby we know that he abideth in us, by the Spirit which he hath given us. Beloved, believe not every spirit, but try* the spirits whether they are of God: because many false prophets are gone out into the world. Hereby know ye the Spirit of God: Every spirit that confesseth that Jesus Christ is come in the flesh is of God: And every spirit that confesseth not that Jesus Christ is come in the flesh is not of God: and this is that spirit of antichrist, whereof ye have heard that it should come; and even now already is it in the world. Ye are of God, little children, and have overcome them: because greater is he that is in you, than he that is in the world. They are of the world: therefore speak they of the world, and the world heareth them. We are of God: He that knoweth God heareth us; he that is not of God heareth not us. Hereby know we the spirit of truth, and the spirit of error.

1 John 3:23–4:6

16 And I looked, and, behold, a whirlwind came out of the north, a great cloud, and a fire infolding itself, and a brightness was about it, and out of the midst thereof as the colour of amber, out of the midst of the fire. Also out of the midst thereof came the likeness of four living creatures. . . . [Their] appearance was like burning coals of fire, and like the appearance of lamps: it went up and down among the living creatures; and the fire was bright, and out of the fire went forth lightning.

Now as I beheld the living creatures, behold one wheel upon the earth by the living creatures, with his four faces. The appearance of the wheels and their work was like unto the colour of a beryl: and they four had one likeness: and their appearance and their work was as it were a wheel in the middle of a wheel. . . . And when the living creatures went, the wheels went by them: and when the living creatures were lifted up from the earth, the wheels were lifted up. Whithersoever the spirit was to go, they went, thither was their spirit to go; and the wheels were lifted up over against them: for the spirit of the living creature was in the wheels. . . . And when they went, I heard the noise of their wings, like the noise of great waters, as the voice of the Almighty, the voice of speech, as the noise of an host. . . .

This was the appearance of the likeness of the glory of the LORD. And when I saw it, I fell upon my face, and I heard a voice of one that spake. And he said unto me, "Son of man, stand upon thy feet, and I will speak unto thee."

Ezekiel 1:4-5a, 13-16, 19-20, 24a, 28b-2:1

17   And we know that the Son of God is come, and hath given us an understanding, that we may know him that is true, and we are in him that is true, even in his Son Jesus Christ. This is the true God, and eternal life. Little children, keep yourselves from idols. Amen.

1 John 5:20-21

18   And when the people saw that Moses delayed to come down out of the mount, the people gathered themselves together unto Aaron, and said unto him, "Up, make us gods, which shall go before us; for as for this Moses, the man that brought us up out of the land of Egypt, we wot* not what is become of him." And Aaron said unto them, "Break off the golden earrings, which are in the ears of your wives, of your sons, and of your daughters, and bring them unto me." And all the people brake off the golden earrings which were in their ears, and brought them unto Aaron. And he received them at their hand, and fashioned it with a graving tool, after he had made it a molten calf: and they said, "These be thy gods, O Israel, which brought thee up out of the land of Egypt." And when Aaron saw it, he built an altar before it; and Aaron made proclama-

tion, and said, "Tomorrow is a feast to the LORD. And they rose up early on the morrow, and offered burnt offerings, and brought peace offerings; and the people sat down to eat and to drink, and rose up to play.

Exodus 32:1-6

19   Moreover, brethren, I would not that ye should be ignorant, how that all our fathers were under the cloud, and all passed through the sea; And were all baptized unto Moses in the cloud and in the sea; And did all eat the same spiritual meat*; And did all drink the same spiritual drink: for they drank of that spiritual Rock that followed them: and that Rock was Christ. But with many of them God was not well pleased: for they were overthrown in the wilderness. Now these things were our examples, to the intent we should not lust after evil things, as they also lusted. Neither be ye idolaters, as were some of them; as it is written, "The people sat down to eat and drink, and rose up to play." Neither let us commit fornication, as some of them committed, and fell in one day three and twenty thousand. Neither let us tempt Christ, as some of them also tempted, and were destroyed of serpents. Neither murmur ye, as some of them also murmured, and were destroyed of the destroyer. Now all these things happened unto them for ensamples*: and they are written for our admonition, upon whom the ends of the world are come. Wherefore let him that thinketh he standeth take heed lest he fall. There hath no temptation taken you but such as is common to man: but God is faithful, who will not suffer* you to be tempted above that ye are able; but will with the temptation also make a way to escape, that ye may be able to bear it.

1 Corinthians 10:1-13

20 And the LORD said unto Moses, "Go, get thee down; for thy people, which thou broughtest out of the land of Egypt, have corrupted themselves: They have turned aside quickly out of the way which I commanded them: they have made them a molten calf, and have worshipped it, and have sacrificed thereunto, and said, 'These be thy gods, O Israel, which have brought thee up out of the land of Egypt.'" And the LORD said unto Moses, "I have seen this people, and, behold, it is a stiffnecked people: Now therefore let me alone, that my wrath may wax hot against them, and that I may consume them: and I will make of thee a great nation."

Exodus 32:7-10

21 For the wrath of God is revealed from heaven against all ungodliness and unrighteousness of men, who hold the truth in unrighteousness; because that which may be known of God is manifest in them; for God hath shewed it unto them. For the invisible things of him from the creation of the world are clearly seen, being understood by the things that are made, even his eternal power and Godhead; so that they are without excuse: Because that, when they knew God, they glorified him not as God, neither were thankful; but became vain in their imaginations, and their foolish heart was darkened. Professing themselves to be wise, they became fools, and changed the glory of the uncorruptible God into an image made like to corruptible man, and to birds, and fourfooted beasts, and creeping things. Wherefore God also gave them up to uncleanness through the lusts of their own hearts, to dishonour their own bodies between themselves: Who changed the truth of God into a lie, and worshipped and served the creature more than the Creator, who is blessed for ever. Amen. For this cause God gave them up unto vile affections: for even their women did change the natural use into that which is against nature: And likewise also the men, leaving the natural use of the woman, burned in their lust one toward another; men with men working that which is unseemly, and receiving in themselves that recompence of their error which was meet.* And even as they did not like to retain God in their knowledge, God gave them over to a reprobate mind, to do those things which are not convenient*; Being filled with all unrighteousness, fornication, wickedness, covetousness, maliciousness; full of envy, murder, debate, deceit, malignity; whisperers, backbiters, haters of God, despiteful, proud, boasters, inventors of evil things, disobedient to parents, without understanding, covenantbreakers, without natural affection, implacable, unmerciful: Who knowing the judgment of God, that they which commit such things are worthy of death, not only do the same, but have pleasure in them that do them.

Romans 1:18-32

22 And Moses besought the LORD his God, and said, "LORD, why doth thy wrath wax hot against thy people, which thou hast brought forth out of the land of Egypt with great power, and with a mighty hand? Wherefore* should the Egyptians speak, and say, 'For mischief did he bring them out, to slay them in the mountains, and to consume them from the face of the earth?' Turn from thy fierce wrath, and repent of this evil against thy people. Remember Abraham, Isaac, and Israel, thy servants, to whom thou swarest by thine own self, and saidst unto them, 'I will multiply your seed as the stars of heaven, and all this land that I have spoken of will I give unto your seed, and they shall inherit it for ever.'" And the LORD repented of the evil which he thought to do unto his people.

Exodus 32:11-14

23   Now concerning spiritual gifts, brethren, I would not have you ignorant.
Ye know that ye were Gentiles, carried away unto these dumb idols, even
as ye were led. Wherefore I give you to understand, that no man speaking
by the Spirit of God calleth Jesus accursed: and that no man can say that
Jesus is the Lord, but by the Holy Ghost.

1 Corinthians 12:1-3

24   Not unto us, O LORD, not unto us,
     But unto thy name give glory,
     For thy mercy, and for thy truth's sake.
Wherefore* should the heathen say,
     Where is now their God?
But our God is in the heavens;
     He hath done whatsoever he hath pleased.
Their idols are silver and gold,
     The work of men's hands.
They have mouths, but they speak not:
     Eyes have they, but they see not:
They have ears, but they hear not:
     Noses have they, but they smell not:
They have hands, but they handle not:
     Feet have they, but they walk not:
     Neither speak they through their throat.
They that make them are like unto them;
     So is every one that trusteth in them.
O Israel, trust thou in the LORD:
     He is their help and their shield.
O house of Aaron, trust in the LORD:

He is their help and their shield.
Ye that fear the LORD, trust in the LORD:
   He is their help and their shield.

Psalm 115:1-11

25   And Moses turned, and went down from the mount, and the two tables of the testimony were in his hand: the tables were written on both their sides; on the one side and on the other were they written. And the tables were the work of God, and the writing was the writing of God, graven upon the tables. And when Joshua heard the noise of the people as they shouted, he said unto Moses, "There is a noise of war in the camp." And he said, "It is not the voice of them that shout for mastery, neither is it the voice of them that cry for being overcome: but the noise of them that sing do I hear." And it came to pass, as soon as he came nigh unto the camp, that he saw the calf, and the dancing: and Moses' anger waxed hot, and he cast the tables out of his hands, and brake them beneath the mount. And he took the calf which they had made, and burnt it in the fire, and ground it to powder, and strewed it upon the water, and made the children of Israel drink of it.

Exodus 32:15-20

26   And the Lord said, "Whereunto then shall I liken the men of this generation? and to what are they like? They are like unto children sitting in the marketplace, and calling one to another, and saying,

   'We have piped unto you, and ye have not danced;
     We have mourned to you, and ye have not wept.'

For John the Baptist came neither eating bread nor drinking wine; and ye say, 'He hath a devil.' The Son of man is come eating and drinking; and ye say, 'Behold a gluttonous man, and a winebibber, a friend of publicans and sinners!' But wisdom is justified of all her children."

Luke 7:31-35

27 And Moses said unto Aaron, "What did this people unto thee, that thou hast brought so great a sin upon them?" And Aaron said, "Let not the anger of my lord wax hot: thou knowest the people, that they are set on mischief. For they said unto me, 'Make us gods, which shall go before us: for as for this Moses, the man that brought us up out of the land of Egypt, we wot* not what is become of him.' And I said unto them, 'Whosoever hath any gold, let them break it off.' So they gave it me: then I cast it into the fire, and there came out this calf."

Exodus 32:21-24

28 For I would not, brethren, that ye should be ignorant of this mystery, lest ye should be wise in your own conceits; that blindness in part is happened to Israel, until the fulness of the Gentiles be come in. And so all Israel shall be saved: as it is written,

"There shall come out of Sion* the Deliverer,
    And shall turn away ungodliness from Jacob":
"For this is my covenant unto them,
    When I shall take away their sins."

Romans 11:25-27

29   For my people is foolish,
>   they have not known me;
> They are sottish* children,
>   And they have none understanding:
> They are wise to do evil,
>   But to do good they have no knowledge.
> I beheld the earth, and, lo, it was without form, and void;
>   And the heavens, and they had no light.
> I beheld the mountains, and, lo, they trembled,
>   And all the hills moved lightly.
> I beheld, and, lo, there was no man, and all the birds of the heavens
>   were fled.
> I beheld, and, lo, the fruitful place was a wilderness,
>   And all the cities thereof were broken down
>   At the presence of the LORD, and by his fierce anger.
> For thus hath the LORD said, "The whole land shall be desolate;
>   yet will I not make a full end.
> For this shall the earth mourn,
>   And the heavens above be black:
> Because I have spoken it, I have purposed it,
>   And will not repent, neither will I turn back from it."

Jeremiah 4:22-28

30   O the depth of the riches both of the wisdom and knowledge of God!
> How unsearchable are his judgments, and his ways past finding out!
>
>   "For who hath known the mind of the Lord?
>   Or who hath been his counsellor?

24

> Or who hath first given to him, and it shall be recompensed
>> unto him again?"

For of him, and through him, and to him, are all things: to whom be
glory for ever. Amen.

Romans 11:33-36

31 And [the LORD] said, "Go, and tell this people,
   'Hear ye indeed, but understand not;
      And see ye indeed, but perceive not.'
   Make the heart of this people fat,
      And make their ears heavy,
      And shut their eyes;
   Lest they see with their eyes,
      And hear with their ears,
   And understand with their heart,
      And convert, and be healed."
Then said I, "Lord, how long?" And he answered,
   "Until the cities be wasted*
      Without inhabitant,
   And the houses without man,
      And the land be utterly desolate,
   And the LORD have removed men far away,
      And there be a great forsaking
      In the midst of the land.
   But yet in it shall be a tenth, and it shall return,
      And shall be eaten:
   As a teil* tree, and as an oak,

Whose substance is in them, when they cast their leaves:
So the holy seed shall be the substance thereof."

Isaiah 6:9-13

32 And when [Jesus] was alone, they that were about him with the twelve
asked of him the parable. And he said unto them, "Unto you it is given to
know the mystery of the kingdom of God: but unto them that are without, all these things are done in parables: That seeing they may see, and
not perceive; and hearing they may hear, and not understand; lest at any
time they should be converted, and their sins should be forgiven them."

Mark 4:10-12

33 Behold, the LORD maketh the earth empty, and maketh it waste,
    And turneth it upside down, and scattereth abroad the
        inhabitants thereof.

Isaiah 24:1

34 Finally, my brethren, be strong in the Lord, and in the power of his
might. Put on the whole armour of God, that ye may be able to stand
against the wiles of the devil. For we wrestle not against flesh and blood,
but against principalities, against powers, against the rulers of the darkness of this world, against spiritual wickedness in high places. Wherefore
take unto you the whole armour of God, that ye may be able to withstand
in the evil day, and having done all, to stand. Stand therefore, having your

loins girt about with truth, and having on the breastplate of righteousness; and your feet shod with the preparation of the gospel of peace. Above all, taking the shield of faith, wherewith ye shall be able to quench all the fiery darts of the wicked. And take the helmet of salvation, and the sword of the Spirit, which is the word of God: Praying always with all prayer and supplication in the Spirit, and watching thereunto with all perseverance and supplication for all saints.

Ephesians 6:10-18

35 And Hezekiah prayed unto the LORD, saying, "O LORD of hosts, God of Israel, that dwellest between the cherubims, thou art the God, even thou alone, of all the kingdoms of the earth: thou hast made heaven and earth."

Isaiah 37:15-16

36 And after these things I heard a great voice of much people in heaven, saying,

"Alleluia; Salvation, and glory, and honour, and power,
     unto the Lord our God:
   For true and righteous are his judgments:
   For he hath judged the great whore, which did corrupt the earth
     With her fornication,
   And hath avenged the blood of his servants at her hand."

And again they said,

"Alleluia. And her smoke rose up for ever and ever."

And the four and twenty elders and the four beasts fell down and worshipped God that sat on the throne, saying, "Amen; Alleluia."
And a voice came out of the throne, saying,

"Praise our God, all ye his servants,
And ye that fear him, both small and great."

Revelation 19:1-5

37 And thou shalt remember all the way which the LORD thy God led thee these forty years in the wilderness, to humble thee, and to prove* thee, to know what was in thine heart, whether thou wouldest keep his commandments, or no. And he humbled thee, and suffered* thee to hunger, and fed thee with manna, which thou knewest not, neither did thy fathers know; that he might make thee know that man doth not live by bread only, but by every word that proceedeth out of the mouth of the LORD doth man live.

Deuteronomy 8:2-3

38 And Jesus being full of the Holy Ghost returned from Jordan, and was led by the Spirit into the wilderness, being forty days tempted of the devil. And in those days he did eat nothing: and when they were ended, he afterward hungered.

And the devil said unto him, "If thou be the Son of God, command this stone that it be made bread." And Jesus answered him, saying, "It is written,

'That man shall not live by bread alone,
    But by every word of God.'"

And the devil, taking him up into an high mountain, shewed unto him all the kingdoms of the world in a moment of time. And the devil said unto him, "All this power will I give thee, and the glory of them: for that is delivered unto me; and to whomsoever I will I give it. If thou therefore wilt worship me, all shall be thine." And Jesus answered and said unto him, "Get thee behind me, Satan: for it is written,

'Thou shalt worship the Lord thy God,
    And him only shalt thou serve.'"

And he brought him to Jerusalem, and set him on a pinnacle of the temple, and said unto him, "If thou be the Son of God, cast thyself down from hence: For it is written,

'He shall give his angels charge over thee, to keep thee:
    And in their hands they shall bear thee up,
    Lest at any time thou dash thy foot against a stone.'"

And Jesus answering said unto him, "It is said, 'Thou shalt not tempt the Lord thy God.'" And when the devil had ended all the temptation, he departed from him for a season.

Luke 4:1-13

39 For he shall give his angels charge over thee,
     To keep thee in all thy ways.
   They shall bear thee up in their hands,
     Lest thou dash thy foot against a stone.
   Thou shalt tread upon the lion and adder:
     The young lion and the dragon shalt thou trample under feet.

Psalm 91:11-13

40 The words of the Preacher, the son of David, king in Jerusalem:
     Vanity of vanities, saith the Preacher,
     Vanity of vanities; all is vanity.
   What profit hath a man of all his labour
     Which he taketh under the sun?
   One generation passeth away, and another generation cometh:
     But the earth abideth for ever.
   The sun also ariseth, and the sun goeth down,
     And hasteth to his place where he arose.
   The wind goeth toward the south,
     And turneth about unto the north;
   It whirleth about continually,
     And the wind returneth again according to his circuits.
   All the rivers run into the sea;
     Yet the sea is not full;
   Unto the place from whence the rivers come,
     Thither they return again.
   All things are full of labour;
     Man cannot utter it:
   The eye is not satisfied with seeing,

  Nor the ear filled with hearing.
 The thing that hath been, it is that which shall be;
   And that which is done is that which shall be done:
   And there is no new thing under the sun.
 Is there any thing whereof it may be said,
   "See, this is new?"
 It hath been already of old time,
   Which was before us.
 There is no remembrance of former things;
 Neither shall there be any remembrance
   Of things that are to come
   with those that shall come after.

Ecclesiastes 1:1-11

41 The voice said, "Cry."
   And he said, "What shall I cry?"
  All flesh is grass,
   And all the goodliness thereof is as the flower of the field:
  The grass withereth, the flower fadeth:
   Because the spirit of the LORD bloweth upon it:
   Surely the people is grass.
  The grass withereth, the flower fadeth:
   But the word of our God shall stand for ever.

Isaiah 40:6-8

42 My flesh is clothed with worms and clods of dust;
       My skin is broken, and become loathsome.
    My days are swifter than a weaver's shuttle,
       And are spent without hope.
    O remember that my life is wind:
       Mine eye shall no more see good.
    The eye of him that hath seen me shall see me no more:
       Thine eyes are upon me, and I am not.
    As the cloud is consumed and vanisheth away:
       So he that goeth down to the grave shall come up no more.
    He shall return no more to his house,
       Neither shall his place know him any more.

Job 7:5-10

43 For I reckon that the sufferings of this present time are not worthy to be compared with the glory which shall be revealed in us. For the earnest expectation of the creature* waiteth for the manifestation of the sons of God. For the creature was made subject to vanity, not willingly, but by reason of him who hath subjected the same in hope, because the creature itself also shall be delivered from the bondage of corruption into the glorious liberty of the children of God. For we know that the whole creation groaneth and travaileth in pain together until now. And not only they, but ourselves also, which have the firstfruits of the Spirit, even we ourselves groan within ourselves, waiting for the adoption, to wit, the redemption of our body. For we are saved by hope: but hope that is seen is not hope: for what a man seeth, why doth he yet hope for? But if we hope for that we see not, then do we with patience wait for it.

Romans 8:18-25

44   "Remember this, and shew yourselves men:
    Bring it again to mind, O ye transgressors.
    Remember the former things of old:
  For I am God, and there is none else;
    I am God, and there is none like me,
  Declaring the end from the beginning,
    And from ancient times the things that are not yet done,
  Saying, My counsel shall stand,
    And I will do all my pleasure:
  Calling a ravenous bird from the east,
    The man that executeth my counsel from a far country:
  Yea, I have spoken it, I will also bring it to pass;
    I have purposed it, I will also do it."

Isaiah 46:8-11

45   For the Son of God, Jesus Christ, who was preached among you by us, even by me and Silvanus and Timotheus, was not yea and nay, but in him was yea. For all the promises of God in him are yea, and in him Amen, unto the glory of God by us. Now he which stablisheth us with you in Christ, and hath anointed us, is God; who hath also sealed us, and given the earnest of the Spirit in our hearts.

2 Corinthians 1:19-22

46   "Am I a God at hand," saith the LORD, "and not a God afar off? Can any hide himself in secret places that I shall not see him?" saith the LORD. "Do not I fill heaven and earth?" saith the LORD.

Jeremiah 23:23-24

47 After this I looked, and, behold, a door was opened in heaven: and the first voice which I heard was as it were of a trumpet talking with me; which said, "Come up hither, and I will shew thee things which must be hereafter." And immediately I was in the spirit: and, behold, a throne was set in heaven, and one sat on the throne. And he that sat was to look upon like a jasper and a sardine stone: and there was a rainbow round about the throne, in sight like unto an emerald. And round about the throne were four and twenty seats: and upon the seats I saw four and twenty elders sitting, clothed in white raiment; and they had on their heads crowns of gold. And out of the throne proceeded lightnings and thunderings and voices: and there were seven lamps of fire burning before the throne, which are the seven Spirits of God.

Revelation 4:1-5

48 For we have not followed cunningly devised fables, when we made known unto you the power and coming of our Lord Jesus Christ, but were eyewitnesses of his majesty.

2 Peter 1:16

49 Then cometh Jesus from Galilee to Jordan unto John, to be baptized of him. But John forbad him, saying, "I have need to be baptized of thee, and comest thou to me?" And Jesus answering said unto him, "Suffer* it to be so now: for thus it becometh us to fulfil all righteousness." Then he suffered him. And Jesus, when he was baptized, went up straightway out of the water: and, lo, the heavens were opened unto him, and he saw the Spirit of God descending like a dove, and lighting upon him: And lo a voice from heaven, saying, "This is my beloved Son, in whom I am well pleased."

Matthew 3:13-17

50 Behold my servant, whom I uphold;
    Mine elect, in whom my soul delighteth;
I have put my spirit upon him:
    He shall bring forth judgment to the Gentiles.
He shall not cry, nor lift up, nor cause his voice to be heard
        in the street.
A bruised reed shall he not break,
    And the smoking flax shall he not quench:
    He shall bring forth judgment unto truth.
He shall not fail nor be discouraged,
    Till he have set judgment in the earth:
    And the isles shall wait for his law.

Isaiah 42:1-4

51 Likewise the Spirit also helpeth our infirmities: for we know not what we should pray for as we ought: but the Spirit itself maketh intercession for us with groanings which cannot be uttered. And he that searcheth the hearts knoweth what is the mind of the Spirit, because he maketh intercession for the saints according to the will of God.

Romans 8:26-27

52 For since the beginning of the world men have not heard, nor perceived by the ear, neither hath the eye seen, O God, beside thee, what he hath prepared for him that waiteth for him.

Isaiah 64:4

53 And when the day of Pentecost was fully come, they were all with one accord in one place. And suddenly there came a sound from heaven as of a rushing mighty wind, and it filled all the house where they were sitting. And there appeared unto them cloven tongues like as of fire, and it sat upon each of them. And they were all filled with the Holy Ghost, and began to speak with other tongues, as the Spirit gave them utterance. And there were dwelling at Jerusalem Jews, devout men, out of every nation under heaven. Now when this was noised abroad, the multitude came together, and were confounded, because that every man heard them speak in his own language. And they were all amazed and marvelled, saying one to another, "Behold, are not all these which speak Galilaeans? And how hear we every man in our own tongue, wherein we were born?"

Acts 2:1-8

54 For as many as are led by the Spirit of God, they are the sons of God. For ye have not received the spirit of bondage again to fear; but ye have received the Spirit of adoption, whereby we cry, "Abba, Father." The Spirit itself beareth witness with our spirit, that we are the children of God: And if children, then heirs; heirs of God, and joint-heirs with Christ; if so be that we suffer with him, that we may be also glorified together.

Romans 8:14-17

55 And [Jesus] saith unto them, "My soul is exceeding sorrowful unto death: tarry ye here, and watch." And he went forward a little, and fell on the ground, and prayed that, if it were possible, the hour might pass from him. And he said, "Abba, Father, all things are possible unto thee; take away this cup from me: nevertheless not what I will, but what thou wilt."

Mark 14:34-36

56 Out of the depths have I cried unto thee, O LORD.
      Lord, hear my voice:
    Let thine ears be attentive
      To the voice of my supplications.
    If thou, LORD, shouldest mark iniquities,
      O Lord, who shall stand?
    But there is forgiveness with thee,
      That thou mayest be feared.
    I wait for the LORD, my soul doth wait,
      And in his word do I hope.
    My soul waiteth for the Lord
      More than they that watch for the morning:
      I say, more than they that watch for the morning.
    Let Israel hope in the LORD:
      For with the LORD there is mercy,
      And with him is plenteous redemption.
    And he shall redeem Israel
      From all his iniquities.

Psalm 130:1-8

57 "These things have I spoken unto you, being yet present with you. But the Comforter, which is the Holy Ghost, whom the Father will send in my name, he shall teach you all things, and bring all things to your remembrance, whatsoever I have said unto you. Peace I leave with you, my peace I give unto you: not as the world giveth, give I unto you. Let not your heart be troubled, neither let it be afraid."

John 14:25-27

58 In the year that king Uzziah died I saw also the LORD sitting upon a throne, high and lifted up, and his train filled the temple. Above it stood the seraphims: each one had six wings; with twain* he covered his face, and with twain he covered his feet, and with twain he did fly. And one cried unto another, and said,

"Holy, holy, holy, is the LORD of hosts:
The whole earth is full of his glory."

And the posts of the door moved at the voice of him that cried, and the house was filled with smoke. Then said I, "Woe is me! For I am undone; because I am a man of unclean lips, and I dwell in the midst of a people of unclean lips: for mine eyes have seen the King, the LORD of hosts."

Isaiah 6:1-5

59 For this cause I bow my knees unto the Father of our Lord Jesus Christ, of whom the whole family in heaven and earth is named, that he would grant you, according to the riches of his glory, to be strengthened with might by his Spirit in the inner man; that Christ may dwell in your hearts

by faith; that ye, being rooted and grounded in love, may be able to comprehend with all saints what is the breadth, and length, and depth, and height; and to know the love of Christ, which passeth knowledge, that ye might be filled with all the fulness of God. Now unto him that is able to do exceeding abundantly above all that we ask or think, according to the power that worketh in us, unto him be glory in the church by Christ Jesus throughout all ages, world without end. Amen.

Ephesians 3:14-21

60   Then flew one of the seraphims unto me, having a live coal in his hand, which he had taken with the tongs from off the altar: And he laid it upon my mouth, and said, "Lo, this hath touched thy lips; and thine iniquity is taken away, and thy sin purged." Also I heard the voice of the Lord, saying, "Whom shall I send, and who will go for us?" Then said I, "Here am I; send me."

Isaiah 6:6-8

61   At that time Jesus answered and said, "I thank thee, O Father, Lord of heaven and earth, because thou hast hid these things from the wise and prudent, and hast revealed them unto babes. Even so, Father: for so it seemed good in thy sight. All things are delivered unto me of my Father: and no man knoweth the Son, but the Father; neither knoweth any man the Father, save the Son, and he to whomsoever the Son will reveal him."

Matthew 11:25-27

62 All this have I proved by wisdom: I said, "I will be wise"; but it was far
from me. That which is far off, and exceeding deep, who can find it out?

Ecclesiastes 7:23-24

63 Wherefore the Lord said,
    "Forasmuch as this people draw near me with their mouth,
        And with their lips do honour me,
        But have removed their heart far from me,
    And their fear toward me is taught by the precept of men:
    Therefore, behold, I will proceed
        To do a marvellous work among this people,
        Even a marvellous work and a wonder:
    For the wisdom of their wise men shall perish,
        And the understanding of their prudent men shall be hid."

Isaiah 29:13-14

64 And I [Paul], brethren, when I came to you, came not with excellency of
speech or of wisdom, declaring unto you the testimony of God. For I determined not to know any thing among you, save Jesus Christ, and him
crucified. And I was with you in weakness, and in fear, and in much
trembling. And my speech and my preaching was not with enticing
words of man's wisdom, but in demonstration of the Spirit and of power:
That your faith should not stand in the wisdom of men, but in the power
of God.

1 Corinthians 2:1-5

65   Canst thou by searching find out God?
      Canst thou find out the Almighty unto perfection?
   It is as high as heaven; what canst thou do?
      Deeper than hell; what canst thou know?
   The measure thereof is longer than the earth,
      And broader than the sea.
   If he cut off, and shut up, or gather together,
      Then who can hinder him?
   For he knoweth vain men:
      He seeth wickedness also;
      Will he not then consider it?
   For vain man would be wise,
      Though man be born like a wild ass's colt.

Job 11:7-12

66   Seek ye the LORD while he may be found,
      Call ye upon him while he is near:
   Let the wicked forsake his way,
      And the unrighteous man his thoughts:
   And let him return unto the LORD,
      And he will have mercy upon him;
   And to our God,
      For he will abundantly pardon.
   For my thoughts are not your thoughts,
      Neither are your ways my ways, saith the LORD.
   For as the heavens are higher than the earth,
      So are my ways higher than your ways,
      And my thoughts than your thoughts.

Isaiah 55:6-9

67 Who is a wise man and endued with knowledge among you? Let him shew out of a good conversation his works with meekness of wisdom. But if ye have bitter envying and strife in your hearts, glory not, and lie not against the truth. This wisdom descendeth not from above, but is earthly, sensual, devilish. For where envying and strife is, there is confusion and every evil work. But the wisdom that is from above is first pure, then peaceable, gentle, and easy to be intreated, full of mercy and good fruits, without partiality, and without hypocrisy. And the fruit of righteousness is sown in peace of them that make peace.

James 3:13-18

68 "But where shall wisdom be found?
    And where is the place of understanding?
Man knoweth not the price thereof;
    Neither is it found in the land of the living.
The depth saith, It is not in me:
    And the sea saith, It is not with me.
It cannot be gotten for gold,
    Neither shall silver be weighed for the price thereof. . . .
God understandeth the way thereof,
    And he knoweth the place thereof.
For he looketh to the ends of the earth,
    And seeth under the whole heaven;
To make the weight for the winds;
    And he weigheth the waters by measure.
When he made a decree for the rain,
    And a way for the lightning of the thunder:
Then did he see it, and declare it;

He prepared it, yea, and searched it out.
And unto man he said,
'Behold, the fear of the LORD, that is wisdom;
 And to depart from evil is understanding.'"

Job 28:12-15, 23-28

69   Howbeit* we speak wisdom among them that are perfect: yet not the wisdom of this world, nor of the princes of this world, that come to nought: But we speak the wisdom of God in a mystery, even the hidden wisdom, which God ordained before the world unto our glory: Which none of the princes of this world knew: for had they known it, they would not have crucified the Lord of glory. But as it is written,

"Eye hath not seen, nor ear heard,
Neither have entered into the heart of man,
The things which God hath prepared for them that love him."

But God hath revealed them unto us by his Spirit: for the Spirit searcheth all things, yea, the deep things of God. For what man knoweth the things of a man, save the spirit of man which is in him? Even so the things of God knoweth no man, but the Spirit of God. Now we have received, not the spirit of the world, but the spirit which is of God; that we might know the things that are freely given to us of God. Which things also we speak, not in the words which man's wisdom teacheth, but which the Holy Ghost teacheth; comparing spiritual things with spiritual.

1 Corinthians 2:6-13

70 And the LORD said unto Moses, "I will do this thing also that thou hast spoken: for thou hast found grace in my sight, and I know thee by name." And he said, "I beseech thee, shew me thy glory." And he said, "I will make all my goodness pass before thee, and I will proclaim the name of the LORD before thee; and will be gracious to whom I will be gracious, and will shew mercy on whom I will shew mercy." And he said, "Thou canst not see my face: for there shall no man see me, and live." And the LORD said, "Behold, there is a place by me, and thou shalt stand upon a rock: And it shall come to pass, while my glory passeth by, that I will put thee in a cleft of the rock, and will cover thee with my hand while I pass by: And I will take away mine hand, and thou shalt see my back parts: but my face shall not be seen."

Exodus 33:17-23

71 Verily thou art a God that hidest thyself,
     O God of Israel, the Saviour.

Isaiah 45:15

72 For the preaching of the cross is to them that perish foolishness; but unto us which are saved it is the power of God. For it is written,

"I will destroy the wisdom of the wise,
And will bring to nothing the understanding of the prudent."

Where is the wise? Where is the scribe? Where is the disputer of this world? Hath not God made foolish the wisdom of this world? For after that in the wisdom of God the world by wisdom knew not God, it

44

pleased God by the foolishness of preaching to save them that believe. For the Jews require a sign, and the Greeks seek after wisdom: But we preach Christ crucified, unto the Jews a stumbling-block, and unto the Greeks foolishness; but unto them which are called, both Jews and Greeks, Christ the power of God, and the wisdom of God. Because the foolishness of God is wiser than men; and the weakness of God is stronger than men. For ye see your calling, brethren, how that not many wise men after the flesh, not many mighty, not many noble, are called: But God hath chosen the foolish things of the world to confound the wise; and God hath chosen the weak things of the world to confound the things which are mighty; and base things of the world, and things which are despised, hath God chosen, yea, and things which are not, to bring to nought things that are: That no flesh should glory in his presence. But of him are ye in Christ Jesus, who of God is made unto us wisdom, and righteousness, and sanctification, and redemption: That, according as it is written, He that glorieth, let him glory in the Lord.

1 Corinthians 1:18-31

73 Wherefore David blessed the LORD before all the congregation: and David said, "Blessed be thou, LORD God of Israel our father, for ever and ever. Thine, O LORD, is the greatness, and the power, and the glory, and the victory, and the majesty: for all that is in the heaven and in the earth is thine; thine is the kingdom, O LORD, and thou art exalted as head above all."

1 Chronicles 29:10-11

74 I will extol thee, my God, O king;
   And I will bless thy name for ever and ever.
   Every day will I bless thee;
   And I will praise thy name for ever and ever.
   Great is the LORD, and greatly to be praised;
   And his greatness is unsearchable.
   One generation shall praise thy works to another,
   And shall declare thy mighty acts.
   I will speak of the glorious honour of thy majesty,
   And of thy wondrous works.
   And men shall speak of the might of thy terrible acts:
   And I will declare thy greatness.
   They shall abundantly utter the memory of thy great goodness,
   And shall sing of thy righteousness.
   The LORD is gracious, and full of compassion;
   Slow to anger, and of great mercy.
   The LORD is good to all:
   And his tender mercies are over all his works.

Psalm 145:1-9

75 Hearken unto me, O Jacob,
   And Israel, my called;
   I am he; I am the first,
   I also am the last.
   Mine hand also hath laid the foundation of the earth,
   And my right hand hath spanned the heavens:
   When I call unto them,
   They stand up together.

Isaiah 48:12-13

76   I am Alpha and Omega, the beginning and the ending, saith the Lord, which is, and which was, and which is to come, the Almighty.

Revelation 1:8

The First Day

Darkness and Light

Obscurity and Clarity

Discernment

Call and Response

Vows and Consequences

MOST OF US GREET a new morning by opening our eyes to light superseding night's darkness. Likewise, in Genesis, God begins creation by throwing on the light. Light defines the darkness beyond its purview. This initial division of day from night fixes the template to which the Creator adheres for the next six Days.

Light and darkness are primary metaphors for human conduct and understanding. An idea "dawns." Actions "come to light." "Sorry," one says, "I'm still in the dark." Scripture develops these metaphors manifold. Most interesting is its inversion of sensory and religious perception. The blind demonstrate greater insight than those with clear vision, even as perfect hearing may prove deaf to God's voice.

Creation's first Day introduces the instrument by which God creates: speech. As God speaks, so it is. This pattern permeates Scripture, notably in its depictions of God's involvement with mortals. A call occurs at the Creator's initiative. It may issue in adulthood, in youth, even during prenatal gestation. Like divine vocation, human discernment is a spiritual gift, not a native ability. At first fumbling, responses to God's call acquire greater precision with benefit of hindsight. Once uttered, however, some words are impossible to take back.

77   And God said, "Let there be light: and there was light." And God saw the light, that it was good: and God divided the light from the darkness. And God called the light Day, and the darkness he called Night. And the evening and the morning were the first day.

Genesis 1:3-5

78   In [the Word] was life;

      And the life was the light of men.

And the light shineth in darkness;

      And the darkness comprehended it not.

There was a man sent from God, whose name was John. The same came for a witness, to bear witness of the Light, that all men through him might believe. He was not that Light, but was sent to bear witness of that Light.

That was the true Light,

      Which lighteth every man that cometh into the world.

He was in the world,

      And the world was made by him,

      And the world knew him not.

He came unto his own,

      And his own received him not.

But as many as received him,

      To them gave he power to become the sons of God,

      Even to them that believe on his name:

Which were born, not of blood,

      Nor of the will of the flesh, nor of the will of man,

      But of God.

John 1:4-13

79 How excellent is thy lovingkindness, O God!
    Therefore the children of men put their trust
        Under the shadow of thy wings.
    They shall be abundantly satisfied with the fatness of thy house;
        And thou shalt make them drink of the river of thy pleasures.
    For with thee is the fountain of life:
        In thy light shall we see light.

Psalm 36:7-9

80 My days are past, my purposes are broken off,
        Even the thoughts of my heart.
    They change the night into day:
        The light is short because of darkness.
    If I wait, the grave is mine house:
        I have made my bed in the darkness.
    I have said to corruption, 'Thou art my father':
        To the worm, 'Thou are my mother, and my sister.'
    And where is now my hope?
        As for my hope, who shall see it?
    They shall go down to the bars of the pit,
        When our rest together is in the dust.

Job 17:11-16

81 And it came to pass, that when Isaac was old, and his eyes were dim, so
    that he could not see, he called Esau his eldest son. . . . And Rebekah
    heard when Isaac spake to Esau his son. And Esau went to the field to

hunt for venison, and to bring it. And Rebekah spake unto Jacob her son, saying, "Behold, I heard thy father speak unto Esau thy brother, saying, 'Bring me venison, and make me savoury meat, that I may eat, and bless thee before the LORD before my death.' Now therefore, my son, obey my voice according to that which I command thee. Go now to the flock, and fetch me from thence two good kids of the goats; and I will make them savoury meat for thy father, such as he loveth: And thou shalt bring it to thy father, that he may eat, and that he may bless thee before his death." And Jacob said to Rebekah his mother, "Behold, Esau my brother is a hairy man, and I am a smooth man: My father peradventure* will feel me, and I shall seem to him as a deceiver; and I shall bring a curse upon me, and not a blessing." And his mother said unto him, "Upon me be thy curse, my son: only obey my voice, and go fetch me them." And he went, and fetched, and brought them to his mother: and his mother made savoury meat, such as his father loved. And Rebekah took goodly raiment of her eldest son Esau, which were with her in the house, and put them upon Jacob her younger son: And she put the skins of the kids of the goats upon his hands, and upon the smooth of his neck: And she gave the savoury meat and the bread, which she had prepared, into the hand of her son Jacob.

Genesis 27:1a, 5-17

82 "The light of the body is the eye: if therefore thine eye be single*, thy whole body shall be full of light. But if thine eye be evil, thy whole body shall be full of darkness. If therefore the light that is in thee be darkness, how great is that darkness!"

Matthew 6:22-23

83 And [Jacob] came unto his father, and said, "My father": and he said, "Here am I; who art thou, my son?" And Jacob said unto his father, "I am Esau thy first born; I have done according as thou badest me: arise, I pray thee, sit and eat of my venison, that thy soul may bless me." And Isaac said unto his son, "How is it that thou hast found it so quickly, my son?" And he said, "Because the LORD thy God brought it to me." And Isaac said unto Jacob, "Come near, I pray thee, that I may feel thee, my son, whether thou be my very son Esau or not." And Jacob went near unto Isaac his father; and he felt him, and said, "The voice is Jacob's voice, but the hands are the hands of Esau." And he discerned him not, because his hands were hairy, as his brother Esau's hands: so he blessed him. And he said, "Art thou my very son Esau?" And he said, "I am." And he said, "Bring it near to me, and I will eat of my son's venison, that my soul may bless thee." And he brought it near to him, and he did eat: and he brought him wine and he drank. And his father Isaac said unto him, "Come near now, and kiss me, my son." And he came near, and kissed him: and he smelled the smell of his raiment, and blessed him, and said,

> "See, the smell of my son
>> Is as the smell of a field which the LORD hath blessed:
> Therefore God give thee of the dew of heaven,
>> And the fatness of the earth,
>> And plenty of corn* and wine:
> Let people serve thee,
>> And nations bow down to thee:
> Be lord over thy brethren,
>> And let thy mother's sons bow down to thee:
> Cursed be every one that curseth thee,
>> And blessed be he that blesseth thee."

Genesis 27:18-29

84 But above all things, my brethren, swear not, neither by heaven, neither by the earth, neither by any other oath: but let your yea be yea; and your nay, nay; lest ye fall into condemnation.

James 5:12

85 Then the Spirit of the LORD came upon Jephthah, and he passed over Gilead, and Manasseh, and passed over Mizpeh of Gilead, and from Mizpeh of Gilead he passed over unto the children of Ammon. And Jephthah vowed a vow unto the LORD, and said, "If thou shalt without fail deliver the children of Ammon into mine hands, then it shall be, that whatsoever cometh forth of the doors of my house to meet me, when I return in peace from the children of Ammon, shall surely be the LORD's, and I will offer it up for a burnt offering." So Jephthah passed over unto the children of Ammon to fight against them; and the LORD delivered them into his hands. And he smote them from Aroer, even till thou come to Minnith, even twenty cities, and unto the plain of the vineyards, with a very great slaughter. Thus the children of Ammon were subdued before the children of Israel.

Judges 11:29-33

86 And it came to pass, as soon as Isaac had made an end of blessing Jacob, and Jacob was yet scarce gone out from the presence of Isaac his father, that Esau his brother came in from his hunting. And he also had made savoury meat, and brought it unto his father, and said unto his father, "Let my father arise, and eat of his son's venison, that thy soul may bless me." And Isaac his father said unto him, "Who art thou?" And he said, "I am thy son, thy firstborn Esau." And Isaac trembled very exceedingly, and said, "Who? Where is he that hath taken venison, and brought it me, and I have eaten of all before thou camest, and have blessed him? Yea, and he shall be blessed." And when Esau heard the words of his father, he cried with a great and exceeding bitter cry, and said unto his father, "Bless me, even me also, O my father." And he said, "Thy brother came with subtilty*, and hath taken away thy blessing." And he said, "Is not he rightly named Jacob? For he hath supplanted me these two times: he took away my birthright; and, behold, now he hath taken away my blessing." And he said, "Hast thou not reserved a blessing for me?" And Isaac answered and said unto Esau, "Behold, I have made him thy lord, and all his brethren have I given to him for servants; and with corn* and wine have I sustained him: and what shall I do now unto thee, my son?" And Esau said unto his father, "Hast thou but one blessing, my father? Bless me, even me also, O my father." And Esau lifted up his voice, and wept. And Isaac his father answered and said unto him,

"Behold, thy dwelling shall be the fatness of the earth,
    And of the dew of heaven from above;
And by thy sword shalt thou live,
    And shalt serve thy brother;
And it shall come to pass when thou shalt have the dominion,
    That thou shalt break his yoke from off thy neck."

And Esau hated Jacob because of the blessing wherewith his father blessed him: and Esau said in his heart, "The days of mourning for my father are at hand; then will I slay my brother Jacob." And these words of Esau her elder son were told to Rebekah: and she sent and called Jacob her younger son, and said unto him, "Behold, thy brother Esau, as touching* thee, doth comfort himself, purposing to kill thee. Now therefore, my son, obey my voice; and arise, flee thou to Laban my brother to

Haran; and tarry with him a few days, until thy brother's fury turn away;
Until thy brother's anger turn away from thee, and he forget that which
thou hast done to him: then I will send, and fetch thee from thence: why
should I be deprived also of you both in one day?"

Genesis 27:30-45

87   O LORD God of my salvation,
    I have cried day and night before thee:
Let my prayer come before thee:
    Incline thine ear unto my cry;
For my soul is full of troubles:
    And my life draweth nigh unto the grave.
I am counted with them that go down into the pit:
    I am as a man that hath no strength:
Free among the dead,
    Like the slain that lie in the grave,
Whom thou rememberest no more:
    And they are cut off from thy hand.
Thou hast laid me in the lowest pit,
    In darkness, in the deeps.
Thy wrath lieth hard upon me,
    And thou hast afflicted me with all thy waves. *Selah**.

Psalm 88:1-7

88 And Jephthah came to Mizpeh unto his house, and, behold, his daughter came out to meet him with timbrels and with dances: and she was his only child; beside her he had neither son nor daughter. And it came to pass, when he saw her, that he rent his clothes, and said, "Alas, my daughter! Thou hast brought me very low, and thou art one of them that trouble me: for I have opened my mouth unto the LORD, and I cannot go back." And she said unto him, "My father, if thou hast opened thy mouth unto the LORD, do to me according to that which hath proceeded out of thy mouth; forasmuch as the LORD hath taken vengeance for thee of thine enemies, even of the children of Ammon." And she said unto her father, "Let this thing be done for me: let me alone two months, that I may go up and down upon the mountains, and bewail my virginity, I and my fellows." And he said, "Go." And he sent her away for two months: and she went with her companions, and bewailed her virginity upon the mountains. And it came to pass at the end of two months, that she returned unto her father, who did with her according to his vow which he had vowed: and she knew no man. And it was a custom in Israel, that the daughters of Israel went yearly to lament the daughter of Jephthah the Gileadite four days in a year.

Judges 11:34-40

89 But unto thee have I cried, O LORD;
    And in the morning shall my prayer prevent* thee.
  LORD, why castest thou off my soul?
    Why hidest thou thy face from me?
  I am afflicted and ready to die from my youth up:
    While I suffer thy terrors I am distracted.
  Thy fierce wrath goeth over me;

Thy terrors have cut me off.
They came round about me daily like water;
    They compassed me about together.
Lover and friend hast thou put far from me,
    And mine acquaintance into darkness.

Psalm 88:13-18

90   And Jacob went out from Beersheba, and went toward Haran. And he lighted upon a certain place, and tarried there all night, because the sun was set; and he took of the stones of that place, and put them for his pillows, and lay down in that place to sleep. And he dreamed, and behold a ladder set up on the earth, and the top of it reached to heaven: and behold the angels of God ascending and descending on it. And, behold, the LORD stood above it, and said, "I am the LORD God of Abraham thy father, and the God of Isaac: the land whereon thou liest, to thee will I give it, and to thy seed; and thy seed shall be as the dust of the earth, and thou shalt spread abroad to the west, and to the east, and to the north, and to the south: and in thee and in thy seed shall all the families of the earth be blessed. And, behold, I am with thee, and will keep thee in all places whither thou goest, and will bring thee again into this land; for I will not leave thee, until I have done that which I have spoken to thee of." And Jacob awaked out of his sleep, and he said, "Surely the LORD is in this place; and I knew it not." And he was afraid, and said, "How dreadful* is this place! This is none other but the house of God, and this is the gate of heaven."

Genesis 28:10-17

91 The day following Jesus would go forth into Galilee, and findeth Philip, and saith unto him, "Follow me." Now Philip was of Bethsaida, the city of Andrew and Peter. Philip findeth Nathanael, and saith unto him, "We have found him, of whom Moses in the law, and the prophets, did write, Jesus of Nazareth, the son of Joseph." And Nathanael said unto him, "Can there any good thing come out of Nazareth?" Philip saith unto him, "Come and see." Jesus saw Nathanael coming to him, and saith of him, "Behold an Israelite indeed, in whom is no guile!" Nathanael saith unto him, "Whence knowest thou me?" Jesus answered and said unto him, "Before that Philip called thee, when thou wast under the fig tree, I saw thee." Nathanael answered and saith unto him, "Rabbi, thou art the Son of God; thou art the King of Israel." Jesus answered and said unto him, "Because I said unto thee, I saw thee under the fig tree, believest thou? thou shalt see greater things than these." And he saith unto him, "Verily, verily, I say unto you, Hereafter ye shall see heaven open, and the angels of God ascending and descending upon the Son of man."

John 1:43-51

92 And [Jacob] rose up that night, and took his two wives, and his two womenservants, and his eleven sons, and passed over the ford Jabbok. And he took them, and sent them over the brook, and sent over that he had. And Jacob was left alone; and there wrestled a man with him until the breaking of the day. And when he saw that he prevailed not against him, he touched the hollow of his thigh; and the hollow of Jacob's thigh was out of joint, as he wrestled with him. And he said, "Let me go, for the day breaketh." And he said, "I will not let thee go, except thou bless me." And he said unto him, "What is thy name?" And he said, "Jacob." And he said, "Thy name shall be called no more Jacob, but Israel: for as a prince hast thou power with God and with men, and hast prevailed." And Jacob asked him, and said, "Tell me, I pray thee, thy name." And he said, "Wherefore* is it that thou dost ask after my name?" And he blessed him there. And Jacob called the name of the place Peniel: "For I have seen God face to face, and my life is preserved." And as he passed over Penuel the sun rose upon him, and he halted upon his thigh. Therefore the children of Israel eat not of the sinew which shrank, which is upon the hollow of the thigh, unto this day: because he touched the hollow of Jacob's thigh in the sinew that shrank.

Genesis 32:22-32

93 "Moreover if thy brother shall trespass against thee, go and tell him his fault between thee and him alone: if he shall hear thee, thou hast gained thy brother. But if he will not hear thee, then take with thee one or two more, that in the mouth of two or three witnesses every word may be established. And if he shall neglect to hear them, tell it unto the church: but if he neglect to hear the church, let him be unto thee as an heathen man and a publican. Verily I say unto you, Whatsoever ye shall bind on earth shall be bound in heaven: and whatsoever ye shall loose on earth shall be loosed in heaven. Again I say unto you, that if two of you shall agree on earth as touching* any thing that they shall ask, it shall be done for them of my Father which is in heaven. For where two or three are gathered together in my name, there am I in the midst of them."

Then came Peter to him, and said, "Lord, how oft shall my brother sin against me, and I forgive him? Till seven times?" Jesus saith unto him, "I say not unto thee, Until seven times: but, Until seventy times seven."

Matthew 18:15-22

94 And Jacob lifted up his eyes, and looked, and, behold, Esau came, and with him four hundred men. And he divided the children unto Leah, and unto Rachel, and unto the two handmaids. And he put the handmaids and their children foremost, and Leah and her children after, and Rachel and Joseph hindermost. And he passed over before them, and bowed himself to the ground seven times, until he came near to his brother. And Esau ran to meet him, and embraced him, and fell on his neck, and kissed him: and they wept. And he lifted up his eyes, and saw the women and the children; and said, "Who are those with thee?" And he said, "The children which God hath graciously given thy servant." Then the handmaidens came near, they and their children, and they bowed themselves. And Leah also with her children came near, and bowed themselves: and after came Joseph near and Rachel, and they bowed themselves. And he said, "What meanest thou by all this drove which I met?" And he said, "These are to find grace in the sight of my lord." And Esau said, "I have enough, my brother; keep that thou hast unto thyself." And Jacob said, "Nay, I pray thee, if now I have found grace in thy sight, then receive my present at my hand: for therefore I have seen thy face, as though I had seen the face of God, and thou wast pleased with me. Take, I pray thee, my blessing that is brought to thee; because God hath dealt graciously with me, and because I have enough." And he urged him, and he took it.

Genesis 33:1-11

95 Though I speak with the tongues of men and of angels, and have not charity*, I am become as sounding brass, or a tinkling cymbal. And though I have the gift of prophecy, and understand all mysteries, and all knowledge; and though I have all faith, so that I could remove moun-

tains, and have not charity, I am nothing. And though I bestow all my goods to feed the poor, and though I give my body to be burned, and have not charity, it profiteth me nothing.

Charity suffereth long, and is kind; charity envieth not; charity vaunteth not itself, is not puffed up, doth not behave itself unseemly, seeketh not her own, is not easily provoked, thinketh no evil; rejoiceth not in iniquity, but rejoiceth in the truth; beareth all things, believeth all things, hopeth all things, endureth all things.

Charity never faileth: but whether there be prophecies, they shall fail; whether there be tongues, they shall cease; whether there be knowledge, it shall vanish away. For we know in part, and we prophesy in part. But when that which is perfect is come, then that which is in part shall be done away. When I was a child, I spake as a child, I understood as a child, I thought as a child: but when I became a man, I put away childish things. For now we see through a glass, darkly; but then face to face: now I know in part; but then shall I know even as also I am known. And now abideth faith, hope, charity, these three; but the greatest of these is charity.

1 Corinthians 13:1-13

96   But the path of the just is as the shining light,
     That shineth more and more unto the perfect day.
   The way of the wicked is as darkness:
     They know not at what they stumble.

Proverbs 4:18-19

97 "There is another that beareth witness of me; and I know that the witness which he witnesseth of me is true. Ye sent unto John, and he bare witness unto the truth. But I receive not testimony from man: but these things I say, that ye might be saved. He was a burning and a shining light: and ye were willing for a season to rejoice in his light. But I have greater witness than that of John: for the works which the Father hath given me to finish, the same works that I do, bear witness of me, that the Father hath sent me."

John 5:32-36

98 Thy word is a lamp unto my feet,
  And a light unto my path.

Psalm 119:105

99 And [Jesus] cometh to Bethsaida; and they bring a blind man unto him, and besought him to touch him. And he took the blind man by the hand, and led him out of the town; and when he had spit on his eyes, and put his hands upon him, he asked him if he saw ought. And he looked up, and said, "I see men as trees, walking." After that he put his hands again upon his eyes, and made him look up: and he was restored, and saw every man clearly. And he sent him away to his house, saying, "Neither go into the town, nor tell it to any in the town."

Mark 8:22-26

100   Do not err, my beloved brethren. Every good gift and every perfect gift is from above, and cometh down from the Father of lights, with whom is no variableness, neither shadow of turning.

James 1:16-17

101   "I am the LORD, and there is none else,
        There is no God beside me:
        I girded thee, though thou hast not known me:
   That they may know from the rising of the sun,
        And from the west, that there is none beside me.
        I am the LORD, and there is none else.
   I form the light, and create darkness:
        I make peace, and create evil:
        I the LORD do all these things."

Isaiah 45:5-7

102   And as Jesus passed by, he saw a man which was blind from his birth. And his disciples asked him, saying, "Master, who did sin, this man, or his parents, that he was born blind?" Jesus answered, "Neither hath this man sinned, nor his parents: but that the works of God should be made manifest in him. I must work the works of him that sent me, while it is day: the night cometh, when no man can work. As long as I am in the world, I am the light of the world." When he had thus spoken, he spat on the ground, and made clay of the spittle, and he anointed the eyes of the blind man with the clay, and said unto him, "Go, wash in the pool of Siloam," (which is by interpretation, Sent). He went his way therefore, and washed, and came seeing. . . . Then again called [the Pharisees] the man that was blind, and said unto him, "Give God the praise: we know that this man is a sinner." He answered and said, "Whether he be a sinner or no, I know not: one thing I know, that, whereas I was blind, now I see."

John 9:1-7, 24-25

103 Rejoice not against me, O mine enemy:
        When I fall, I shall arise;
    When I sit in darkness,
        The LORD shall be a light unto me.
    I will bear the indignation of the LORD,
        Because I have sinned against him,
    Until he plead my cause,
        And execute judgment for me:
    He will bring me forth to the light,
        And I shall behold his righteousness.

Micah 7:8-9

104 For God so loved the world, that he gave his only begotten Son, that whosoever believeth in him should not perish, but have everlasting life. For God sent not his Son into the world to condemn the world; but that the world through him might be saved. He that believeth on him is not condemned: but he that believeth not is condemned already, because he hath not believed in the name of the only begotten Son of God. And this is the condemnation, that light is come into the world, and men loved

darkness rather than light, because their deeds were evil. For every one that doeth evil hateth the light, neither cometh to the light, lest his deeds should be reproved. But he that doeth truth cometh to the light, that his deeds may be made manifest, that they are wrought in God.

John 3:16-21

105 Whither shall I go from thy spirit?
     Or whither shall I flee from thy presence?
If I ascend up into heaven, thou art there:
     If I make my bed in hell, behold, thou art there.
If I take the wings of the morning,
     And dwell in the uttermost parts of the sea;
Even there shall thy hand lead me,
     And thy right hand shall hold me.
If I say, "Surely the darkness shall cover me;
     Even the night shall be light about me."
Yea, the darkness hideth not from thee;
     But the night shineth as the day:
     The darkness and the light are both alike to thee.

Psalm 139:7-12

106 This then is the message which we have heard of him, and declare unto you, that God is light, and in him is no darkness at all. If we say that we have fellowship with him, and walk in darkness, we lie, and do not the truth: But if we walk in the light, as he is in the light, we have fellowship one with another, and the blood of Jesus Christ his Son cleanseth us from all sin.

1 John 1:5-7

107 "Hear, ye deaf;
    And look, ye blind, that ye may see.
Who is blind, but my servant?
    Or deaf, as my messenger that I sent?
Who is blind as he that is perfect,
    And blind as the LORD's servant?
Seeing many things, but thou observest not;
    Opening the ears, but he heareth not."

Isaiah 42:18-20

108 And they bring unto [Jesus] one that was deaf, and had an impediment in his speech; and they beseech him to put his hand upon him. And he took him aside from the multitude, and put his fingers into his ears, and he spit, and touched his tongue; and looking up to heaven, he sighed, and saith unto him, "Ephphatha," that is, "Be opened." And straightway his ears were opened, and the string of his tongue was loosed, and he spake plain. And he charged them that they should tell no man: but the more he charged them, so much the more a great deal they published it; and were beyond measure astonished, saying, "He hath done all things well: he maketh both the deaf to hear, and the dumb to speak."

Mark 7:32-37

109 Now Moses kept the flock of Jethro his father in law, the priest of Midian: and he led the flock to the backside of the desert, and came to the mountain of God, even to Horeb. And the angel of the LORD appeared unto him in a flame of fire out of the midst of a bush: and he looked, and, behold, the bush burned with fire, and the bush was not consumed. And Moses said, "I will now turn aside, and see this great sight, why the bush is not burnt." And when the LORD saw that he turned aside to see, God called unto him out of the midst of the bush, and said, "Moses, Moses." And he said, "Here am I." And he said, "Draw not nigh hither: Put off thy shoes from off thy feet, for the place whereon thou standest is holy ground." Moreover he said, "I am the God of thy father, the God of Abraham, the God of Isaac, and the God of Jacob." And Moses hid his face; for he was afraid to look upon God. And the LORD said, "I have surely seen the affliction of my people which are in Egypt, and have heard their cry by reason of their taskmasters; for I know their sorrows; and I am come down to deliver them out of the hand of the Egyptians, and to bring them up out of that land unto a good land and a large, unto a land flowing with milk and honey; unto the place of the Canaanites, and the Hittites, and the Amorites, and the Perizzites, and the Hivites, and the Jebusites. Now therefore, behold, the cry of the children of Israel is come unto me: and I have also seen the oppression wherewith the Egyptians oppress them. Come now therefore, and I will send thee unto Pharaoh, that thou mayest bring forth my people the children of Israel out of Egypt." And Moses said unto God, "Who am I, that I should go unto Pharaoh, and that I should bring forth the children of Israel out of Egypt?" And he said, "Certainly I will be with thee; and this shall be a token unto thee, that I have sent thee: When thou hast brought forth the people out of Egypt, ye shall serve God upon this mountain."

And Moses said unto God, "Behold, when I come unto the children of Israel, and shall say unto them, 'The God of your fathers hath sent me unto you'; and they shall say to me, 'What is his name?' what shall I say unto them?" And God said unto Moses, "I AM THAT I AM": and he said, "Thus shalt thou say unto the children of Israel, I AM hath sent me unto you."

Exodus 3:1-14

110   The LORD is slow to anger, and great in power,
          And will not at all acquit the wicked:
      The LORD hath his way in the whirlwind and in the storm,
          And the clouds are the dust of his feet.
      He rebuketh the sea, and maketh it dry,
          And drieth up all the rivers:
      Bashan languisheth, and Carmel,
          And the flower of Lebanon languisheth.
      The mountains quake at him,
          And the hills melt,
      And the earth is burned at his presence,
          Yea, the world, and all that dwell therein.

Nahum 1:3-5

111   And it came to pass, when Moses came down from Mount Sinai with the
      two tables of testimony in Moses' hand, when he came down from the
      mount, that Moses wist* not that the skin of his face shone while he
      talked with him. And when Aaron and all the children of Israel saw Mo-
      ses, behold, the skin of his face shone; and they were afraid to come nigh
      him. And Moses called unto them; and Aaron and all the rulers of the
      congregation returned unto him: and Moses talked with them. And af-
      terward all the children of Israel came nigh: and he gave them in com-
      mandment all that the LORD had spoken with him in mount Sinai. And
      till Moses had done speaking with them, he put a vail* on his face. But
      when Moses went in before the LORD to speak with him, he took the vail
      off, until he came out. And he came out, and spake unto the children of
      Israel that which he was commanded. And the children of Israel saw the

face of Moses, that the skin of Moses' face shone: and Moses put the vail upon his face again, until he went in to speak with him.

Exodus 34:29-35

112 Seeing then that we have such hope, we use great plainness of speech: And not as Moses, which put a vail* over his face, that the children of Israel could not stedfastly look to the end of that which is abolished: But their minds were blinded: for until this day remaineth the same vail untaken away in the reading of the old testament; which vail is done away in Christ. But even unto this day, when Moses is read, the vail is upon their heart. Nevertheless when it shall turn to the Lord, the vail shall be taken away. Now the Lord is that Spirit: and where the Spirit of the Lord is, there is liberty. But we all, with open face beholding as in a glass the glory of the Lord, are changed into the same image from glory to glory, even as by the Spirit of the Lord.

2 Corinthians 3:12-18

113 And [Elijah] arose, and did eat and drink, and went in the strength of that meat* forty days and forty nights unto Horeb the mount of God. And he came thither unto a cave, and lodged there; and, behold, the word of the LORD came to him, and he said unto him, "What doest thou here, Elijah?" And he said, "I have been very jealous* for the LORD God of hosts: for the children of Israel have forsaken thy covenant, thrown down thine altars, and slain thy prophets with the sword; and I, even I only, am left; and they seek my life, to take it away." And he said, "Go forth, and stand upon the mount before the LORD." And, behold, the

LORD passed by, and a great and strong wind rent the mountains, and brake in pieces the rocks before the LORD; but the LORD was not in the wind: and after the wind an earthquake; but the LORD was not in the earthquake: And after the earthquake a fire; but the LORD was not in the fire: and after the fire a still small voice. And it was so, when Elijah heard it, that he wrapped his face in his mantle, and went out, and stood in the entering in of the cave. . . . And the LORD said unto him, "Go, return on thy way to the wilderness of Damascus: and when thou comest, anoint Hazael to be king over Syria: And Jehu the son of Nimshi shalt thou anoint to be king over Israel: and Elisha the son of Shaphat of Abel-meholah shalt thou anoint to be prophet in thy room. And it shall come to pass, that him that escapeth the sword of Hazael shall Jehu slay: and him that escapeth from the sword of Jehu shall Elisha slay. Yet I have left me seven thousand in Israel, all the knees which have not bowed unto Baal, and every mouth which hath not kissed him."

1 Kings 19:8-13a, 15-18

114   I say then, Hath God cast away his people? God forbid. For I also am an Israelite, of the seed of Abraham, of the tribe of Benjamin. God hath not cast away his people which he foreknew. Wot* ye not what the scripture saith of Elias*? How he maketh intercession to God against Israel, saying, "Lord, they have killed thy prophets, and digged down thine altars; and I am left alone, and they seek my life." But what saith the answer of God unto him? "I have reserved to myself seven thousand men, who have not bowed the knee to the image of Baal." Even so then at this present time also there is a remnant according to the election of grace. And if by grace, then is it no more of works: otherwise grace is no more grace. But if it be of works, then is it no more grace: otherwise work is no more work.

Romans 11:1-6

115 And it came to pass about an eight days after these sayings, he took Peter and John and James, and went up into a mountain to pray. And as he prayed, the fashion of his countenance was altered, and his raiment was white and glistering. And, behold, there talked with him two men, which were Moses and Elias*: Who appeared in glory, and spake of his decease which he should accomplish at Jerusalem. But Peter and they that were with him were heavy with sleep: and when they were awake, they saw his glory, and the two men that stood with him. And it came to pass, as they departed from him, Peter said unto Jesus, "Master, it is good for us to be here: and let us make three tabernacles*; one for thee, and one for Moses, and one for Elias": not knowing what he said. While he thus spake, there came a cloud, and overshadowed them: and they feared as they entered into the cloud. And there came a voice out of the cloud, saying, "This is my beloved Son: hear him." And when the voice was past, Jesus was found alone. And they kept it close, and told no man in those days any of those things which they had seen.

Luke 9:28-36

116 For he received from God the Father honour and glory, when there came such a voice to him from the excellent glory, "This is my beloved Son, in whom I am well pleased." And this voice which came from heaven we heard, when we were with him in the holy mount. We have also a more sure word of prophecy; whereunto ye do well that ye take heed, as unto a light that shineth in a dark place, until the day dawn, and the day star arise in your hearts.

2 Peter 1:17-19

117 Nevertheless the dimness shall not be such as was in [Judah's] vexation, when at the first he lightly afflicted the land of Zebulun and the land of Naphtali, and afterward did more grievously afflict her by the way of the sea, beyond Jordan, in Galilee of the nations.

> The people that walked in darkness
>> Have seen a great light:
> They that dwell in the land of the shadow of death,
>> Upon them hath the light shined.

Isaiah 9:1-2

118 Now when Jesus had heard that John was cast into prison, he departed into Galilee; and leaving Nazareth, he came and dwelt in Capernaum, which is upon the sea coast, in the borders of Zabulon and Nephthalim: That it might be fulfilled which was spoken by Esaias* the prophet, saying,

> "The land of Zabulon, and the land of Nephthalim,
>> By the way of the sea, beyond Jordan,
>> Galilee of the Gentiles;
> The people which sat in darkness
>> Saw great light;
> And to them which sat in the region and shadow of death
>> Light is sprung up.

From that time Jesus began to preach, and to say, "Repent: for the kingdom of heaven is at hand."

Matthew 4:12-17

119 The Spirit of the Lord GOD is upon me;
    Because the LORD hath anointed me
To preach good tidings unto the meek;
    He hath sent me to bind up the brokenhearted,
To proclaim liberty to the captives,
    And the opening of the prison to them that are bound;
To proclaim the acceptable year of the LORD,
    And the day of vengeance of our God;
    To comfort all that mourn;
To appoint unto them that mourn in Zion,
    To give unto them beauty for ashes,
The oil of joy for mourning,
    The garment of praise for the spirit of heaviness;
That they might be called trees of righteousness,
    The planting of the LORD, that he might be glorified.

Isaiah 61:1-3

120 And [Jesus] came to Nazareth, where he had been brought up: and, as his custom was, he went into the synagogue on the sabbath day, and stood up for to read. And there was delivered unto him the book of the prophet Esaias*. And when he had opened the book, he found the place where it was written,

"The Spirit of the Lord is upon me,
Because he hath anointed me to preach the gospel to the poor;
He hath sent me to heal the brokenhearted,
To preach deliverance to the captives,
And recovering of sight to the blind,

>To set at liberty them that are bruised,
>To preach the acceptable year of the Lord."

And he closed the book, and he gave it again to the minister, and sat down. And the eyes of all them that were in the synagogue were fastened on him. And he began to say unto them, "This day is this scripture fulfilled in your ears."

Luke 4:16-21

121   Listen, O isles, unto me;
>And hearken, ye people, from far;
The LORD hath called me from the womb;
>From the bowels* of my mother hath he made mention
>>of my name.
And he hath made my mouth like a sharp sword;
>In the shadow of his hand hath he hid me,
And made me a polished shaft;
>In his quiver hath he hid me;
And said unto me, "Thou art my servant,
>O Israel, in whom I will be glorified."

Isaiah 49:1-3

122   And all bare [Jesus] witness, and wondered at the gracious words which proceeded out of his mouth. And they said, "Is not this Joseph's son?" And he said unto them, "Ye will surely say unto me this proverb, 'Physician, heal thyself: whatsoever we have heard done in Capernaum, do also

here in thy country.'" And he said, "Verily I say unto you, No prophet is accepted in his own country. But I tell you of a truth, many widows were in Israel in the days of Elias*, when the heaven was shut up three years and six months, when great famine was throughout all the land; but unto none of them was Elias sent, save unto Sarepta, a city of Sidon, unto a woman that was a widow. And many lepers were in Israel in the time of Eliseus* the prophet; and none of them was cleansed, saving Naaman the Syrian." And all they in the synagogue, when they heard these things, were filled with wrath, and rose up, and thrust him out of the city, and led him unto the brow of the hill whereon their city was built, that they might cast him down headlong. But he passing through the midst of them went his way.

Luke 4:22-30

123   Then I said, "I have laboured in vain,
    I have spent my strength for nought, and in vain:
Yet surely my judgment is with the LORD,
    And my work with my God."
And now, saith the LORD
    That formed me from the womb
      To be his servant,
To bring Jacob again to him,
    Though Israel be not gathered,
Yet shall I be glorious in the eyes of the LORD,
    And my God shall be my strength.
And he said,
"It is a light thing that thou shouldest be my servant
    To raise up the tribes of Jacob,

And to restore the preserved of Israel:
I will also give thee for a light to the Gentiles,
  That thou mayest be my salvation unto the end of the earth."

Isaiah 49:4-6

124 Then the eleven disciples went away into Galilee, into a mountain where Jesus had appointed them. And when they saw him, they worshipped him: but some doubted. And Jesus came and spake unto them, saying, "All power is given unto me in heaven and in earth. Go ye therefore, and teach all nations, baptizing them in the name of the Father, and of the Son, and of the Holy Ghost: Teaching them to observe all things whatsoever I have commanded you: and, lo, I am with you always, even unto the end of the world. Amen."

Matthew 28:16-20

125 Then the word of the LORD came unto me, saying,
    "Before I formed thee in the belly
        I knew thee;
    And before thou camest forth out of the womb
        I sanctified thee,
    And I ordained thee a prophet unto the nations."
Then said I, "Ah, Lord GOD! Behold, I cannot speak:
        for I am a child." But the LORD said unto me,
    "Say not, 'I am a child':
    For thou shalt go to all that I shall send thee,
    And whatsoever I command thee thou shalt speak.

Be not afraid of their faces:
>For I am with thee to deliver thee," saith the LORD.
Then the LORD put forth his hand, and touched my mouth.
>And the LORD said unto me,
"Behold, I have put my words in thy mouth.
>See, I have this day set thee over the nations and over
>>the kingdoms,
>To root out, and to pull down,
>And to destroy, and to throw down,
>To build, and to plant."

Jeremiah 1:4-10

126 But I [Paul] certify you, brethren, that the gospel which was preached of me is not after man. For I neither received it of man, neither was I taught it, but by the revelation of Jesus Christ. For ye have heard of my conversation in time past in the Jews' religion, how that beyond measure I persecuted the church of God, and wasted* it: and profited in the Jews' religion above many my equals in mine own nation, being more exceedingly zealous of the traditions of my fathers. But when it pleased God, who separated me from my mother's womb, and called me by his grace, to reveal his Son in me, that I might preach him among the heathen; immediately I conferred not with flesh and blood: Neither went I up to Jerusalem to them which were apostles before me; but I went into Arabia, and returned again unto Damascus.

Galatians 1:11-17

127 And Job spake, and said,

"Let the day perish wherein I was born,
    And the night in which it was said,
    'There is a man child conceived.'
Let that day be darkness;
    Let not God regard it from above,
    Neither let the light shine upon it.
Let darkness and the shadow of death stain it;
    Let a cloud dwell upon it;
    Let the blackness of the day terrify it.
As for that night, let darkness seize upon it;
    Let it not be joined unto the days of the year,
    Let it not come into the number of the months.
Lo, let that night be solitary,
    Let no joyful voice come therein.
Let them curse it that curse the day,
    Who are ready to raise up their mourning.
Let the stars of the twilight thereof be dark;
    Let it look for light, but have none;
    Neither let it see the dawning of the day:
Because it shut not up the doors of my mother's womb,
    Nor hid sorrow from mine eyes."

Job 3:2-10

128 If any other man thinketh that he hath whereof he might trust in the flesh, I [Paul] more: Circumcised the eighth day, of the stock of Israel, of the tribe of Benjamin, an Hebrew of the Hebrews; as touching* the law, a Pharisee; Concerning zeal, persecuting the church; touching the righteousness which is in the law, blameless. But what things were gain to me, those I counted loss for Christ. Yea doubtless, and I count all things but loss for the excellency of the knowledge of Christ Jesus my Lord: for whom I have suffered the loss of all things, and do count them but dung, that I may win Christ, and be found in him, not having mine own righteousness, which is of the law, but that which is through the faith of Christ, the righteousness which is of God by faith: That I may know him, and the power of his resurrection, and the fellowship of his sufferings, being made conformable unto his death; If by any means I might attain unto the resurrection of the dead.

Philippians 3:4b-11

129 For thou hast possessed my reins:
    Thou hast covered me in my mother's womb.
I will praise thee; for I am fearfully and wonderfully made:
    Marvellous are thy works;
    And that my soul knoweth right well.
My substance was not hid from thee,
    When I was made in secret,
    And curiously wrought in the lowest parts of the earth.

Psalm 139:13-15

130 And Saul, yet breathing out threatenings and slaughter against the disciples of the Lord, went unto the high priest, and desired of him letters to
Damascus to the synagogues, that if he found any of this way, whether
they were men or women, he might bring them bound unto Jerusalem.
And as he journeyed, he came near Damascus: and suddenly there shined
round about him a light from heaven: And he fell to the earth, and heard
a voice saying unto him, "Saul, Saul, why persecutest thou me?" And he
said, "Who art thou, Lord?" And the Lord said, "I am Jesus whom thou
persecutest: it is hard for thee to kick against the pricks." And he trembling and astonished said, "Lord, what wilt thou have me to do?" And
the Lord said unto him, "Arise, and go into the city, and it shall be told
thee what thou must do." And the men which journeyed with him stood
speechless, hearing a voice, but seeing no man. And Saul arose from the
earth; and when his eyes were opened, he saw no man: but they led him
by the hand, and brought him into Damascus. And he was three days
without sight, and neither did eat nor drink.

Acts 9:1-9

131 And the child Samuel ministered unto the LORD before Eli. And the
word of the LORD was precious* in those days; there was no open vision.
And it came to pass at that time, when Eli was laid down in his place, and
his eyes began to wax dim, that he could not see; and ere the lamp of God
went out in the temple of the LORD, where the ark of God was, and Samuel was laid down to sleep; that the LORD called, "Samuel": and he answered, "Here am I." And he ran unto Eli, and said, "Here am I; for thou
calledst me." And he said, "I called not; lie down again." And he went
and lay down. And the LORD called yet again, "Samuel." And Samuel
arose and went to Eli, and said, "Here am I; for thou didst call me." And

he answered, "I called not, my son; lie down again." Now Samuel did not yet know the LORD, neither was the word of the LORD yet revealed unto him. And the LORD called Samuel again the third time. And he arose and went to Eli, and said, "Here am I; for thou didst call me." And Eli perceived that the LORD had called the child. Therefore Eli said unto Samuel, "Go, lie down: and it shall be, if he call thee, that thou shalt say, 'Speak, LORD; for thy servant heareth.'" So Samuel went and lay down in his place.

1 Samuel 3:1-9

132 And there was a certain disciple at Damascus, named Ananias; and to him said the Lord in a vision, "Ananias." And he said, "Behold, I am here, Lord." And the Lord said unto him, "Arise, and go into the street which is called Straight, and inquire in the house of Judas for one called Saul, of Tarsus: for, behold, he prayeth, and hath seen in a vision a man named Ananias coming in, and putting his hand on him, that he might receive his sight." Then Ananias answered, "Lord, I have heard by many of this man, how much evil he hath done to thy saints at Jerusalem: And here he hath authority from the chief priests to bind all that call on thy name." But the Lord said unto him, "Go thy way: for he is a chosen vessel unto me, to bear my name before the Gentiles, and kings, and the children of Israel: For I will shew him how great things he must suffer for my name's sake." And Ananias went his way, and entered into the house; and putting his hands on him said, "Brother Saul, the Lord, even Jesus, that appeared unto thee in the way as thou camest, hath sent me, that thou mightest receive thy sight, and be filled with the Holy Ghost." And immediately there fell from his eyes as it had been scales: and he received sight forthwith, and arose, and was baptized. And when he had received meat*, he was strengthened. Then was Saul certain days with the disciples which were at Damascus

Acts 9:10-19

133   And the LORD came, and stood, and called as at other times, "Samuel, Samuel." Then Samuel answered, "Speak; for thy servant heareth." And the LORD said to Samuel, "Behold, I will do a thing in Israel, at which both the ears of every one that heareth it shall tingle. In that day I will perform against Eli all things which I have spoken concerning his house: when I begin, I will also make an end. For I have told him that I will judge his house for ever for the iniquity which he knoweth; because his sons made themselves vile, and he restrained them not. And therefore I have sworn unto the house of Eli, that the iniquity of Eli's house shall not be purged with sacrifice nor offering for ever." And Samuel lay until the morning, and opened the doors of the house of the LORD. And Samuel feared to shew Eli the vision. Then Eli called Samuel, and said, "Samuel, my son." And he answered, "Here am I." And he said, "What is the thing that the LORD hath said unto thee? I pray thee hide it not from me: God do so to thee, and more also, if thou hide any thing from me of all the things that he said unto thee." And Samuel told him every whit, and hid nothing from him. And he said, "It is the LORD: let him do what seemeth him good."

1 Samuel 3:10-18

134 "But I say unto you which hear, Love your enemies, do good to them which hate you, bless them that curse you, and pray for them which despitefully use you. And unto him that smiteth thee on the one cheek offer also the other; and him that taketh away thy cloke* forbid not to take thy coat also. Give to every man that asketh of thee; and of him that taketh away thy goods ask them not again. And as ye would that men should do to you, do ye also to them likewise."

Luke 6:27-31

135 For the day of the LORD is near upon all the heathen:
　　As thou hast done, it shall be done unto thee:
　　Thy reward shall return upon thine own head.

Obadiah 15

136 Woe unto you that desire the day of the LORD!
　　To what end is it for you?
The day of the LORD is darkness, and not light.
　　As if a man did flee from a lion,
　　and a bear met him;
Or went into the house, and leaned his hand on the wall,
　　And a serpent bit him.
Shall not the day of the LORD be darkness, and not light?
　　Even very dark, and no brightness in it?

Amos 5:18-20

137 For yourselves know perfectly that the day of the Lord so cometh as a thief in the night. For when they shall say, "Peace and safety"; then sudden destruction cometh upon them, as travail upon a woman with child; and they shall not escape. But ye, brethren, are not in darkness, that that day should overtake you as a thief. Ye are all the children of light, and the children of the day: we are not of the night, nor of darkness. Therefore let us not sleep, as do others; but let us watch and be sober. For they that sleep sleep in the night; and they that be drunken are drunken in the night. But let us, who are of the day, be sober, putting on the breastplate of faith and love; and for an helmet, the hope of salvation. For God hath not appointed us to wrath, but to obtain salvation by our Lord Jesus Christ, who died for us, that, whether we wake or sleep, we should live together with him. Wherefore comfort yourselves together, and edify one another, even as also ye do.

1 Thessalonians 5:2-11

138 Then came there two women, that were harlots, unto [Solomon] the king, and stood before him. And the one woman said, "O my lord, I and this woman dwell in one house; and I was delivered of a child with her in the house. And it came to pass the third day after that I was delivered, that this woman was delivered also: and we were together; there was no stranger with us in the house, save we two in the house. And this woman's child died in the night; because she overlaid* it. And she arose at midnight, and took my son from beside me, while thine handmaid slept, and laid it in her bosom, and laid her dead child in my bosom. And when I rose in the morning to give my child suck, behold, it was dead: but when I had considered it in the morning, behold, it was not my son, which I did bear." And the other woman said, "Nay; but the living is my son, and the dead is thy son." And this said, "No; but the dead is thy son, and the living is my son." Thus they spake before the king. Then said the king, "The one saith, 'This is my son that liveth, and thy son is the dead': and the other saith, 'Nay; but thy son is the dead, and my son is the living.'" And the king said, "Bring me a sword." And they brought a sword before the king.

1 Kings 3:16-24

139 "Then shall the kingdom of heaven be likened unto ten virgins, which took their lamps, and went forth to meet the bridegroom. And five of them were wise, and five were foolish. They that were foolish took their lamps, and took no oil with them: But the wise took oil in their vessels with their lamps. While the bridegroom tarried, they all slumbered and slept. And at midnight there was a cry made, 'Behold, the bridegroom cometh; go ye out to meet him.' Then all those virgins arose, and trimmed their lamps. And the foolish said unto the wise, 'Give us of your oil; for our lamps are gone out.' But the wise answered, saying, 'Not so; lest there be not enough for us and you: but go ye rather to them that sell, and buy for yourselves.' And while they went to buy, the bridegroom came; and they that were ready went in with him to the marriage: and the door was shut. Afterward came also the other virgins, saying, 'Lord, Lord, open to us.' But he answered and said, 'Verily I say unto you, I know you not.' Watch therefore, for ye know neither the day nor the hour wherein the Son of man cometh."

Matthew 25:1-13

140   And the king said, "Divide the living child in two, and give half to the
one, and half to the other." Then spake the woman whose the living child
was unto the king, for her bowels* yearned upon her son, and she said,
"O my lord, give her the living child, and in no wise* slay it." But the
other said, "Let it be neither mine nor thine, but divide it." Then the
king answered and said, "Give her the living child, and in no wise slay it:
she is the mother thereof." And all Israel heard of the judgment which
the king had judged; and they feared the king: for they saw that the wisdom of God was in him, to do judgment.

1 Kings 3:25-28

141   Awake thou that sleepest, and arise from the dead,
        And Christ shall give thee light.

Ephesians 5:14

142   "For as the rain cometh down, and the snow from heaven,
        And returneth not thither, but watereth the earth,
    And maketh it bring forth and bud,
        That it may give seed to the sower, and bread to the eater:
    So shall my word be that goeth forth out of my mouth:
        It shall not return unto me void,
    But it shall accomplish that which I please,
        And it shall prosper in the thing whereto I sent it."

Isaiah 55:10-11

The Second Day

A Divine Ecology

Judgment and Separation

Shelter and Protection

God's Kingdom and Mundane Principalities

Covenant, Passover, and Atonement

WHY IS THE SKY BLUE? Because, reasoned the Hebrew people, there's water up there. Then why doesn't it rain nonstop? Because, they supposed, God has installed a celestial, transparent dome with windows, which at divine discretion are opened for rain and snow to replenish the earth's lakes and seas.

At the heart of this ingenious notion of a firmament lies an important confession: God is committed to creation's maintenance. The many social covenants that the Creator initiates with his creatures — with Noah and his family, with Abraham and his sons Ishmael and Isaac, with Moses and a wilderness people, with David and his lineage, with Jeremiah and a deported Israel, with Jesus and his church — testify to God's relentless bonding of himself to creation's health and well-being. Human ecology coheres with God's beneficent coordination of the natural world.

Contracts with mortal flesh are broken all too easily. Thirsting for God, human beings repeatedly look for springs of eternal life in all the wrong places. Humanity's annulment of divine covenants yields devastating consequences: watery chaos, exile, and death. Because God is God, judgment creates surprising occasions for merciful renewal of a wayward creation to which the Almighty has irrevocably committed himself.

143   And God said, "Let there be a firmament in the midst of the waters, and
      let it divide the waters from the waters." And God made the firmament,
      and divided the waters which were under the firmament from the waters
      which were above the firmament: and it was so. And God called the fir-
      mament Heaven. And the evening and the morning were the second day.

Genesis 1:6-8

144   The heavens declare the glory of God;
          And the firmament sheweth his handywork.
      Day unto day uttereth speech,
          And night unto night sheweth knowledge.
      There is no speech nor language,
          Where their voice is not heard. . . .
      Who can understand his errors?
          Cleanse thou me from secret faults.
      Keep back thy servant also from presumptuous sins;
          Let them not have dominion over me:
      Then shall I be upright,
          And I shall be innocent from the great transgression.
      Let the words of my mouth, and the meditation of my heart,
          Be acceptable in thy sight,
      O LORD, my strength, and my redeemer.

Psalm 19:1-3, 12-14

145 And GOD saw that the wickedness of man was great in the earth, and that every imagination of the thoughts of his heart was only evil continually. And it repented the LORD that he had made man on the earth, and it grieved him at his heart. And the LORD said, "I will destroy man whom I have created from the face of the earth; both man, and beast, and the creeping thing, and the fowls of the air; for it repenteth me that I have made them." But Noah found grace in the eyes of the LORD.

Genesis 6:5-8

146 The fool hath said in his heart,
　　"There is no God."
They are corrupt,
　　They have done abominable works,
　　There is none that doeth good.
The LORD looked down from heaven
　　Upon the children of men,
To see if there were any that did understand,
　　And seek God.
They are all gone aside, they are all together become filthy:
　　There is none that doeth good, no, not one.

Psalm 14:1-3

147 What then? Are we better than they? No, in no wise*: for we have before proved both Jews and Gentiles, that they are all under sin; . . . But now the righteousness of God without the law is manifested, being witnessed by the law and the prophets; even the righteousness of God which is by faith of Jesus Christ unto all and upon all them that believe: for there is no difference: For all have sinned, and come short of the glory of God; being justified freely by his grace through the redemption that is in Christ Jesus: Whom God hath set forth to be a propitiation through faith in his blood, to declare his righteousness for the remission of sins that are past, through the forbearance of God; To declare, I say, at this time his righteousness: that he might be just, and the justifier of him which believeth in Jesus.

Romans 3:9, 21-26

148 And the LORD said unto Noah, "Come thou and all thy house into the ark; for thee have I seen righteous before me in this generation. Of every clean beast thou shalt take to thee by sevens, the male and his female: and of beasts that are not clean by two, the male and his female. Of fowls also of the air by sevens, the male and the female; to keep seed alive upon the face of all the earth. For yet seven days, and I will cause it to rain upon the earth forty days and forty nights; and every living substance that I have made will I destroy from off the face of the earth." And Noah did according unto all that the LORD commanded him. . . . And it came to pass after seven days, that the waters of the flood were upon the earth. In the six hundredth year of Noah's life, in the second month, the seventeenth day of the month, the same day were all the fountains of the great deep broken up, and the windows of heaven were opened. . . . And the flood was forty days upon the earth; and the waters increased, and bare up the ark, and it was lift up above the earth.

Genesis 7:1-5, 10-11, 17

149 "Behold, God is great, and we know him not,
    Neither can the number of his years be searched out.
For he maketh small the drops of water:
    They pour down rain according to the vapour thereof:
Which the clouds do drop
    And distil upon man abundantly. . . .
At this also my heart trembleth,
    And is moved out of his place.
Hear attentively the noise of his voice,
    And the sound that goeth out of his mouth.
He directeth it under the whole heaven,
    And his lightning unto the ends of the earth.
After it a voice roareth:
    He thundereth with the voice of his excellency;
    And he will not stay them when his voice is heard.
God thundereth marvellously with his voice;
    Great things doeth he, which we cannot comprehend."

Job 36:26-28; 37:1-5

150 "When the Son of man shall come in his glory, and all the holy angels
with him, then shall he sit upon the throne of his glory: And before him
shall be gathered all nations: and he shall separate them one from another, as a shepherd divideth his sheep from the goats: And he shall set
the sheep on his right hand, but the goats on the left. Then shall the King
say unto them on his right hand, 'Come, ye blessed of my Father, inherit
the kingdom prepared for you from the foundation of the world: For I
was an hungred, and ye gave me meat*: I was thirsty, and ye gave me
drink: I was a stranger, and ye took me in: Naked, and ye clothed me: I

was sick, and ye visited me: I was in prison, and ye came unto me.' Then shall the righteous answer him, saying, 'Lord, when saw we thee an hungred, and fed thee? Or thirsty, and gave thee drink? When saw we thee a stranger, and took thee in? Or naked, and clothed thee? Or when saw we thee sick, or in prison, and came unto thee?' And the King shall answer and say unto them, 'Verily I say unto you, Inasmuch as ye have done it unto one of the least of these my brethren, ye have done it unto me.' Then shall he say also unto them on the left hand, 'Depart from me, ye cursed, into everlasting fire, prepared for the devil and his angels: For I was an hungred, and ye gave me no meat: I was thirsty, and ye gave me no drink: I was a stranger, and ye took me not in: naked, and ye clothed me not: sick, and in prison, and ye visited me not.' Then shall they also answer him, saying, 'Lord, when saw we thee an hungred, or athirst, or a stranger, or naked, or sick, or in prison, and did not minister unto thee?' Then shall he answer them, saying, 'Verily I say unto you, Inasmuch as ye did it not to one of the least of these, ye did it not to me.' And these shall go away into everlasting punishment: but the righteous into life eternal."

Matthew 25:31-46

151   Save me, O God;
> For the waters are come in unto my soul.

I sink in deep mire,
> Where there is no standing:

I am come into deep waters,
> Where the floods overflow me.

I am weary of my crying:
> My throat is dried:
> Mine eyes fail while I wait for my God.

Psalm 69:1-3

152 And the waters prevailed, and were increased greatly upon the earth; and the ark went upon the face of the waters. And the waters prevailed exceedingly upon the earth; and all the high hills, that were under the whole heaven, were covered. . . . And all flesh died that moved upon the earth, both of fowl, and of cattle, and of beast, and of every creeping thing that creepeth upon the earth, and every man: All in whose nostrils was the breath of life, of all that was in the dry land, died. And every living substance was destroyed which was upon the face of the ground, both man, and cattle, and the creeping things, and the fowl of the heaven; and they were destroyed from the earth: and Noah only remained alive, and they that were with him in the ark.

Genesis 7:18-19, 21-23

153 Deep calleth unto deep
    At the noise of thy waterspouts:
All thy waves and thy billows
    Are gone over me.
Yet the LORD will command his lovingkindness in the day time,
    And in the night his song shall be with me,
    And my prayer unto the God of my life.
I will say unto God my rock, "Why hast thou forgotten me?
    Why go I mourning because of the oppression of the enemy?"
As with a sword in my bones,
    Mine enemies reproach me;
While they say daily unto me,
    "Where is thy God?"
Why art thou cast down, O my soul?
    And why art thou disquieted within me?

Hope thou in God: for I shall yet praise him,
    Who is the health of my countenance, and my God.

Psalm 42:7-11

154   And it came to pass at the end of forty days, that Noah opened the window of the ark which he had made: And he sent forth a raven, which went forth to and fro, until the waters were dried up from off the earth. Also he sent forth a dove from him, to see if the waters were abated from off the face of the ground; but the dove found no rest for the sole of her foot, and she returned unto him into the ark, for the waters were on the face of the whole earth: then he put forth his hand, and took her, and pulled her in unto him into the ark. And he stayed yet other seven days; and again he sent forth the dove out of the ark; and the dove came in to him in the evening; and, lo, in her mouth was an olive leaf pluckt off: so Noah knew that the waters were abated from off the earth. And he stayed yet other seven days; and sent forth the dove; which returned not again unto him any more. And it came to pass in the six hundredth and first year, in the first month, the first day of the month, the waters were dried up from off the earth: and Noah removed the covering of the ark, and looked, and, behold, the face of the ground was dry.

Genesis 8:6-13

155   "Or who shut up the sea with doors, when it brake forth,
        As if it had issued out of the womb?
    When I made the cloud the garment thereof,
        And thick darkness a swaddlingband for it,

And brake up for it my decreed place,
    And set bars and doors,
And said, 'Hitherto shalt thou come, but no further:
    And here shall thy proud waves be stayed?' . . .
Knowest thou the ordinances of heaven?
    Canst thou set the dominion thereof in the earth?"

Job 38:8-11, 33

156 And Noah builded an altar unto the LORD; and took of every clean beast, and of every clean fowl, and offered burnt offerings on the altar. And the LORD smelled a sweet savour; and the LORD said in his heart, "I will not again curse the ground any more for man's sake; for the imagination of man's heart is evil from his youth; neither will I again smite any more every thing living, as I have done. While the earth remaineth, seedtime and harvest, and cold and heat, and summer and winter, and day and night shall not cease."

Genesis 8:20-22

157 "The LORD is my rock, and my fortress, and my deliverer;
    The God of my rock; in him will I trust:
He is my shield, and the horn of my salvation,
    My high tower, and my refuge,
    My saviour; thou savest me from violence.
I will call on the LORD, who is worthy to be praised:
    So shall I be saved from mine enemies.
When the waves of death compassed me,

    The floods of ungodly men made me afraid;
The sorrows of hell compassed me about;
    The snares of death prevented* me;
In my distress I called upon the LORD,
    And cried to my God.
And he did hear my voice out of his temple,
    And my cry did enter into his ears."

2 Samuel 22:2-7

158   And God spake unto Noah, and to his sons with him, saying, "And I, behold, I establish my covenant with you, and with your seed after you; and with every living creature that is with you, of the fowl, of the cattle, and of every beast of the earth with you; from all that go out of the ark, to every beast of the earth. And I will establish my covenant with you; neither shall all flesh be cut off any more by the waters of a flood; neither shall there any more be a flood to destroy the earth." And God said, "This is the token of the covenant which I make between me and you and every living creature that is with you, for perpetual generations: I do set my bow in the cloud, and it shall be for a token of a covenant between me and the earth. And it shall come to pass, when I bring a cloud over the earth, that the bow shall be seen in the cloud: And I will remember my covenant, which is between me and you and every living creature of all flesh; and the waters shall no more become a flood to destroy all flesh."

Genesis 9:8-15

159 "For this is as the waters of Noah unto me:
For as I have sworn that the waters of Noah
Should no more go over the earth;
So have I sworn that I would not be wroth* with thee,
Nor rebuke thee.
For the mountains shall depart,
And the hills be removed;
But my kindness shall not depart from thee,
Neither shall the covenant of my peace be removed,"
saith the LORD that hath mercy on thee.

Isaiah 54:9-10

160 "But if from thence thou shalt seek the LORD thy God, thou shalt find him, if thou seek him with all thy heart and with all thy soul. When thou art in tribulation, and all these things are come upon thee, even in the latter days, if thou turn to the LORD thy God, and shalt be obedient unto his voice; For the LORD thy God is a merciful God; he will not forsake thee, neither destroy thee, nor forget the covenant of thy fathers which he sware unto them."

Deuteronomy 4:29-31

161 For it is better, if the will of God be so, that ye suffer for well doing, than for evil doing. For Christ also hath once suffered for sins, the just for the unjust, that he might bring us to God, being put to death in the flesh, but quickened* by the Spirit: By which also he went and preached unto the spirits in prison; which sometime were disobedient, when once the longsuffering of God waited in the days of Noah, while the ark was a preparing, wherein few, that is, eight souls were saved by water. The like figure whereunto even baptism doth also now save us, not the putting away of the filth of the flesh, but the answer of a good conscience toward God, by the resurrection of Jesus Christ: Who is gone into heaven, and is on the right hand of God; angels and authorities and powers being made subject unto him.

1 Peter 3:17-22

162   "And thou shalt speak and say before the LORD thy God, 'A Syrian ready to perish was my father, and he went down into Egypt, and sojourned there with a few, and became there a nation, great, mighty, and populous: And the Egyptians evil entreated us, and afflicted us, and laid upon us hard bondage: And when we cried unto the LORD God of our fathers, the LORD heard our voice, and looked on our affliction, and our labour, and our oppression: And the LORD brought us forth out of Egypt with a mighty hand, and with an outstretched arm, and with great terribleness, and with signs, and with wonders: And he hath brought us into this place, and hath given us this land, even a land that floweth with milk and honey.'"

Deuteronomy 26:5-9

163   And it came to pass, that, as he was praying in a certain place, when he ceased, one of his disciples said unto him, "Lord, teach us to pray, as John also taught his disciples." And he said unto them, "When ye pray, say, 'Our Father which art in heaven, hallowed be thy name. Thy kingdom come. Thy will be done, as in heaven, so in earth. Give us day by day our daily bread. And forgive us our sins; for we also forgive every one that is indebted to us. And lead us not into temptation; but deliver us from evil.'"

Luke 11:1-4

164 And when Pharaoh drew nigh, the children of Israel lifted up their eyes, and, behold, the Egyptians marched after them; and they were sore afraid: and the children of Israel cried out unto the LORD. And they said unto Moses, "Because there were no graves in Egypt, hast thou taken us away to die in the wilderness? Wherefore* hast thou dealt thus with us, to carry us forth out of Egypt? Is not this the word that we did tell thee in Egypt, saying, 'Let us alone, that we may serve the Egyptians?' For it had been better for us to serve the Egyptians, than that we should die in the wilderness." And Moses said unto the people, "Fear ye not, stand still, and see the salvation of the LORD, which he will shew to you to day: for the Egyptians whom ye have seen to day, ye shall see them again no more for ever. The LORD shall fight for you, and ye shall hold your peace."

Exodus 14:10-14

165 And they were in the way going up to Jerusalem; and Jesus went before them: and they were amazed; and as they followed, they were afraid. And he took again the twelve, and began to tell them what things should happen unto him, saying, "Behold, we go up to Jerusalem; and the Son of man shall be delivered unto the chief priests, and unto the scribes; and they shall condemn him to death, and shall deliver him to the Gentiles:

And they shall mock him, and shall scourge him, and shall spit upon him, and shall kill him: and the third day he shall rise again."

And James and John, the sons of Zebedee, come unto him, saying, "Master, we would that thou shouldest do for us whatsoever we shall desire." And he said unto them, "What would ye that I should do for you?" They said unto him, "Grant unto us that we may sit, one on thy right hand, and the other on thy left hand, in thy glory." But Jesus said unto them, "Ye know not what ye ask: Can ye drink of the cup that I drink of? And be baptized with the baptism that I am baptized with?" And they said unto him, "We can." And Jesus said unto them, "Ye shall indeed drink of the cup that I drink of; and with the baptism that I am baptized withal shall ye be baptized: But to sit on my right hand and on my left hand is not mine to give; but it shall be given to them for whom it is prepared."

Mark 10:32-40

166 And Moses stretched out his hand over the sea; and the LORD caused the sea to go back by a strong east wind all that night, and made the sea dry land, and the waters were divided. And the children of Israel went into the midst of the sea upon the dry ground: and the waters were a wall unto them on their right hand, and on their left. . . . And the LORD said unto Moses, "Stretch out thine hand over the sea, that the waters may come again upon the Egyptians, upon their chariots, and upon their horsemen." . . . And the waters returned, and covered the chariots, and the horsemen, and all the host of Pharaoh that came into the sea after them; there remained not so much as one of them.

Exodus 14:21-22, 26, 28

167 What shall we say then? Shall we continue in sin, that grace may abound? God forbid. How shall we, that are dead to sin, live any longer therein? Know ye not, that so many of us as were baptized into Jesus Christ were baptized into his death? Therefore we are buried with him by baptism into death: that like as Christ was raised up from the dead by the glory of the Father, even so we also should walk in newness of life. For if we have been planted together in the likeness of his death, we shall be also in the likeness of his resurrection: Knowing this, that our old man is crucified with him, that the body of sin might be destroyed, that henceforth we should not serve sin. For he that is dead is freed from sin. Now if we be dead with Christ, we believe that we shall also live with him: Knowing that Christ being raised from the dead dieth no more; death hath no more dominion over him. For in that he died, he died unto sin once: but in that he liveth, he liveth unto God. Likewise reckon ye also yourselves to be dead indeed unto sin, but alive unto God through Jesus Christ our Lord.

Romans 6:1-11

168 Then sang Moses and the children of Israel this song unto the LORD, and spake, saying,

> "I will sing unto the LORD, for he hath triumphed gloriously:
>   The horse and his rider hath he thrown into the sea.
> The LORD is my strength and song,
>   And he is become my salvation:
> He is my God, and I will prepare him an habitation;
>   My father's God, and I will exalt him.
> The LORD is a man of war:
>   The LORD is his name. . . .

Thou didst blow with thy wind, the sea covered them:
   They sank as lead in the mighty waters.
Who is like unto thee, O LORD, among the gods?
   Who is like thee, glorious in holiness, fearful in praises,
      doing wonders? . . .
Till thy people pass over, O LORD,
   Till the people pass over, which thou hast purchased.
Thou shalt bring them in, and plant them in the mountain
      of thine inheritance,
   In the place, O LORD, which thou hast made for thee
      to dwell in,
   In the Sanctuary, O LORD, which thy hands have established.
The LORD shall reign for ever and ever."

Exodus 15:1-3, 10-11, 16cd-18

169   Then went the Pharisees, and took counsel how they might entangle [Jesus] in his talk. And they sent out unto him their disciples with the Herodians, saying, "Master, we know that thou art true, and teachest the way of God in truth, neither carest thou for any man: for thou regardest not the person of men. Tell us therefore, What thinkest thou? Is it lawful to give tribute unto Caesar, or not?" But Jesus perceived their wickedness, and said, "Why tempt ye me, ye hypocrites? Shew me the tribute money." And they brought unto him a penny. And he saith unto them, "Whose is this image and superscription?" They say unto him, "Caesar's." Then saith he unto them, "Render therefore unto Caesar the things which are Caesar's; and unto God the things that are God's." When they had heard these words, they marvelled, and left him, and went their way.

Matthew 22:15-22

170   Nebuchadnezzar the king made an image of gold, whose height was threescore cubits*, and the breadth thereof six cubits: he set it up in the plain of Dura, in the province of Babylon. . . . Then Nebuchadnezzar in his rage and fury commanded to bring Shadrach, Meshach, and Abednego. Then they brought these men before the king. Nebuchadnezzar spake and said unto them, "Is it true, O Shadrach, Meshach, and Abednego, do not ye serve my gods, nor worship the golden image which I have set up? Now if ye be ready that at what time ye hear the sound of the cornet, flute, harp, sackbut*, psaltery*, and dulcimer, and all kinds of musick, ye fall down and worship the image which I have made; well: but if ye worship not, ye shall be cast the same hour into the midst of a burning fiery furnace; and who is that God that shall deliver you out of my hands?" Shadrach, Meshach, and Abednego, answered and said to the king, "O Nebuchadnezzar, we are not careful* to answer thee in this matter. If it be so, our God whom we serve is able to deliver us from the burning fiery furnace, and he will deliver us out of thine hand, O king. But if not, be it known unto thee, O king, that we will not serve thy gods, nor worship the golden image which thou hast set up." Then was Nebuchadnezzar full of fury, and the form of his visage was changed against Shadrach, Meshach, and Abednego: therefore he spake, and commanded that they should heat the furnace one seven times more than it was wont to be heated. And he commanded the most mighty men that were in his army to bind Shadrach, Meshach, and Abednego, and to cast them into the burning fiery furnace. Then these men were bound in their coats, their hosen*, and their hats, and their other garments, and were cast into the midst of the burning fiery furnace.

Daniel 3:1, 13-21

171   But now thus saith the LORD that created thee, O Jacob,
   And he that formed thee, O Israel,
"Fear not: for I have redeemed thee,
   I have called thee by thy name; thou art mine.
When thou passest through the waters, I will be with thee;
   And through the rivers, they shall not overflow thee:
When thou walkest through the fire,
   Thou shalt not be burned;
   Neither shall the flame kindle upon thee.
For I am the LORD thy God,
   The Holy One of Israel, thy Saviour."

Isaiah 43:1-3b

172   Then Nebuchadnezzar the king was astonied*, and rose up in haste, and spake, and said unto his counsellors, "Did not we cast three men bound into the midst of the fire?" They answered and said unto the king, "True, O king." He answered and said, "Lo, I see four men loose, walking in the midst of the fire, and they have no hurt; and the form of the fourth is like the Son of God." Then Nebuchadnezzar came near to the mouth of the burning fiery furnace, and spake, and said, "Shadrach, Meshach, and Abednego, ye servants of the most high God, come forth, and come hither." Then Shadrach, Meshach, and Abednego, came forth of the midst of the fire. And the princes, governors, and captains, and the king's counsellors, being gathered together, saw these men, upon whose bodies the fire had no power, nor was an hair of their head singed, neither were their coats changed, nor the smell of fire had passed on them. Then Nebuchadnezzar spake, and said, "Blessed be the God of Shadrach, Meshach, and Abednego, who hath sent his angel, and delivered his servants that trusted in him, and have changed the king's word, and yielded their bodies, that they might not serve nor worship any god, except their own God. Therefore I make a decree, That every people, nation, and language, which speak any thing amiss against the God of Shadrach, Meshach, and Abednego, shall be cut in pieces, and their houses shall be made a dunghill: because there is no other God that can deliver after this sort."

Daniel 3:24-29

173   And when [the temple guard] had brought [the apostles], they set them before the council: and the high priest asked them, saying, "Did not we straitly* command you that ye should not teach in this name? And, behold, ye have filled Jerusalem with your doctrine, and intend to bring this man's blood upon us." Then Peter and the other apostles answered and said, "We ought to obey God rather than men. The God of our fathers raised up Jesus, whom ye slew and hanged on a tree. Him hath God exalted with his right hand to be a Prince and a Saviour, for to give repentance to Israel, and forgiveness of sins. And we are his witnesses of these things; and so is also the Holy Ghost, whom God hath given to them that obey him."

Acts 5:27-32

174   Now when Daniel knew that the writing was signed, he went into his house; and his windows being open in his chamber toward Jerusalem, he kneeled upon his knees three times a day, and prayed, and gave thanks before his God, as he did aforetime. Then these men assembled, and

found Daniel praying and making supplication before his God. Then they came near, and spake before the king concerning the king's decree; "Hast thou not signed a decree, that every man that shall ask a petition of any God or man within thirty days, save of thee, O king, shall be cast into the den of lions?" The king answered and said, "The thing is true, according to the law of the Medes and Persians, which altereth not." Then answered they and said before the king, "That Daniel, which is of the children of the captivity of Judah, regardeth not thee, O king, nor the decree that thou hast signed, but maketh his petition three times a day." Then the king, when he heard these words, was sore displeased with himself, and set his heart on Daniel to deliver him: and he laboured till the going down of the sun to deliver him. Then these men assembled unto the king, and said unto the king, "Know, O king, that the law of the Medes and Persians is, That no decree nor statute which the king establisheth may be changed." Then the king commanded, and they brought Daniel, and cast him into the den of lions. Now the king spake and said unto Daniel, "Thy God whom thou servest continually, he will deliver thee." And a stone was brought and laid upon the mouth of the den; and the king sealed it with his own signet, and with the signet of his lords; that the purpose might not be changed concerning Daniel. Then the king went to his palace, and passed the night fasting: neither were instruments of musick brought before him: and his sleep went from him.

Daniel 6:10-18

175 And it came to pass, as we went to prayer, a certain damsel possessed with a spirit of divination met us, which brought her masters much gain by soothsaying: The same followed Paul and us, and cried, saying, "These men are the servants of the most high God, which shew unto us the way

of salvation." And this did she many days. But Paul, being grieved, turned and said to the spirit, "I command thee in the name of Jesus Christ to come out of her." And he came out the same hour. And when her masters saw that the hope of their gains was gone, they caught Paul and Silas, and drew them into the marketplace unto the rulers, and brought them to the magistrates, saying, "These men, being Jews, do exceedingly trouble our city, and teach customs, which are not lawful for us to receive, neither to observe, being Romans." And the multitude rose up together against them: and the magistrates rent off their clothes, and commanded to beat them. And when they had laid many stripes* upon them, they cast them into prison, charging the jailor to keep them safely: Who, having received such a charge, thrust them into the inner prison, and made their feet fast in the stocks.

Acts 16:16-24

176   Then the king arose very early in the morning, and went in haste unto the den of lions. And when he came to the den, he cried with a lamentable voice unto Daniel: and the king spake and said to Daniel, "O Daniel, servant of the living God, is thy God, whom thou servest continually, able to deliver thee from the lions?" Then said Daniel unto the king, "O king, live for ever. My God hath sent his angel, and hath shut the lions' mouths, that they have not hurt me: forasmuch as before him innocency was found in me; and also before thee, O king, have I done no hurt." Then was the king exceeding glad for him, and commanded that they should take Daniel up out of the den. So Daniel was taken up out of the den, and no manner of hurt was found upon him, because he believed in his God. And the king commanded, and they brought those men which had accused Daniel, and they cast them into the den of lions, them, their

children, and their wives; and the lions had the mastery of them, and brake all their bones in pieces or ever they came at the bottom of the den.

Daniel 6:19-24

177   And at midnight Paul and Silas prayed, and sang praises unto God: and the prisoners heard them. And suddenly there was a great earthquake, so that the foundations of the prison were shaken: and immediately all the doors were opened, and every one's bands were loosed. And the keeper of the prison awaking out of his sleep, and seeing the prison doors open, he drew out his sword, and would have killed himself, supposing that the prisoners had been fled. But Paul cried with a loud voice, saying, "Do thyself no harm: for we are all here." Then he called for a light, and sprang in, and came trembling, and fell down before Paul and Silas, and brought them out, and said, "Sirs, what must I do to be saved?" And they said, "Believe on the Lord Jesus Christ, and thou shalt be saved, and thy house." And they spake unto him the word of the Lord, and to all that were in his house. And he took them the same hour of the night, and washed their stripes*; and was baptized, he and all his, straightway. And when he had brought them into his house, he set meat* before them, and rejoiced, believing in God with all his house.

Acts 16:25-34

178   Belshazzar, whiles* he tasted the wine, commanded to bring the golden and silver vessels which his father Nebuchadnezzar had taken out of the temple which was in Jerusalem; that the king, and his princes, his wives, and his concubines, might drink therein. . . . In the same hour came forth

fingers of a man's hand, and wrote over against the candlestick upon the plaister* of the wall of the king's palace: and the king saw the part of the hand that wrote. Then the king's countenance was changed, and his thoughts troubled him, so that the joints of his loins were loosed, and his knees smote one against another. The king cried aloud to bring in the astrologers, the Chaldeans, and the soothsayers. And the king spake, and said to the wise men of Babylon, "Whosoever shall read this writing, and shew me the interpretation thereof, shall be clothed with scarlet, and have a chain of gold about his neck, and shall be the third ruler in the kingdom." Then came in all the king's wise men: but they could not read the writing, nor make known to the king the interpretation thereof.

Daniel 5:2, 5-8

179 Surely men of low degree are vanity,
   And men of high degree are a lie:
  To be laid in the balance,
   They are altogether lighter than vanity.
  Trust not in oppression,
   And become not vain in robbery:
   If riches increase, set not your heart upon them.
  God hath spoken once;
   Twice have I heard this;
  That power belongeth unto God.
   Also unto thee, O Lord, belongeth mercy:
   For thou renderest to every man according to his work.

Psalm 62:9-12

180 Then Daniel answered and said before the king, "Let thy gifts be to thyself, and give thy rewards to another; yet I will read the writing unto the king, and make known to him the interpretation. . . . And thou his son, O Belshazzar, hast not humbled thine heart, though thou knewest all this; But hast lifted up thyself against the LORD of heaven; and they have brought the vessels of his house before thee, and thou, and thy lords, thy wives, and thy concubines, have drunk wine in them; and thou hast praised the gods of silver, and gold, of brass, iron, wood, and stone, which see not, nor hear, nor know: and the God in whose hand thy breath is, and whose are all thy ways, hast thou not glorified: Then was the part of the hand sent from him; and this writing was written.

> And this is the writing that was written, MENE, MENE,
>   TEKEL, UPHARSIN.
> This is the interpretation of the thing:
> MENE; God hath numbered thy kingdom, and finished it.
> TEKEL; Thou art weighed in the balances, and art
>   found wanting.
> PERES; Thy kingdom is divided, and given to the Medes
>   and Persians."

Then commanded Belshazzar, and they clothed Daniel with scarlet, and put a chain of gold about his neck, and made a proclamation concerning him, that he should be the third ruler in the kingdom. In that night was Belshazzar the king of the Chaldeans slain. And Darius the Median took the kingdom, being about threescore and two years old.

Daniel 5:17, 22-31

181 Then Jacob went on his journey, and came into the land of the people of the east. And he looked, and behold a well in the field, and, lo, there were three flocks of sheep lying by it; for out of that well they watered the flocks.

Genesis 29:1-2

182 Then cometh [Jesus] to a city of Samaria, which is called Sychar, near to the parcel of ground that Jacob gave to his son Joseph. Now Jacob's well was there. Jesus therefore, being wearied with his journey, sat thus on the well: and it was about the sixth hour. There cometh a woman of Samaria to draw water: Jesus saith unto her, "Give me to drink." (For his disciples were gone away unto the city to buy meat*.) Then saith the woman of Samaria unto him, "How is it that thou, being a Jew, askest drink of me, which am a woman of Samaria?" For the Jews have no dealings with the Samaritans. Jesus answered and said unto her, "If thou knewest the gift of God, and who it is that saith to thee, 'Give me to drink'; thou wouldest have asked of him, and he would have given thee living water." The woman saith unto him, "Sir, thou hast nothing to draw with, and the well is deep: from whence then hast thou that living water? Art thou greater than our father Jacob, which gave us the well, and drank thereof himself, and his children, and his cattle?" Jesus answered and said unto her, "Whosoever drinketh of this water shall thirst again: But whosoever drinketh of the water that I shall give him shall never thirst; but the water that I shall give him shall be in him a well of water springing up into everlasting life." The woman saith unto him, "Sir, give me this water, that I thirst not, neither come hither to draw."

John 4:5-15

183 And Jacob said unto them, "My brethren, whence be ye?" And they said, "Of Haran are we." And he said unto them, "Know ye Laban the son of Nahor?" And they said, "We know him." And he said unto them, "Is he well?" And they said, "He is well: and, behold, Rachel his daughter cometh with the sheep." . . . And while he yet spake with them, Rachel came with her father's sheep: for she kept them. And it came to pass, when Jacob saw Rachel the daughter of Laban his mother's brother, and the sheep of Laban his mother's brother, that Jacob went near, and rolled the stone from the well's mouth, and watered the flock of Laban his mother's brother. And Jacob kissed Rachel, and lifted up his voice, and wept. And Jacob told Rachel that he was her father's brother, and that he was Rebekah's son: and she ran and told her father.

Genesis 29:4-6, 9-12

184 Jesus saith unto her, "Go, call thy husband, and come hither." The woman answered and said, "I have no husband." Jesus said unto her, "Thou hast well said, 'I have no husband': For thou hast had five husbands; and he whom thou now hast is not thy husband: in that saidst thou truly." The woman saith unto him, "Sir, I perceive that thou art a prophet. Our fathers worshipped in this mountain; and ye say, that in Jerusalem is the place where men ought to worship." Jesus saith unto her, "Woman, believe me, the hour cometh, when ye shall neither in this mountain, nor yet at Jerusalem, worship the Father. Ye worship ye know not what: we know what we worship: for salvation is of the Jews. But the hour cometh, and now is, when the true worshippers shall worship the Father in spirit and in truth: for the Father seeketh such to worship him. God is a Spirit: and they that worship him must worship him in spirit and in truth." The woman saith unto him, "I know that Messias* cometh, which is called Christ: when he is come, he will tell us all things." Jesus saith unto her, "I that speak unto thee am he."

And upon this came his disciples, and marvelled that he talked with the woman: yet no man said, "What seekest thou?" or, "Why talkest thou with her?" The woman then left her waterpot, and went her way into the city, and saith to the men, "Come, see a man, which told me all things that ever I did: is not this the Christ?" Then they went out of the city, and came unto him.

John 4:16-30

185 Happy is the man that findeth wisdom,
     And the man that getteth understanding.
For the merchandise of it is better than the merchandise of silver,
     And the gain thereof than fine gold.
She is more precious than rubies:
     And all the things thou canst desire are not to be compared
       unto her.

Proverbs 3:13-15

186 The next day John seeth Jesus coming unto him, and saith, "Behold the Lamb of God, which taketh away the sin of the world. This is he of whom I said, 'After me cometh a man which is preferred before me: for he was before me.' And I knew him not: but that he should be made manifest to Israel, therefore am I come baptizing with water." And John bare record, saying, "I saw the Spirit descending from heaven like a dove, and it abode upon him. And I knew him not: but he that sent me to baptize

with water, the same said unto me, 'Upon whom thou shalt see the Spirit descending, and remaining on him, the same is he which baptizeth with the Holy Ghost.' And I saw, and bare record that this is the Son of God." Again the next day after John stood, and two of his disciples; and looking upon Jesus as he walked, he saith, "Behold the Lamb of God!" And the two disciples heard him speak, and they followed Jesus.

John 1:29-37

187   And the LORD answered me, and said,

> "Write the vision,
> > And make it plain upon tables,
> > That he may run that readeth it.
> For the vision is yet for an appointed time,
> > But at the end it shall speak, and not lie:
> Though it tarry, wait for it;
> > Because it will surely come, it will not tarry.
> Behold, his soul which is lifted up is not upright in him:
> > But the just shall live by his faith."

Habakkuk 2:2-4

188   And when Abram was ninety years old and nine, the LORD appeared to Abram, and said unto him, "I am the Almighty God; walk before me, and be thou perfect. And I will make my covenant between me and thee, and will multiply thee exceedingly." And Abram fell on his face: and God talked with him, saying, "As for me, behold, my covenant is with thee,

and thou shalt be a father of many nations. Neither shall thy name any more be called Abram, but thy name shall be Abraham; for a father of many nations have I made thee. And I will make thee exceeding fruitful, and I will make nations of thee, and kings shall come out of thee. And I will establish my covenant between me and thee and thy seed after thee in their generations for an everlasting covenant, to be a God unto thee, and to thy seed after thee. And I will give unto thee, and to thy seed after thee, the land wherein thou art a stranger, all the land of Canaan, for an everlasting possession; and I will be their God."

Genesis 17:1-8

189   For I am not ashamed of the gospel of Christ: for it is the power of God unto salvation to every one that believeth; to the Jew first, and also to the Greek. For therein is the righteousness of God revealed from faith to faith: as it is written, "The just shall live by faith."

Romans 1:16-17

190   Now Sarai Abram's wife bare him no children: and she had an handmaid, an Egyptian, whose name was Hagar. And Sarai said unto Abram, "Behold now, the LORD hath restrained me from bearing: I pray thee, go in unto my maid; it may be that I may obtain children by her." And Abram hearkened to the voice of Sarai. . . . And he went in unto Hagar, and she conceived: and when she saw that she had conceived, her mistress was despised in her eyes.

Genesis 16:1-2, 4

191 "Think not that I am come to send peace on earth: I came not to send peace, but a sword. For I am come to set a man at variance against his father, and the daughter against her mother, and the daughter in law against her mother in law. And a man's foes shall be they of his own household."

Matthew 10:34-36

192 And the LORD visited Sarah as he had said, and the LORD did unto Sarah as he had spoken. For Sarah conceived, and bare Abraham a son in his old age, at the set time of which God had spoken to him. And Abraham called the name of his son that was born unto him, whom Sarah bare to him, Isaac. . . . And Sarah saw [Ishmael] the son of Hagar the Egyptian, which she had born unto Abraham, mocking. Wherefore she said unto Abraham, "Cast out this bondwoman and her son: for the son of this bondwoman shall not be heir with my son, even with Isaac." And the thing was very grievous in Abraham's sight because of his son. And God said unto Abraham, "Let it not be grievous in thy sight because of the lad, and because of thy bondwoman; in all that Sarah hath said unto thee, hearken unto her voice; for in Isaac shall thy seed be called. And also of the son of the bondwoman will I make a nation, because he is thy seed." And Abraham rose up early in the morning, and took bread, and a bottle of water, and gave it unto Hagar, putting it on her shoulder, and the child, and sent her away: and she departed, and wandered in the wilderness of Beersheba.

Genesis 21:1-3, 9-14

193 And when the hour was come, [Jesus] sat down, and the twelve apostles with him. And he said unto them, "With desire I have desired to eat this Passover with you before I suffer: For I say unto you, I will not any more eat thereof, until it be fulfilled in the kingdom of God." And he took the cup, and gave thanks, and said, "Take this, and divide it among yourselves: For I say unto you, I will not drink of the fruit of the vine, until the kingdom of God shall come." And he took bread, and gave thanks, and brake it, and gave unto them, saying, "This is my body which is given for you: this do in remembrance of me." Likewise also the cup after supper, saying, "This cup is the new testament in my blood, which is shed for you. But, behold, the hand of him that betrayeth me is with me on the table. And truly the Son of man goeth, as it was determined: but woe unto that man by whom he is betrayed!" And they began to inquire among themselves, which of them it was that should do this thing.

Luke 22:14-23

194 And it came to pass after these things, that God did tempt Abraham, and said unto him, "Abraham": and he said, "Behold, here I am." And he said, "Take now thy son, thine only son Isaac, whom thou lovest, and get thee into the land of Moriah; and offer him there for a burnt offering upon one of the mountains which I will tell thee of." And Abraham rose up early in the morning, and saddled his ass, and took two of his young men with him, and Isaac his son, and clave the wood for the burnt offering, and rose up, and went unto the place of which God had told him. Then on the third day Abraham lifted up his eyes, and saw the place afar off. And Abraham said unto his young men, "Abide ye here with the ass; and I and the lad will go yonder and worship, and come again to you." And Abraham took the wood of the burnt offering, and laid it upon

Isaac his son; and he took the fire in his hand, and a knife; and they went both of them together. And Isaac spake unto Abraham his father, and said, "My father": and he said, "Here am I, my son." And he said, "Behold the fire and the wood: but where is the lamb for a burnt offering?" And Abraham said, "My son, God will provide himself a lamb for a burnt offering": so they went both of them together. And they came to the place which God had told him of; and Abraham built an altar there, and laid the wood in order, and bound Isaac his son, and laid him on the altar upon the wood. And Abraham stretched forth his hand, and took the knife to slay his son. And the angel of the LORD called unto him out of heaven, and said, "Abraham, Abraham": and he said, "Here am I." And he said, "Lay not thine hand upon the lad, neither do thou any thing unto him: for now I know that thou fearest God, seeing thou hast not withheld thy son, thine only son from me." And Abraham lifted up his eyes, and looked, and behold behind him a ram caught in a thicket by his horns: and Abraham went and took the ram, and offered him up for a burnt offering in the stead of his son.

Genesis 22:1-13

195 The cup of blessing which we bless, is it not the communion of the blood of Christ? The bread which we break, is it not the communion of the body of Christ? For we being many are one bread, and one body: for we are all partakers of that one bread.

1 Corinthians 10:16-17

196   And I looked for some to take pity,
>But there was none;

And for comforters,
>But I found none.

They gave me also gall for my meat*;
>And in my thirst they gave me vinegar to drink.

Psalm 69:20b-21

197   And [Jesus] bearing his cross went forth into a place called the place of a skull, which is called in the Hebrew Golgotha: Where they crucified him, and two other with him, on either side one, and Jesus in the midst. . . . After this, Jesus knowing that all things were now accomplished, that the scripture might be fulfilled, saith, "I thirst." Now there was set a vessel full of vinegar: and they filled a spunge with vinegar, and put it upon hyssop, and put it to his mouth. When Jesus therefore had received the vinegar, he said, "It is finished": and he bowed his head, and gave up the ghost.

John 19:17-18, 28-30

198   Then Moses called for all the elders of Israel, and said unto them, "Draw out and take you a lamb according to your families, and kill the Passover. And ye shall take a bunch of hyssop, and dip it in the blood that is in the bason, and strike the lintel and the two side posts with the blood that is in the bason; and none of you shall go out at the door of his house until the morning. For the LORD will pass through to smite the Egyptians; and when he seeth the blood upon the lintel, and on the two side posts, the LORD will pass over the door, and will not suffer* the destroyer to come in unto your houses to smite you. And ye shall observe this thing for an ordinance to thee and to thy sons for ever. And it shall come to pass, when ye be come to the land which the LORD will give you, according as he hath promised, that ye shall keep this service. And it shall come to pass, when your children shall say unto you, 'What mean ye by this service?' That ye shall say, 'It is the sacrifice of the LORD's Passover, who passed over the houses of the children of Israel in Egypt, when he smote the Egyptians, and delivered our houses.'" And the people bowed the head and worshipped.

Exodus 12:21-27

199 For when Moses had spoken every precept to all the people according to the law, he took the blood of calves and of goats, with water, and scarlet wool, and hyssop, and sprinkled both the book, and all the people, saying, "This is the blood of the testament which God hath enjoined unto you." Moreover he sprinkled with blood both the tabernacle*, and all the vessels of the ministry. And almost all things are by the law purged with blood; and without shedding of blood is no remission.

Hebrews 9:19-22

200 For even Christ our Passover is sacrificed for us: Therefore let us keep the feast, not with old leaven, neither with the leaven of malice and wickedness; but with the unleavened bread of sincerity and truth.

1 Corinthians 5:7b-8

201 The burden of the word of the LORD for Israel, saith the LORD, which stretcheth forth the heavens, and layeth the foundation of the earth, and formeth the spirit of man within him.... "And I will pour upon the house of David, and upon the inhabitants of Jerusalem, the spirit of grace and of supplications: and they shall look upon me whom they have pierced, and they shall mourn for him, as one mourneth for his only son, and shall be in bitterness for him, as one that is in bitterness for his firstborn."

Zechariah 12:1, 10

202 The Jews therefore, because it was the preparation [for Passover], that the bodies should not remain upon the cross on the sabbath day, (for that sabbath day was an high day,) besought Pilate that their legs might be broken, and that they might be taken away. Then came the soldiers, and brake the legs of the first, and of the other which was crucified with him. But when they came to Jesus, and saw that he was dead already, they brake not his legs: But one of the soldiers with a spear pierced his side, and forthwith came there out blood and water. And he that saw it bare record, and his record is true: and he knoweth that he saith true, that ye might believe. For these things were done, that the scripture should be fulfilled, "A bone of him shall not be broken." And again another scripture saith, "They shall look on him whom they pierced."

John 19:31-37

203 Many are the afflictions of the righteous:
        But the LORD delivereth him out of them all.
    He keepeth all his bones:

Not one of them is broken.
Evil shall slay the wicked:
  And they that hate the righteous shall be desolate.
The LORD redeemeth the soul of his servants:
  And none of them that trust in him shall be desolate.

Psalm 34:19-22

204   And after this Joseph of Arimathaea, being a disciple of Jesus, but secretly for fear of the Jews, besought Pilate that he might take away the body of Jesus: and Pilate gave him leave. He came therefore, and took the body of Jesus. And there came also Nicodemus, which at the first came to Jesus by night, and brought a mixture of myrrh and aloes, about an hundred pound weight. Then took they the body of Jesus, and wound it in linen clothes with the spices, as the manner of the Jews is to bury. Now in the place where he was crucified there was a garden; and in the garden a new sepulchre, wherein was never man yet laid. There laid they Jesus therefore because of the Jews' preparation day; for the sepulchre was nigh at hand.

John 19:38-42

205   Set me as a seal upon thine heart,
    As a seal upon thine arm:
For love is strong as death;
    Jealousy is cruel as the grave:
The coals thereof are coals of fire,
    Which hath a most vehement flame.

Many waters cannot quench love,
  Neither can the floods drown it:
If a man would give all the substance of his house for love,
  It would utterly be contemned.

Song of Songs 8:6-7

206   And I beheld, and, lo, in the midst of the throne and of the four beasts, and in the midst of the elders, stood a Lamb as it had been slain, having seven horns and seven eyes, which are the seven Spirits of God sent forth into all the earth. And he came and took the book out of the right hand of him that sat upon the throne. And when he had taken the book, the four beasts and four and twenty elders fell down before the Lamb, having every one of them harps, and golden vials full of odours, which are the prayers of saints. And they sung a new song, saying,

  "Thou art worthy to take the book, and to open the seals
      thereof:
  For thou wast slain, and hast redeemed us to God by thy blood
  Out of every kindred, and tongue, and people, and nation;
  And hast made us unto our God kings and priests:
  And we shall reign on the earth."

Revelation 5:6-10

207   For Christ is not entered into the holy places made with hands, which are the figures of the true; but into heaven itself, now to appear in the presence of God for us: Nor yet that he should offer himself often, as the

high priest entereth into the holy place every year with blood of others; for then must he often have suffered since the foundation of the world: but now once in the end of the world hath he appeared to put away sin by the sacrifice of himself. . . . [We] are sanctified through the offering of the body of Jesus Christ once for all.

Hebrews 9:24-26; 10:10

208   "'I am the LORD thy God, which brought thee out of the land of Egypt, from the house of bondage.

Thou shalt have none other gods before me.

Thou shalt not make thee any graven image, or any likeness of any thing that is in heaven above, or that is in the earth beneath, or that is in the waters beneath the earth: Thou shalt not bow down thyself unto them, nor serve them: for I the LORD thy God am a jealous God, visiting the iniquity of the fathers upon the children unto the third and fourth generation of them that hate me, and shewing mercy unto thousands of them that love me and keep my commandments.

Thou shalt not take the name of the LORD thy God in vain: for the LORD will not hold him guiltless that taketh his name in vain.

Keep the sabbath day to sanctify it, as the LORD thy God hath commanded thee. Six days thou shalt labour, and do all thy work: But the seventh day is the sabbath of the LORD thy God: in it thou shalt not do any work, thou, nor thy son, nor thy daughter, nor thy manservant, nor thy maidservant, nor thine ox, nor thine ass, nor any of thy cattle, nor thy stranger that is within thy gates; that thy manservant and thy maidservant may rest as well as thou. And remember that thou wast a servant in the land of Egypt, and that the LORD thy God brought thee out thence through a mighty hand and by a stretched out arm: therefore the LORD thy God commanded thee to keep the sabbath day.

Honour thy father and thy mother, as the LORD thy God hath commanded thee; that thy days may be prolonged, and that it may go well with thee, in the land which the LORD thy God giveth thee.

Thou shalt not kill.

Neither shalt thou commit adultery.

Neither shalt thou steal.

Neither shalt thou bear false witness against thy neighbour.

Neither shalt thou desire thy neighbour's wife, neither shalt thou covet thy neighbour's house, his field, or his manservant, or his maidservant, his ox, or his ass, or any thing that is thy neighbour's.'

"These words the LORD spake unto all your assembly in the mount out of the midst of the fire, of the cloud, and of the thick darkness, with a great voice: and he added no more. And he wrote them in two tables of stone, and delivered them unto me."

Deuteronomy 5:6-22

209 "Behold, the days come," saith the LORD, "that I will make a new covenant with the house of Israel, and with the house of Judah: Not according to the covenant that I made with their fathers in the day that I took them by the hand to bring them out of the land of Egypt; which my covenant they brake, although I was an husband unto them," saith the LORD: "But this shall be the covenant that I will make with the house of Israel; After those days," saith the LORD, "I will put my law in their inward parts, and write it in their hearts; and will be their God, and they shall be my people. And they shall teach no more every man his neighbour, and every man his brother, saying, 'Know the LORD': for they shall all know me, from the least of them unto the greatest of them," saith the LORD; "for I will forgive their iniquity, and I will remember their sin no more."

Thus saith the LORD,
Which giveth the sun for a light by day,
   And the ordinances of the moon and of the stars for a light
      by night,
Which divideth the sea when the waves thereof roar;
   The LORD of hosts is his name.

Jeremiah 31:31-35

210   And every priest standeth daily ministering and offering oftentimes the same sacrifices, which can never take away sins: But this man, after he had offered one sacrifice for sins for ever, sat down on the right hand of God; from henceforth expecting till his enemies be made his footstool. For by one offering he hath perfected for ever them that are sanctified. Whereof the Holy Ghost also is a witness to us: for after that he had said before,

"'This is the covenant that I will make with them
After those days,' saith the Lord,
'I will put my laws into their hearts,
   And in their minds will I write them;
And their sins and iniquities will I remember no more.'"

Now where remission of these is, there is no more offering for sin.

Hebrews 10:11-18

211   Sing unto the LORD, all the earth;
          Shew forth from day to day his salvation.
      Declare his glory among the heathen;
          His marvellous works among all nations.
      For great is the LORD, and greatly to be praised:
          He also is to be feared above all gods.
      For all the gods of the people are idols:
          But the LORD made the heavens.
      Glory and honour are in his presence; strength and gladness
              are in his place.

1 Chronicles 16:23-27

212   What time I am afraid,
          I will trust in thee.
      In God I will praise his word,
          In God I have put my trust;
          I will not fear what flesh can do unto me.

Psalm 56:3-4

213   Now unto him that is able to keep you from falling, and to present you
      faultless before the presence of his glory with exceeding joy, to the only
      wise God our Saviour, be glory and majesty, dominion and power, both
      now and ever. Amen.

Jude 24-25

The Third Day

Distinctions and Differences

Seeds, Plants, and Trees

Vegetation and Decay

Marriage and Its Adulterations

Impurity and Holiness

THE THIRD DAY OF CREATION *is for separation and gathering, so that seed may sprout and vegetation grow lush. This is a Day for contemplating cultural distinctions and their qualification by various means of bonding. In this, as in so much, Christian Scripture speaks with many voices, not one. So, too, have its communities of readers.*

Returning to the metaphor in Genesis: Many seeds yield a proliferation of fruit — some nourishing, others quizzical, still others toxic. Which social boundaries are wholesome? When have standards become barricades? Rarely for Israel and the church were the answers immediately clear. Let the reader beware: Disclosed by this Day are magnificent beauty and staggering ugliness. Here one encounters companionship and bigotry, innocence and hubris, trust and treachery, gift and theft, wedding and divorce, intimacy and incest, tenderness and rape — even a heinous episode of gangrape. Scripture holds for its readers a mirror true to life. Occasionally the reflection seems unbearable. If one can bear to gaze, penetrating it all is the God who sees and understands, who suffers the cracks within creation in order to heal them.

214   And God said, "Let the waters under the heaven be gathered together unto one place, and let the dry land appear": and it was so. And God called the dry land Earth; and the gathering together of the waters called he Seas: And God saw that it was good. And God said, "Let the earth bring forth grass, the herb yielding seed, and the fruit tree yielding fruit after his kind, whose seed is in itself, upon the earth": and it was so. And the earth brought forth grass, and herb yielding seed after his kind, and the tree yielding fruit, whose seed was in itself, after his kind: and God saw that it was good. And the evening and the morning were the third day.

Genesis 1:9-13

215   For the LORD is a great God,
     And a great King above all gods.
  In his hand are the deep places of the earth:
     The strength of the hills is his also.
  The sea is his, and he made it:
     And his hands formed the dry land.

Psalm 95:3-5

216   "Therefore thou shalt keep the commandments of the LORD thy God, to walk in his ways, and to fear him. For the LORD thy God bringeth thee into a good land, a land of brooks of water, of fountains and depths that spring out of valleys and hills; a land of wheat, and barley, and vines, and fig trees, and pomegranates; a land of oil olive, and honey; a land wherein thou shalt eat bread without scarceness, thou shalt not lack any thing in

it; a land whose stones are iron, and out of whose hills thou mayest dig brass. When thou hast eaten and art full, then thou shalt bless the LORD thy God for the good land which he hath given thee."

Deuteronomy 8:6-10

217 These are the generations of the heavens and of the earth when they were created, in the day that the LORD God made the earth and the heavens, and every plant of the field before it was in the earth, and every herb of the field before it grew: for the LORD God had not caused it to rain upon the earth, and there was not a man to till the ground. But there went up a mist from the earth, and watered the whole face of the ground. And the LORD God formed man of the dust of the ground, and breathed into his nostrils the breath of life; and man became a living soul. And the LORD God planted a garden eastward in Eden; and there he put the man whom he had formed. And out of the ground made the LORD God to grow every tree that is pleasant to the sight, and good for food; the tree of life also in the midst of the garden, and the tree of knowledge of good and evil. And a river went out of Eden to water the garden; and from thence it was parted, and became into four heads.

Genesis 2:4-10

218 And so it is written, "The first man Adam was made a living soul"; the last Adam was made a quickening* spirit. Howbeit* that was not first which is spiritual, but that which is natural; and afterward that which is spiritual. The first man is of the earth, earthy: the second man is the Lord from heaven. As is the earthy, such are they also that are earthy: and as is the heavenly, such are they also that are heavenly. And as we have borne the image of the earthy, we shall also bear the image of the heavenly. Now this I say, brethren, that flesh and blood cannot inherit the kingdom of God; neither doth corruption inherit incorruption.

1 Corinthians 15:45-50

219 And the LORD God took the man, and put him into the Garden of Eden to dress it and to keep it. And the LORD God commanded the man, saying, "Of every tree of the garden thou mayest freely eat: But of the tree of the knowledge of good and evil, thou shalt not eat of it: for in the day that thou eatest thereof thou shalt surely die."

Genesis 2:15-17

220 Honour the LORD with thy substance,
    And with the firstfruits of all thine increase:
So shall thy barns be filled with plenty,
    And thy presses shall burst out with new wine.
My son, despise not the chastening of the LORD;
    Neither be weary of his correction:
For whom the LORD loveth he correcteth;
    Even as a father the son in whom he delighteth.

Proverbs 3:9-12

221 And the LORD God said, "It is not good that the man should be alone; I will make him an help meet* for him." And out of the ground the LORD God formed every beast of the field, and every fowl of the air; and brought them unto Adam to see what he would call them: and whatsoever Adam called every living creature, that was the name thereof. And Adam gave names to all cattle, and to the fowl of the air, and to every beast of the field; but for Adam there was not found an help meet for him. And the LORD God caused a deep sleep to fall upon Adam and he slept: and he took one of his ribs, and closed up the flesh instead thereof; And the rib, which the LORD God had taken from man, made he a woman, and brought her unto the man. And Adam said,

"This is now bone of my bones,
    And flesh of my flesh:
She shall be called Woman,
    Because she was taken out of Man."

Therefore shall a man leave his father and his mother, and shall cleave* unto his wife: and they shall be one flesh. And they were both naked, the man and his wife, and were not ashamed.

Genesis 2:18-25

222 And the Pharisees came to him, and asked him, "Is it lawful for a man to put away his wife?" tempting him. And he answered and said unto them, "What did Moses command you?" And they said, "Moses suffered* to write a bill of divorcement, and to put her away." And Jesus answered and said unto them, "For the hardness of your heart he wrote you this precept. But from the beginning of the creation God made them male and female. For this cause shall a man leave his father and mother, and cleave* to his wife; And they twain* shall be one flesh: so then they are no more twain, but one flesh. What therefore God hath joined together, let not man put asunder."

Mark 10:2-9

223   Now the serpent was more subtil* than any beast of the field which the LORD God had made. And he said unto the woman, "Yea, hath God said, 'Ye shall not eat of every tree of the garden'?" And the woman said unto the serpent, "We may eat of the fruit of the trees of the garden: But of the fruit of the tree which is in the midst of the garden, God hath said, 'Ye shall not eat of it, neither shall ye touch it, lest ye die.'" And the serpent said unto the woman, "Ye shall not surely die: For God doth know that in the day ye eat thereof, then your eyes shall be opened, and ye shall be as gods, knowing good and evil." And when the woman saw that the tree was good for food, and that it was pleasant to the eyes, and a tree to be desired to make one wise, she took of the fruit thereof, and did eat, and gave also unto her husband with her; and he did eat. And the eyes of them both were opened, and they knew that they were naked; and they sewed fig leaves together, and made themselves aprons.

Genesis 3:1-7

224   All these things spake Jesus unto the multitude in parables; and without a parable spake he not unto them: That it might be fulfilled which was spoken by the prophet, saying,

    "I will open my mouth in parables;

I will utter things which have been kept secret
From the foundation of the world."

Matthew 13:34-35

225 And they heard the voice of the LORD God walking in the garden in the cool of the day: and Adam and his wife hid themselves from the presence of the LORD God amongst the trees of the garden. And the LORD God called unto Adam, and said unto him, "Where art thou?" And he said, "I heard thy voice in the garden, and I was afraid, because I was naked; and I hid myself." And he said, "Who told thee that thou wast naked? Hast thou eaten of the tree, whereof I commanded thee that thou shouldest not eat?" And the man said, "The woman whom thou gavest to be with me, she gave me of the tree, and I did eat." And the LORD God said unto the woman, "What is this that thou hast done?" And the woman said, "The serpent beguiled me, and I did eat."

Genesis 3:8-13

226 Let the woman learn in silence with all subjection. But I suffer* not a woman to teach, nor to usurp authority over the man, but to be in silence. For Adam was first formed, then Eve. And Adam was not deceived, but the woman being deceived was in the transgression. Notwithstanding she shall be saved in childbearing, if they continue in faith and charity* and holiness with sobriety.

1 Timothy 2:11-15

227   And the Lord God said unto the serpent,

"Because thou hast done this,
  Thou art cursed above all cattle,
  And above every beast of the field;
Upon thy belly shalt thou go,
  And dust shalt thou eat
  All the days of thy life:
And I will put enmity between thee and the woman,
  And between thy seed and her seed;
It shall bruise thy head,
  And thou shalt bruise his heel."

Unto the woman he said,

"I will greatly multiply thy sorrow and thy conception;
  In sorrow thou shalt bring forth children;
And thy desire shall be to thy husband,
  And he shall rule over thee."

And unto Adam he said,

"Because thou hast hearkened unto the voice of thy wife,
  And hast eaten of the tree,
Of which I commanded thee, saying,
  'Thou shalt not eat of it':
Cursed is the ground for thy sake;
  In sorrow shalt thou eat of it all the days of thy life;
Thorns also and thistles shall it bring forth to thee;
  And thou shalt eat the herb of the field;
In the sweat of thy face
  Shalt thou eat bread,

Till thou return unto the ground;
    For out of it wast thou taken:
For dust thou art,
    And unto dust shalt thou return."

Genesis 3:14-19

228   Wherefore, as by one man sin entered into the world, and death by sin; and so death passed upon all men, for that all have sinned. . . . But not as the offence, so also is the free gift. For if through the offence of one many be dead, much more the grace of God, and the gift by grace, which is by one man, Jesus Christ, hath abounded unto many. And not as it was by one that sinned, so is the gift: for the judgment was by one to condemnation, but the free gift is of many offences unto justification. For if by one man's offence death reigned by one; much more they which receive abundance of grace and of the gift of righteousness shall reign in life by one, Jesus Christ. Therefore as by the offence of one judgment came upon all men to condemnation; even so by the righteousness of one the free gift came upon all men unto justification of life. For as by one man's disobedience many were made sinners, so by the obedience of one shall many be made righteous. . . . But where sin abounded, grace did much more abound: That as sin hath reigned unto death, even so might grace reign through righteousness unto eternal life by Jesus Christ our Lord.

Romans 5:12, 15-19, 20b-21

229   God is our refuge and strength,
        A very present help in trouble.
      Therefore will not we fear, though the earth be removed,
        And though the mountains be carried into the midst of the sea;
      Though the waters thereof roar and be troubled,
        Though the mountains shake with the swelling thereof. *Selah**.
      There is a river, the streams whereof shall make glad the city of God,
        The holy place of the tabernacles* of the most High.
      God is in the midst of her; she shall not be moved:
        God shall help her, and that right early. . . .
      "Be still, and know that I am God:
        I will be exalted among the heathen,
        I will be exalted in the earth."
      The LORD of hosts is with us;
        The God of Jacob is our refuge. *Selah**

Psalm 46:1-5, 10-11

230   And [an angel] shewed me a pure river of water of life, clear as crystal,
      proceeding out of the throne of God and of the Lamb. In the midst of
      the street of it, and on either side of the river, was there the tree of life,
      which bare twelve manner of fruits, and yielded her fruit every month:
      and the leaves of the tree were for the healing of the nations. And there
      shall be no more curse: but the throne of God and of the Lamb shall be in
      it; and his servants shall serve him: And they shall see his face; and his
      name shall be in their foreheads. And there shall be no night there; and
      they need no candle, neither light of the sun; for the Lord God giveth
      them light: and they shall reign for ever and ever.

Revelation 22:1-5

231 And Adam called his wife's name Eve; because she was the mother of all living. Unto Adam also and to his wife did the LORD God make coats of skins, and clothed them. And the LORD God said, "Behold, the man is become as one of us, to know good and evil: and now, lest he put forth his hand, and take also of the tree of life, and eat, and live for ever": Therefore the LORD God sent him forth from the Garden of Eden, to till the ground from whence he was taken. So he drove out the man; and he placed at the east of the Garden of Eden Cherubims, and a flaming sword which turned every way, to keep the way of the tree of life.

Genesis 3:20-24

232 But now is Christ risen from the dead, and become the firstfruits of them that slept. For since by man came death, by man came also the resurrection of the dead. For as in Adam all die, even so in Christ shall all be made alive.

1 Corinthians 15:20-22

233 They that go down to the sea in ships,
    That do business in great waters;
These see the works of the LORD,
    And his wonders in the deep.
For he commandeth, and raiseth the stormy wind,
    Which lifteth up the waves thereof.
They mount up to the heaven, they go down again to the depths:
    Their soul is melted because of trouble.
They reel to and fro, and stagger like a drunken man,

And are at their wit's end.
Then they cry unto the LORD in their trouble,
  And he bringeth them out of their distresses.
He maketh the storm a calm,
  So that the waves thereof are still.
Then are they glad because they be quiet;
  So he bringeth them unto their desired haven.
Oh that men would praise the LORD for his goodness,
  And for his wonderful works to the children of men!

Psalm 107:23-31

234 And the same day, when the even* was come, he saith unto them, "Let us pass over unto the other side." And when they had sent away the multitude, they took him even as he was in the ship. And there were also with him other little ships. And there arose a great storm of wind, and the waves beat into the ship, so that it was now full. And he was in the hinder part of the ship, asleep on a pillow: and they awake him, and say unto him, "Master, carest thou not that we perish?" And he arose, and rebuked the wind, and said unto the sea, "Peace, be still." And the wind ceased, and there was a great calm. And he said unto them, "Why are ye so fearful? How is it that ye have no faith?" And they feared exceedingly, and said one to another, "What manner of man is this, that even the wind and the sea obey him?"

Mark 4:35-41

235   Thou art the God that doest wonders:
>   Thou hast declared thy strength among the people.
> Thou hast with thine arm redeemed thy people,
>   The sons of Jacob and Joseph. *Selah**.
> The waters saw thee, O God,
>   The waters saw thee;
> They were afraid:
>   The depths also were troubled.
> The clouds poured out water:
>   The skies sent out a sound:
>   Thine arrows also went abroad.
> The voice of thy thunder was in the heaven:
>   The lightnings lightened the world:
>   The earth trembled and shook.
> Thy way is in the sea,
>   And thy path in the great waters,
>   And thy footsteps are not known.

Psalm 77:14-19

236   And straightway Jesus constrained his disciples to get into a ship, and to go before him unto the other side, while he sent the multitudes away. And when he had sent the multitudes away, he went up into a mountain apart to pray: and when the evening was come, he was there alone. But the ship was now in the midst of the sea, tossed with waves: for the wind was contrary. And in the fourth watch of the night Jesus went unto them, walking on the sea. And when the disciples saw him walking on the sea, they were troubled, saying, "It is a spirit"; and they cried out for fear. But straightway Jesus spake unto them, saying, "Be of good cheer; it

is I; be not afraid." And Peter answered him and said, "Lord, if it be thou, bid me come unto thee on the water." And he said, "Come." And when Peter was come down out of the ship, he walked on the water, to go to Jesus. But when he saw the wind boisterous, he was afraid; and beginning to sink, he cried, saying, "Lord, save me." And immediately Jesus stretched forth his hand, and caught him, and said unto him, "O thou of little faith, wherefore* didst thou doubt?" And when they were come into the ship, the wind ceased. Then they that were in the ship came and worshipped him, saying, "Of a truth thou art the Son of God."

Matthew 14:22-33

237 "Ye shall therefore keep my statutes, and my judgments: which if a man do, he shall live in them: I am the LORD. None of you shall approach to any that is near of kin to him, to uncover their nakedness: I am the LORD."

Leviticus 18:5-6

238 And Lot went up out of Zoar, and dwelt in the mountain, and his two daughters with him; for he feared to dwell in Zoar: and he dwelt in a cave, he and his two daughters. And the firstborn said unto the younger, "Our father is old, and there is not a man in the earth to come in unto us after the manner of all the earth: Come, let us make our father drink wine, and we will lie with him, that we may preserve seed of our father." And they made their father drink wine that night: and the firstborn went in, and lay with her father; and he perceived not when she lay down, nor when she arose. And it came to pass on the morrow, that the firstborn

said unto the younger, "Behold, I lay yesternight with my father: let us make him drink wine this night also; and go thou in, and lie with him, that we may preserve seed of our Father." And they made their father drink wine that night also: and the younger arose, and lay with him; and he perceived not when she lay down, nor when she arose. Thus were both the daughters of Lot with child by their father. And the firstborn bare a son, and called his name Moab: the same is the father of the Moabites unto this day. And the younger, she also bare a son, and called his name Benammi: the same is the father of the children of Ammon unto this day.

Genesis 19:30-38

239 It is reported commonly that there is fornication among you, and such fornication as is not so much as named among the Gentiles, that one should have his father's wife. And ye are puffed up, and have not rather mourned, that he that hath done this deed might be taken away from among you. For I verily, as absent in body, but present in spirit, have judged already, as though I were present, concerning him that hath so done this deed, in the name of our Lord Jesus Christ, when ye are gathered together, and my spirit, with the power of our Lord Jesus Christ, to deliver such an one unto Satan for the destruction of the flesh, that the spirit may be saved in the day of the Lord Jesus.

1 Corinthians 5:1-5

240 "And if a woman have an issue, and her issue in her flesh be blood, she shall be put apart seven days: and whosoever toucheth her shall be unclean until the even*. And every thing that she lieth upon in her separa-

tion shall be unclean: every thing also that she sitteth upon shall be unclean."

Leviticus 15:19-20

241 And a woman having an issue of blood twelve years, which had spent all her living upon physicians, neither could be healed of any, came behind him, and touched the border of his garment: and immediately her issue of blood stanched. And Jesus said, "Who touched me?" When all denied, Peter and they that were with him said, "Master, the multitude throng thee and press thee, and sayest thou, 'Who touched me?'" And Jesus said, "Somebody hath touched me: for I perceive that virtue is gone out of me." And when the woman saw that she was not hid, she came trembling, and falling down before him, she declared unto him before all the people for what cause she had touched him and how she was healed immediately. And he said unto her, "Daughter, be of good comfort: thy faith hath made thee whole; go in peace."

Luke 8:43-48

242 "Sanctify yourselves therefore, and be ye holy: for I am the LORD your God. And ye shall keep my statutes, and do them: I am the LORD which sanctify you.

"For every one that curseth his father or his mother shall be surely put to death: he hath cursed his father or his mother; his blood shall be upon him.

"And the man that committeth adultery with another man's wife, even he that committeth adultery with his neighbour's wife, the adulterer and the adulteress shall surely be put to death.

"And the man that lieth with his father's wife hath uncovered his father's nakedness: both of them shall surely be put to death; their blood shall be upon them.

"And if a man lie with his daughter in law, both of them shall surely be put to death: they have wrought confusion; their blood shall be upon them.

"If a man also lie with mankind, as he lieth with a woman, both of them have committed an abomination: they shall surely be put to death; their blood shall be upon them.

"And if a man take a wife and her mother, it is wickedness: they shall be burnt with fire, both he and they; that there be no wickedness among you."

Leviticus 20:7-14

243 And early in the morning [Jesus] came again into the temple, and all the people came unto him; and he sat down, and taught them. And the scribes and Pharisees brought unto him a woman taken in adultery; and when they had set her in the midst, they say unto him, "Master, this woman was taken in adultery, in the very act. Now Moses in the law commanded us, that such should be stoned: but what sayest thou?" This they said, tempting him, that they might have to accuse him. But Jesus stooped down, and with his finger wrote on the ground, as though he heard them not. So when they continued asking him, he lifted up himself, and said unto them, "He that is without sin among you, let him first cast a stone at her." And again he stooped down, and wrote on the ground. And they which heard it, being convicted by their own con-

science, went out one by one, beginning at the eldest, even unto the last: and Jesus was left alone, and the woman standing in the midst. When Jesus had lifted up himself, and saw none but the woman, he said unto her, "Woman, where are those thine accusers? Hath no man condemned thee?" She said, "No man, Lord." And Jesus said unto her, "Neither do I condemn thee: go, and sin no more."

John 8:2-11

244   And there came two angels to Sodom at even*; and Lot sat in the gate of Sodom: and Lot seeing them rose up to meet them; and he bowed himself with his face toward the ground; And he said, "Behold now, my lords, turn in, I pray you, into your servant's house, and tarry all night, and wash your feet, and ye shall rise up early, and go on your ways." And they said, "Nay; but we will abide in the street all night." And he pressed upon them greatly; and they turned in unto him, and entered into his house; and he made them a feast, and did bake unleavened bread, and they did eat. But before they lay down, the men of the city, even the men of Sodom, compassed the house round, both old and young, all the people from every quarter: And they called unto Lot, and said unto him, "Where are the men which came in to thee this night? Bring them out unto us, that we may know them." And Lot went out at the door unto them, and shut the door after him, and said, "I pray you, brethren, do not so wickedly. Behold now, I have two daughters which have not known man; let me, I pray you, bring them out unto you, and do ye to them as is good in your eyes: only unto these men do nothing; for therefore came they under the shadow of my roof." And they said, "Stand back." And they said again, "This one fellow came in to sojourn, and he will needs be a judge: now will we deal worse with thee, than with them." And they pressed sore upon the man, even Lot, and came near

to break the door. But the men put forth their hand, and pulled Lot into the house to them, and shut to the door. And they smote the men that were at the door of the house with blindness, both small and great: so that they wearied themselves to find the door.

And the men said unto Lot, "Hast thou here any besides? Son in law, and thy sons, and thy daughters, and whatsoever thou hast in the city, bring them out of this place: For we will destroy this place, because the cry of them is waxen great before the face of the LORD; and the LORD hath sent us to destroy it." And Lot went out, and spake unto his sons in law, which married his daughters, and said, "Up, get you out of this place; for the LORD will destroy this city." But he seemed as one that mocked unto his sons in law.

Genesis 19:1-14

245 Why boastest thou thyself in mischief, O mighty man?
    The goodness of God endureth continually.
Thy tongue deviseth mischiefs;
    Like a sharp razor, working deceitfully.
Thou lovest evil more than good;
    And lying rather than to speak righteousness. *Selah**.
Thou lovest all devouring words,
    O thou deceitful tongue.
God shall likewise destroy thee for ever,
    He shall take thee away,
And pluck thee out of thy dwelling place,
    And root thee out of the land of the living. *Selah.*

Psalm 52:1-5

246 "Beware of false prophets, which come to you in sheep's clothing, but inwardly they are ravening wolves. Ye shall know them by their fruits. Do men gather grapes of thorns, or figs of thistles? Even so every good tree bringeth forth good fruit; but a corrupt tree bringeth forth evil fruit. A good tree cannot bring forth evil fruit, neither can a corrupt tree bring forth good fruit. Every tree that bringeth not forth good fruit is hewn down, and cast into the fire. Wherefore by their fruits ye shall know them."

Matthew 7:15-20

247 The heart is deceitful above all things,
And desperately wicked:
Who can know it?

Jeremiah 17:9

248 And it came to pass after this, that Absalom the son of David had a fair sister, whose name was Tamar; and Amnon the son of David loved her. And Amnon was so vexed, that he fell sick for his sister Tamar; for she was a virgin; and Amnon thought it hard for him to do any thing to her. . . . So Amnon lay down, and made himself sick: and when the king was come to see him, Amnon said unto the king, "I pray thee, let Tamar my sister come, and make me a couple of cakes in my sight, that I may eat at her hand." Then David sent home to Tamar, saying, "Go now to thy brother Amnon's house, and dress him meat*." . . .

And Amnon said unto Tamar, "Bring the meat into the chamber, that I may eat of thine hand." And Tamar took the cakes which she had made, and brought them into the chamber to Amnon her brother. And when she had brought them unto him to eat, he took hold of her, and said unto her, "Come lie with me, my sister." And she answered him, "Nay, my brother, do not force me; for no such thing ought to be done in Israel: do not thou this folly. And I, whither shall I cause my shame to go? And as for thee, thou shalt be as one of the fools in Israel. Now therefore, I pray thee, speak unto the king; for he will not withhold me from thee." Howbeit* he would not hearken unto her voice: but, being stronger than she, forced her, and lay with her.

2 Samuel 13:1-2, 6-7, 10-14

249 They that hate me without a cause
    Are more than the hairs of mine head:
They that would destroy me, being mine enemies wrongfully,
    are mighty:
    Then I restored that which I took not away.

Psalm 69:4

250 Then Amnon hated her exceedingly; so that the hatred wherewith he hated her was greater than the love wherewith he had loved her. And Amnon said unto her, "Arise, be gone." And she said unto him, "There is no cause: this evil in sending me away is greater than the other that thou didst unto me." But he would not hearken unto her. Then he called his servant that ministered unto him, and said, "Put now this woman out from me, and bolt the door after her." And she had a garment of divers colours upon her: for with such robes were the king's daughters that were

virgins apparelled. Then his servant brought her out, and bolted the door after her. And Tamar put ashes on her head, and rent her garment of divers colours that was on her, and laid her hand on her head, and went on crying. And Absalom her brother said unto her, "Hath Amnon thy brother been with thee? But hold now thy peace, my sister: he is thy brother; regard not this thing." So Tamar remained desolate in her brother Absalom's house. But when King David heard of all these things, he was very wroth*. And Absalom spake unto his brother Amnon neither good nor bad: for Absalom hated Amnon, because he had forced his sister Tamar.

2 Samuel 13:15-22

251   LORD, how long shall the wicked,
          How long shall the wicked triumph?
      How long shall they utter and speak hard things?
          And all the workers of iniquity boast themselves?

Psalm 94:3-4

252   Now Absalom had commanded his servants, saying, "Mark ye now when Amnon's heart is merry with wine, and when I say unto you, 'Smite Amnon'; then kill him, fear not: have not I commanded you? Be courageous and be valiant." And the servants of Absalom did unto Amnon as Absalom had commanded. Then all the king's sons arose, and every man gat* him up upon his mule, and fled. . . . And Jonadab, the son of Shimeah David's brother, answered and said, "Let not my lord suppose that they have slain all the young men the king's sons; for Amnon only is

dead: for by the appointment of Absalom this hath been determined from the day that he forced his sister Tamar." . . . But Absalom fled, and went to Talmai, the son of Ammihud, king of Geshur. And David mourned for his son every day.

2 Samuel 13:28-29, 32, 37

253 We have sinned with our fathers,
      We have committed iniquity,
      We have done wickedly. . . .
We have done wickedly. . . .
They forgat God their saviour,
      Which had done great things in Egypt;
      Wondrous works in the land of Ham,
      And terrible things by the Red sea. . . .
But were mingled among the heathen,
      And learned their works.
And they served their idols:
      Which were a snare unto them.
Yea, they sacrificed their sons and their daughters unto devils,
      And shed innocent blood,
      Even the blood of their sons and of their daughters,
Whom they sacrificed unto the idols of Canaan:
      And the land was polluted with blood.

Psalm 106:6, 21-22, 35-38

254 Another parable put he forth unto them, saying, "The kingdom of heaven is likened unto a man which sowed good seed in his field: But

while men slept, his enemy came and sowed tares among the wheat, and
went his way. But when the blade was sprung up, and brought forth fruit,
then appeared the tares also. So the servants of the householder came and
said unto him, 'Sir, didst not thou sow good seed in thy field? From
whence then hath it tares?' He said unto them, 'An enemy hath done
this.' The servants said unto him, 'Wilt thou then that we go and gather
them up?' But he said, 'Nay; lest while ye gather up the tares, ye root up
also the wheat with them. Let both grow together until the harvest: and
in the time of harvest I will say to the reapers, "Gather ye together first
the tares, and bind them in bundles to burn them: but gather the wheat
into my barn."'"

Matthew 13:24-30

255 And David numbered the people that were with him, and set captains of
thousands and captains of hundreds over them. And David sent forth a
third part of the people under the hand of Joab, and a third part under
the hand of Abishai the son of Zeruiah, Joab's brother, and a third part
under the hand of Ittai the Gittite. . . . And the king commanded Joab
and Abishai and Ittai, saying, "Deal gently for my sake with the young
man, even with Absalom." And all the people heard when the king gave
all the captains charge concerning Absalom.

2 Samuel 18:1-2, 5

256 Then Jesus sent the multitude away, and went into the house: and his disciples came unto him, saying, "Declare unto us the parable of the tares of the
field." He answered and said unto them, "He that soweth the good seed is

the Son of man; the field is the world; the good seed are the children of the kingdom; but the tares are the children of the wicked one; The enemy that sowed them is the devil; the harvest is the end of the world; and the reapers are the angels. As therefore the tares are gathered and burned in the fire; so shall it be in the end of this world. The Son of man shall send forth his angels, and they shall gather out of his kingdom all things that offend, and them which do iniquity; and shall cast them into a furnace of fire: there shall be wailing and gnashing of teeth. Then shall the righteous shine forth as the sun in the kingdom of their Father. Who hath ears to hear, let him hear."

Matthew 13:36-43

257 And Absalom met the servants of David. And Absalom rode upon a mule, and the mule went under the thick boughs of a great oak, and his head caught hold of the oak, and he was taken up between the heaven and the earth; and the mule that was under him went away. And a certain man saw it, and told Joab, and said, "Behold, I saw Absalom hanged in an oak." And Joab said unto the man that told him, "And, behold, thou sawest him, and why didst thou not smite him there to the ground? And I would have given thee ten shekels of silver, and a girdle*." And the man said unto Joab, "Though I should receive a thousand shekels of silver in mine hand, yet would I not put forth mine hand against the king's son: for in our hearing the king charged thee and Abishai and Ittai, saying, 'Beware that none touch the young man Absalom.' Otherwise I should have wrought falsehood against mine own life: for there is no matter hid from the king, and thou thyself wouldest have set thyself against me." Then said Joab, "I may not tarry thus with thee." And he took three darts in his hand, and thrust them through the heart of Absalom, while he was

yet alive in the midst of the oak. And ten young men that bare Joab's armour compassed about and smote Absalom, and slew him.

2 Samuel 18:9-15

258 "Therefore whosoever heareth these sayings of mine, and doeth them, I will liken him unto a wise man, which built his house upon a rock: And the rain descended, and the floods came, and the winds blew, and beat upon that house; and it fell not: for it was founded upon a rock. And every one that heareth these sayings of mine, and doeth them not, shall be likened unto a foolish man, which built his house upon the sand: And the rain descended, and the floods came, and the winds blew, and beat upon that house; and it fell: and great was the fall of it."

Matthew 7:24-27

259 And, behold, Cushi came; and Cushi said, "Tidings, my lord the king: for the LORD hath avenged thee this day of all them that rose up against thee." And [David] said unto Cushi, "Is the young man Absalom safe?" And Cushi answered, "The enemies of my lord the king, and all that rise against thee to do thee hurt, be as that young man is." And the king was much moved, and went up to the chamber over the gate, and wept: and as he went, thus he said, "O my son Absalom, my son, my son Absalom! Would God I had died for thee, O Absalom, my son, my son!"

2 Samuel 18:31-33

260 Be not deceived; God is not mocked: for whatsoever a man soweth, that shall he also reap. For he that soweth to his flesh shall of the flesh reap corruption; but he that soweth to the Spirit shall of the Spirit reap life everlasting.

Galatians 6:7-8

261 The stone which the builders refused
    Is become the head stone of the corner.
This is the LORD's doing;
    It is marvellous in our eyes.
This is the day which the LORD hath made;
    We will rejoice and be glad in it.

Psalm 118:22-24

262 "Hear another parable: There was a certain householder, which planted a vineyard, and hedged it round about, and digged a winepress in it, and built a tower, and let it out to husbandmen, and went into a far country: And when the time of the fruit drew near, he sent his servants to the husbandmen, that they might receive the fruits of it. And the husbandmen took his servants, and beat one, and killed another, and stoned another. Again, he sent other servants more than the first: and they did unto them likewise. But last of all he sent unto them his son, saying, 'They will reverence my son.' But when the husbandmen saw the son, they said among themselves, 'This is the heir; come, let us kill him, and let us seize on his inheritance.' And they caught him, and cast him out of the vineyard, and slew him. When the lord therefore of the vineyard cometh, what will he do

unto those husbandmen?" They say unto him, "He will miserably destroy those wicked men, and will let out his vineyard unto other husbandmen, which shall render him the fruits in their seasons." Jesus saith unto them, "Did ye never read in the scriptures,

> 'The stone which the builders rejected,
>> The same is become the head of the corner:
> This is the Lord's doing,
>> And it is marvellous in our eyes?'

Therefore say I unto you, The kingdom of God shall be taken from you, and given to a nation bringing forth the fruits thereof. And whosoever shall fall on this stone shall be broken: but on whomsoever it shall fall, it will grind him to powder."

Matthew 21:33-44

263 To whom coming, as unto a living stone, disallowed indeed of men, but chosen of God, and precious, ye also, as lively stones, are built up a spiritual house, an holy priesthood, to offer up spiritual sacrifices, acceptable to God by Jesus Christ. Wherefore also it is contained in the scripture,

> "Behold, I lay in Sion* a chief corner stone, elect, precious:
> And he that believeth on him shall not be confounded."

1 Peter 2:4-6

264 Now will I sing to my wellbeloved a song of my beloved touching*
          his vineyard.
      My wellbeloved hath a vineyard in a very fruitful hill:
      And he fenced it, and gathered out the stones thereof, and planted
          it with the choicest vine,
        And built a tower in the midst of it,
        And also made a winepress therein:
      And he looked that it should bring forth grapes,
        And it brought forth wild grapes.
      And now, O inhabitants of Jerusalem,
        And men of Judah, judge,
      I pray you, betwixt me and my vineyard.
      What could have been done more to my vineyard,
        That I have not done in it?
      Wherefore*, when I looked that it should bring forth grapes,
        Brought it forth wild grapes?
      And now go to;
        I will tell you what I will do to my vineyard:
      I will take away the hedge thereof,
        And it shall be eaten up;
      And break down the wall thereof,
        And it shall be trodden down:
      And I will lay it waste:
        It shall not be pruned, nor digged;
        But there shall come up briers and thorns:
      I will also command the clouds that they rain no rain upon it.
      For the vineyard of the LORD of hosts is the house of Israel,
      And the men of Judah his pleasant plant:
      And he looked for judgment,
        But behold oppression;

For righteousness,
But behold a cry.

Isaiah 5:1-7

265 For I [Paul] speak to you Gentiles, inasmuch as I am the apostle of the Gentiles, I magnify mine office: If by any means I may provoke to emulation them which are my flesh, and might save some of them. For if the casting away of them be the reconciling of the world, what shall the receiving of them be, but life from the dead? For if the firstfruit be holy, the lump is also holy: and if the root be holy, so are the branches. And if some of the branches be broken off, and thou, being a wild olive tree, wert graffed in among them, and with them partakest of the root and fatness of the olive tree; boast not against the branches. But if thou boast, thou bearest not the root, but the root thee. Thou wilt say then, "The branches were broken off, that I might be graffed in." Well; because of unbelief they were broken off, and thou standest by faith. Be not highminded, but fear: For if God spared not the natural branches, take heed lest he also spare not thee. Behold therefore the goodness and severity of God: on them which fell, severity; but toward thee, goodness, if thou continue in his goodness: otherwise thou also shalt be cut off. And they also, if they abide not still in unbelief, shall be graffed in: for God is able to graff them in again. For if thou wert cut out of the olive tree which is wild by nature, and wert graffed contrary to nature into a good olive tree: how much more shall these, which be the natural branches, be graffed into their own olive tree?

Romans 11:13-24

266   And it came to pass after these things, that Naboth the Jezreelite had a vineyard, which was in Jezreel, hard by the palace of Ahab king of Samaria. And Ahab spake unto Naboth, saying, "Give me thy vineyard, that I may have it for a garden of herbs, because it is near unto my house: and I will give thee for it a better vineyard than it; or, if it seem good to thee, I will give thee the worth of it in money." And Naboth said to Ahab, "The LORD forbid it me, that I should give the inheritance of my fathers unto thee." And Ahab came into his house heavy and displeased because of the word which Naboth the Jezreelite had spoken to him: for he had said, "I will not give thee the inheritance of my fathers." And he laid him down upon his bed, and turned away his face, and would eat no bread.

1 Kings 21:1-4

267   And he taught them many things by parables, and said unto them in his doctrine, "Hearken; Behold, there went out a sower to sow: And it came to pass, as he sowed, some fell by the way side, and the fowls of the air came and devoured it up. And some fell on stony ground, where it had not much earth; and immediately it sprang up, because it had no depth of earth: But when the sun was up, it was scorched; and because it had no root, it withered away. And some fell among thorns, and the thorns grew up, and choked it, and it yielded no fruit. And other fell on good ground, and did yield fruit that sprang up and increased; and brought forth, some thirty, and some sixty, and some an hundred." And he said unto them, "He that hath ears to hear, let him hear."

Mark 4:2-9

268   But Jezebel his wife came to him, and said unto him, . . . "Dost thou now govern the kingdom of Israel? Arise, and eat bread, and let thine heart be merry: I will give thee the vineyard of Naboth the Jezreelite." So she wrote letters in Ahab's name, and sealed them with his seal, and sent the letters unto the elders and to the nobles that were in his city, dwelling with Naboth. And she wrote in the letters, saying, "Proclaim a fast, and set Naboth on high among the people: And set two men, sons of Belial, before him, to bear witness against him, saying, 'Thou didst blaspheme God and the king.' And then carry him out, and stone him, that he may die." And the men of his city, even the elders and the nobles who were the inhabitants in his city, did as Jezebel had sent unto them, and as it was written in the letters which she had sent unto them. . . . And it came to pass, when Jezebel heard that Naboth was stoned, and was dead, that Jezebel said to Ahab, "Arise, take possession of the vineyard of Naboth the Jezreelite, which he refused to give thee for money: for Naboth is not alive, but dead." And it came to pass, when Ahab heard that Naboth was dead, that Ahab rose up to go down to the vineyard of Naboth the Jezreelite, to take possession of it.

1 Kings 21:5a, 7-11a, 15-16

269   [Jesus] spake also this parable; "A certain man had a fig tree planted in his vineyard; and he came and sought fruit thereon, and found none. Then said he unto the dresser of his vineyard, 'Behold, these three years I come seeking fruit on this fig tree, and find none: cut it down; why cumbereth it the ground?' And he answering said unto him, 'Lord, let it alone this year also, till I shall dig about it, and dung it: And if it bear fruit, well: and if not, then after that thou shalt cut it down.'"

Luke 13:6-9

270 And the word of the LORD came to Elijah the Tishbite, saying, "Arise, go down to meet Ahab king of Israel, which is in Samaria: behold, he is in the vineyard of Naboth, whither he is gone down to possess it. And thou shalt speak unto him, saying, 'Thus saith the LORD, Hast thou killed, and also taken possession?' And thou shalt speak unto him, saying, 'Thus saith the LORD, In the place where dogs licked the blood of Naboth shall dogs lick thy blood, even thine.'" And Ahab said to Elijah, "Hast thou found me, O mine enemy?" And he answered, "I have found thee: because thou hast sold thyself to work evil in the sight of the LORD. Behold, I will bring evil upon thee, and will take away thy posterity, and will cut off from Ahab him that pisseth against the wall, and him that is shut up and left in Israel, and will make thine house like the house of Jeroboam the son of Nebat, and like the house of Baasha the son of Ahijah, for the provocation wherewith thou hast provoked me to anger, and made Israel to sin." And of Jezebel also spake the LORD, saying, "The dogs shall eat Jezebel by the wall of Jezreel. Him that dieth of Ahab in the city the dogs shall eat; and him that dieth in the field shall the fowls of the air eat."

1 Kings 21:17-24

271 "Among the bushes they brayed;
    Under the nettles they were gathered together.
They were children of fools,
    Yea, children of base men:
    They were viler than the earth.
And now am I their song,
    Yea, I am their byword.
They abhor me, they flee far from me,
    And spare not to spit in my face."

Job 30:7-10

272   For he hath made him to be sin for us, who knew no sin; that we might be made the righteousness of God in him.

2 Corinthians 5:21

273   "And the leper in whom the plague is, his clothes shall be rent, and his head bare, and he shall put a covering upon his upper lip, and shall cry, 'Unclean, unclean.' All the days wherein the plague shall be in him he shall be defiled; he is unclean: he shall dwell alone; without the camp shall his habitation be."

Leviticus 13:45-46

274   And it came to pass, as he went to Jerusalem, that he passed through the midst of Samaria and Galilee. And as he entered into a certain village, there met him ten men that were lepers, which stood afar off: And they lifted up their voices, and said, "Jesus, Master, have mercy on us." And when he saw them, he said unto them, "Go shew yourselves unto the priests." And it came to pass, that, as they went, they were cleansed. And one of them, when he saw that he was healed, turned back, and with a loud voice glorified God, and fell down on his face at his feet, giving him thanks: and he was a Samaritan. And Jesus answering said, "Were there not ten cleansed? But where are the nine? There are not found that returned to give glory to God, save this stranger." And he said unto him, "Arise, go thy way: thy faith hath made thee whole."

Luke 17:11-19

275   "And if a man have committed a sin worthy of death, and he be to be put to death, and thou hang him on a tree: His body shall not remain all night upon the tree, but thou shalt in any wise* bury him that day; (for he that is hanged is accursed of God;) that thy land be not defiled, which the LORD thy God giveth thee for an inheritance."

Deuteronomy 21:22-23

276   Christ hath redeemed us from the curse of the law, being made a curse for us: for it is written, "Cursed is every one that hangeth on a tree": That the blessing of Abraham might come on the Gentiles through Jesus Christ; that we might receive the promise of the Spirit through faith.

Galatians 3:13-14

277   "Whatsoever goeth upon the belly, and whatsoever goeth upon all four, or whatsoever hath more feet among all creeping things that creep upon the earth, them ye shall not eat; for they are an abomination. . . . For I am the LORD that bringeth you up out of the land of Egypt, to be your God: ye shall therefore be holy, for I am holy. This is the law of the beasts, and of the fowl, and of every living creature that moveth in the waters, and of every creature that creepeth upon the earth: To make a difference between the unclean and the clean, and between the beast that may be eaten and the beast that may not be eaten."

Leviticus 11:45-47

278 And when [Jesus] had called all the people unto him, he said unto them, "Hearken unto me every one of you, and understand: There is nothing from without a man, that entering into him can defile him: but the things which come out of him, those are they that defile the man. If any man have ears to hear, let him hear." And when he was entered into the house from the people, his disciples asked him concerning the parable. And he saith unto them, "Are ye so without understanding also? Do ye not perceive, that whatsoever thing from without entereth into the man, it cannot defile him; because it entereth not into his heart, but into the belly, and goeth out into the draught, purging all meats?"

Mark 7:14-19

279 On the morrow, as they went on their journey, and drew nigh unto the city, Peter went up upon the housetop to pray about the sixth hour: And he became very hungry, and would have eaten: but while they made ready, he fell into a trance, and saw heaven opened, and a certain vessel descending upon him, as it had been a great sheet knit at the four corners, and let down to the earth: Wherein were all manner of fourfooted beasts of the earth, and wild beasts, and creeping things, and fowls of the air. And there came a voice to him, "Rise, Peter; kill, and eat." But Peter said, "Not so, Lord; for I have never eaten any thing that is common or unclean." And the voice spake unto him again the second time, "What God hath cleansed, that call not thou common." This was done thrice: and the vessel was received up again into heaven.

Acts 10:9-16

280 For one believeth that he may eat all things: another, who is weak, eateth
herbs. Let not him that eateth despise him that eateth not; and let not
him which eateth not judge him that eateth: for God hath received
him. . . . He that eateth, eateth to the Lord, for he giveth God thanks; and
he that eateth not, to the Lord he eateth not, and giveth God thanks. For
none of us liveth to himself, and no man dieth to himself. For whether
we live, we live unto the Lord; and whether we die, we die unto the Lord:
whether we live therefore, or die, we are the Lord's. . . . Let us not therefore judge one another any more: but judge this rather, that no man put a
stumblingblock or an occasion to fall in his brother's way. I know, and
am persuaded by the Lord Jesus, that there is nothing unclean of itself:
but to him that esteemeth any thing to be unclean, to him it is unclean.
But if thy brother be grieved with thy meat*, now walkest thou not charitably. Destroy not him with thy meat, for whom Christ died. Let not
then your good be evil spoken of: For the kingdom of God is not meat
and drink; but righteousness, and peace, and joy in the Holy Ghost.

Romans 14:2-3, 6b-8, 13-17

281 And the apostles and brethren that were in Judaea heard that the
Gentiles had also received the word of God. And when Peter was come
up to Jerusalem, they that were of the circumcision contended with him,
saying, "Thou wentest in to men uncircumcised, and didst eat with
them." But Peter rehearsed the matter from the beginning, and expounded it by order unto them. . . . "And as I began to speak, the Holy
Ghost fell on them, as on us at the beginning. Then remembered I the
word of the Lord, how that he said, 'John indeed baptized with water;
but ye shall be baptized with the Holy Ghost.' Forasmuch then as God
gave them the like gift as he did unto us, who believed on the Lord Jesus

Christ; what was I, that I could withstand God?" When they heard these things, they held their peace, and glorified God, saying, "Then hath God also to the Gentiles granted repentance unto life."

Acts 11:1-4, 15-18

282 Wherefore remember, that ye being in time past Gentiles in the flesh, who are called Uncircumcision by that which is called the Circumcision in the flesh made by hands; That at that time ye were without Christ, being aliens from the commonwealth of Israel, and strangers from the covenants of promise, having no hope, and without God in the world: But now in Christ Jesus ye who sometimes were far off are made nigh by the blood of Christ. For he is our peace, who hath made both one, and hath broken down the middle wall of partition between us; having abolished in his flesh the enmity, even the law of commandments contained in ordinances; for to make in himself of twain* one new man, so making peace; and that he might reconcile both unto God in one body by the cross, having slain the enmity thereby: And came and preached peace to you which were afar off, and to them that were nigh. For through him we both have access by one Spirit unto the Father. Now therefore ye are no more strangers and foreigners, but fellowcitizens with the saints, and of the household of God.

Ephesians 2:11-19

283 And Naomi had a kinsman of her husband's, a mighty man of wealth, of the family of Elimelech; and his name was Boaz.... Then said Boaz unto Ruth, "Hearest thou not, my daughter? Go not to glean in another field,

neither go from hence, but abide here fast by my maidens: Let thine eyes be on the field that they do reap, and go thou after them: have I not charged the young men that they shall not touch thee? And when thou art athirst, go unto the vessels, and drink of that which the young men have drawn." Then she fell on her face, and bowed herself to the ground, and said unto him, "Why have I found grace in thine eyes, that thou shouldest take knowledge of me, seeing I am a stranger?" And Boaz answered and said unto her, "It hath fully been shewed me, all that thou hast done unto thy mother in law since the death of thine husband: and how thou hast left thy father and thy mother, and the land of thy nativity, and art come unto a people which thou knewest not heretofore. The LORD recompense thy work, and a full reward be given thee of the LORD God of Israel, under whose wings thou art come to trust." Then she said, "Let me find favour in thy sight, my lord; for that thou hast comforted me, and for that thou hast spoken friendly unto thine handmaid, though I be not like unto one of thine handmaidens."

Ruth 2:1, 8-13

284   Wait on the LORD: be of good courage,
         And he shall strengthen thine heart:
         Wait, I say, on the LORD.

Psalm 27:14

285   And [Ruth] went down unto the floor, and did according to all that her
         mother in law bade her. And when Boaz had eaten and drunk, and his
         heart was merry, he went to lie down at the end of the heap of corn*: and

170

she came softly, and uncovered his feet, and laid her down. And it came to pass at midnight, that the man was afraid, and turned himself: and, behold, a woman lay at his feet. And he said, "Who art thou?" And she answered, "I am Ruth thine handmaid: spread therefore thy skirt over thine handmaid; for thou art a near kinsman." And he said, "Blessed be thou of the LORD, my daughter: for thou hast shewed more kindness in the latter end than at the beginning, inasmuch as thou followedst not young men, whether poor or rich. And now, my daughter, fear not; I will do to thee all that thou requirest: for all the city of my people doth know that thou art a virtuous woman. And now it is true that I am thy near kinsman: howbeit* there is a kinsman nearer than I. Tarry this night, and it shall be in the morning, that if he will perform unto thee the part of a kinsman, well; let him do the kinsman's part: but if he will not do the part of a kinsman to thee, then will I do the part of a kinsman to thee, as the LORD liveth: lie down until the morning."

Ruth 3:6-13

286 "Again, the kingdom of heaven is like unto a merchant man, seeking goodly pearls: Who, when he had found one pearl of great price, went and sold all that he had, and bought it.

Matthew 13:45-46

287 So Boaz took Ruth, and she was his wife: and when he went in unto her, the LORD gave her conception, and she bare a son. And the women said unto Naomi, "Blessed be the LORD, which hath not left thee this day without a kinsman, that his name may be famous in Israel. And he shall

be unto thee a restorer of thy life, and a nourisher of thine old age: for thy daughter in law, which loveth thee, which is better to thee than seven sons, hath born him." And Naomi took the child, and laid it in her bosom, and became nurse unto it. And the women her neighbours gave it a name, saying, "There is a son born to Naomi"; and they called his name Obed: he is the father of Jesse, the father of David.

Ruth 4:13-17

288   And Jesus answered them, saying, "The hour is come, that the Son of man should be glorified. Verily, verily, I say unto you, Except a corn* of wheat fall into the ground and die, it abideth alone: but if it die, it bringeth forth much fruit. He that loveth his life shall lose it; and he that hateth his life in this world shall keep it unto life eternal. If any man serve me, let him follow me; and where I am, there shall also my servant be: if any man serve me, him will my Father honour."

John 12:23-26

289   O sing unto the LORD a new song:
           Sing unto the LORD, all the earth.
       Sing unto the LORD, bless his name;
           Shew forth his salvation from day to day.
       Declare his glory among the heathen,
           His wonders among all people.
       For the LORD is great, and greatly to be praised:
           He is to be feared above all gods.
       For all the gods of the nations are idols:

But the LORD made the heavens.
Honour and majesty are before him:
    Strength and beauty are in his sanctuary.
Give unto the LORD, O ye kindreds of the people,
    Give unto the LORD glory and strength.
Give unto the LORD the glory due unto his name:
    Bring an offering, and come into his courts.
O worship the LORD in the beauty of holiness:
    Fear before him, all the earth.
Say among the heathen that the LORD reigneth:
    The world also shall be established that it shall not be moved:
    He shall judge the people righteously.
Let the heavens rejoice,
    And let the earth be glad;
Let the sea roar,
    And the fulness thereof.
Let the field be joyful,
    And all that is therein:
Then shall all the trees of the wood rejoice
    Before the LORD:
For he cometh, for he cometh to judge the earth:
    He shall judge the world with righteousness,
    And the people with his truth.

Psalm 96:1-13

The Fourth Day

Sun and Moon

Stars and Signs

Seasons and Cycles

Sterility and Fruition

The Day of the Lord

FOR THE EXPECTANT MOTHER *every pregnancy is the same —save for its unmistakable differences. So it is with all of life's seasons. Every year witnesses a regular sequence of spring and summer, autumn and winter. So also unfold man-made seasons: school years, religious calendars, business cycles, athletic contests, political phases, even war's oscillation with peace. Each is familiar, none quite the same as before.*

Seasonal rhythm is the hallmark of creation's fourth day. Evening follows morning, as predictably as moonrise attending sunset. Unto Israel is born a child: Moses or Samuel or Jesus? It's hard to say; in Scripture they run together somehow. One Joseph's dreamtime flows into that of another Joseph. Throughout God is at work: always recognizably, ever defying expectation. To what end does all course — a bang or a whimper? Mortals guess and place their bets. God only knows.

290   And God said, "Let there be lights in the firmament of the heaven to divide the day from the night; and let them be for signs, and for seasons, and for days, and years: and let them be for lights in the firmament of the heaven to give light upon the earth": And it was so. And God made two great lights; the greater light to rule the day, and the lesser light to rule the night: he made the stars also. And God set them in the firmament of the heaven to give light upon the earth, and to rule over the day and over the night, and to divide the light from the darkness: And God saw that it was good. And the evening and the morning were the fourth day.

Genesis 1:14-19

291   The mighty God, even the LORD, hath spoken,
> And called the earth from the rising of the sun unto the going
> > down thereof.
Out of Zion, the perfection of beauty,
> God hath shined.

Psalm 50:1-2

292   But of the times and the seasons, brethren, ye have no need that I write unto you.

1 Thessalonians 5:1

293 He appointed the moon for seasons:
     The sun knoweth his going down.
Thou makest darkness, and it is night:
     Wherein all the beasts of the forest do creep forth.
The young lions roar after their prey,
     And seek their meat* from God.
The sun ariseth, they gather themselves together,
     And lay them down in their dens.
Man goeth forth unto his work
     And to his labour until the evening.

Psalm 104:19-23

294 There is an evil which I have seen under the sun, and it is common among men: A man to whom God hath given riches, wealth, and honour, so that he wanteth nothing for his soul of all that he desireth, yet God giveth him not power to eat thereof, but a stranger eateth it: this is vanity, and it is an evil disease. If a man beget an hundred children, and live many years, so that the days of his years be many, and his soul be not filled with good, and also that he have no burial; I say, that an untimely birth is better than he. For he cometh in with vanity, and departeth in darkness, and his name shall be covered with darkness. Moreover he hath not seen the sun, nor known any thing: this hath more rest than the other. Yea, though he live a thousand years twice told, yet hath he seen no good: do not all go to one place?

Ecclesiastes 6:1-6

295 I will lift up mine eyes unto the hills,
  From whence cometh my help.
My help cometh from the LORD,
  Which made heaven and earth.
He will not suffer* thy foot to be moved:
  He that keepeth thee will not slumber.
Behold, he that keepeth Israel
  Shall neither slumber nor sleep.
The LORD is thy keeper:
  The LORD is thy shade upon thy right hand.
The sun shall not smite thee by day,
  Nor the moon by night.
The LORD shall preserve thee from all evil:
  He shall preserve thy soul.
The LORD shall preserve thy going out and thy coming in
  From this time forth, and even for evermore.

Psalm 121:1-8

296 Now there was a certain man of Ramathaim-zophim, of Mount
Ephraim, and his name was Elkanah . . . : And he had two wives; the
name of the one was Hannah, and the name of the other Peninnah: and
Peninnah had children, but Hannah had no children.

1 Samuel 1:1-2

297 There was in the days of Herod, the king of Judaea, a certain priest
named Zacharias, of the course of Abia: and his wife was of the daugh-

ters of Aaron, and her name was Elisabeth. And they were both righteous before God, walking in all the commandments and ordinances of the Lord blameless. And they had no child, because that Elisabeth was barren, and they both were now well stricken in years.

Luke 1:5-7

298 And [Elkanah] went up out of his city yearly to worship and to sacrifice unto the LORD of hosts in Shiloh. And the two sons of Eli, Hophni and Phinehas, the priests of the LORD, were there. And when the time was that Elkanah offered, he gave to Peninnah his wife, and to all her sons and her daughters, portions: But unto Hannah he gave a worthy portion; for he loved Hannah: but the LORD had shut up her womb. And her adversary also provoked her sore, for to make her fret, because the LORD had shut up her womb. And as he did so year by year, when she went up to the house of the LORD, so she provoked her; therefore she wept, and did not eat. Then said Elkanah her husband to her, "Hannah, why weepest thou? And why eatest thou not? And why is thy heart grieved? Am not I better to thee than ten sons?"

1 Samuel 1:3-8

299 And it came to pass, that while [Zacharias] executed the priest's office before God in the order of his course, according to the custom of the priest's office, his lot was to burn incense when he went into the temple of the Lord. And the whole multitude of the people were praying without at the time of incense. And there appeared unto him an angel of the Lord standing on the right side of the altar of incense. And when Zacha-

rias saw him, he was troubled, and fear fell upon him. But the angel said unto him, "Fear not, Zacharias: for thy prayer is heard; and thy wife Elisabeth shall bear thee a son, and thou shalt call his name John.

> And thou shalt have joy and gladness;
>   And many shall rejoice at his birth.
> For he shall be great in the sight of the Lord,
>   And shall drink neither wine nor strong drink;
> And he shall be filled with the Holy Ghost,
>   Even from his mother's womb.
> And many of the children of Israel shall he turn to the
>   Lord their God.
> And he shall go before him in the spirit and power of Elias*,
>   To turn the hearts of the fathers to the children,
>   And the disobedient to the wisdom of the just;
>   To make ready a people prepared for the Lord."

And Zacharias said unto the angel, "Whereby shall I know this? For I am an old man, and my wife well stricken in years." And the angel answering said unto him, "I am Gabriel, that stand in the presence of God; and am sent to speak unto thee, and to shew thee these glad tidings. And, behold, thou shalt be dumb, and not able to speak, until the day that these things shall be performed, because thou believest not my words, which shall be fulfilled in their season." And the people waited for Zacharias, and marvelled that he tarried so long in the temple. And when he came out, he could not speak unto them: and they perceived that he had seen a vision in the temple: for he beckoned unto them, and remained speechless.

Luke 1:8-22

300 So Hannah rose up after they had eaten in Shiloh, and after they had drunk. Now Eli the priest sat upon a seat by a post of the temple of the LORD. And she was in bitterness of soul, and prayed unto the LORD, and wept sore. And she vowed a vow, and said, "O LORD of hosts, if thou wilt indeed look on the affliction of thine handmaid, and remember me, and not forget thine handmaid, but wilt give unto thine handmaid a man child, then I will give him unto the LORD all the days of his life, and there shall no razor come upon his head."

1 Samuel 1:9-11

301 The voice of my beloved!
    Behold, he cometh
Leaping upon the mountains,
    Skipping upon the hills.
My beloved is like a roe
    Or a young hart:
Behold, he standeth
    Behind our wall,
He looketh forth at the windows,
    Shewing himself through the lattice.
My beloved spake,
    And said unto me,
"Rise up, my love, my fair one,
    And come away.
For, lo, the winter is past,
    The rain is over and gone;
The flowers appear on the earth;
    The time of the singing of birds is come,

And the voice of the turtle*
    Is heard in our land;
The fig tree putteth forth her green figs,
    And the vines with the tender grape
    Give a good smell.
Arise, my love, my fair one,
    And come away.
O my dove, that art in the clefts of the rock,
    In the secret places of the stairs,
Let me see thy countenance,
    Let me hear thy voice;
For sweet is thy voice,
    And thy countenance is comely.
Take us the foxes,
    The little foxes,
That spoil the vines:
    For our vines have tender grapes."
My beloved is mine, and I am his:
    He feedeth among the lilies.
Until the day break,
    And the shadows flee away,
Turn, my beloved, and be thou like a roe
    Or a young hart upon the mountains of Bether.

Song of Songs 2:8-17

302 And it came to pass, that, as soon as the days of his ministration were accomplished, [Zacharias] departed to his own house. And after those days
his wife Elisabeth conceived, and hid herself five months, saying, "Thus
hath the Lord dealt with me in the days wherein he looked on me, to take
away my reproach among men."

Luke 1:23-25

303 And it came to pass, as she continued praying before the LORD, that Eli
marked her mouth. Now Hannah, she spake in her heart; only her lips
moved, but her voice was not heard: therefore Eli thought she had been
drunken. And Eli said unto her, "How long wilt thou be drunken? Put
away thy wine from thee." And Hannah answered and said, "No, my
lord, I am a woman of a sorrowful spirit: I have drunk neither wine nor
strong drink, but have poured out my soul before the LORD. Count not
thine handmaid for a daughter of Belial: for out of the abundance of my
complaint and grief have I spoken hitherto." Then Eli answered and said,
"Go in peace: and the God of Israel grant thee thy petition that thou hast
asked of him." And she said, "Let thine handmaid find grace in thy
sight." So the woman went her way, and did eat, and her countenance
was no more sad.

1 Samuel 1:12-18

304 Praise ye the LORD.
Praise, O ye servants of the LORD,
    Praise the name of the LORD.
Blessed be the name of the LORD

From this time forth and for evermore.
From the rising of the sun unto the going down of the same
    The LORD's name is to be praised.
The LORD is high above all nations,
    And his glory above the heavens.
Who is like unto the LORD our God,
    Who dwelleth on high,
Who humbleth himself to behold
    The things that are in heaven, and in the earth!
He raiseth up the poor out of the dust,
    And lifteth the needy out of the dunghill;
That he may set him with princes,
    Even with the princes of his people.
He maketh the barren woman to keep house,
    And to be a joyful mother of children.
Praise ye the LORD.

Psalm 113:1-9

305   And in the sixth month the angel Gabriel was sent from God unto a city of Galilee, named Nazareth, to a virgin espoused to a man whose name was Joseph, of the house of David; and the virgin's name was Mary. And the angel came in unto her, and said, "Hail, thou that art highly favoured, the Lord is with thee: blessed art thou among women." And when she saw him, she was troubled at his saying, and cast in her mind what manner of salutation this should be. And the angel said unto her, "Fear not, Mary: for thou hast found favour with God. And, behold, thou shalt conceive in thy womb, and bring forth a son, and shalt call his name JESUS.

He shall be great, and shall be called the Son of the Highest:
And the Lord God shall give unto him the throne of his
    father David:
And he shall reign over the house of Jacob for ever;
And of his kingdom there shall be no end."

Then said Mary unto the angel, "How shall this be, seeing I know not a man?" And the angel answered and said unto her,

"The Holy Ghost shall come upon thee,
And the power of the Highest shall overshadow thee:
Therefore also that holy thing which shall be born of thee
Shall be called the Son of God.

And, behold, thy cousin Elisabeth, she hath also conceived a son in her old age: and this is the sixth month with her, who was called barren. For with God nothing shall be impossible." And Mary said, "Behold the handmaid of the Lord; be it unto me according to thy word." And the angel departed from her.

Luke 1:26-38

306   And they rose up in the morning early, and worshipped before the LORD, and returned, and came to their house to Ramah: and Elkanah knew Hannah his wife; and the LORD remembered her. Wherefore it came to pass, when the time was come about after Hannah had conceived, that she bare a son, and called his name Samuel, saying, "Because I have asked him of the LORD." And the man Elkanah, and all his house, went up to offer unto the LORD the yearly sacrifice, and his vow. But Hannah went not up; for she said unto her husband, "I will not go up until the child be weaned, and then I will bring him, that he may appear before the LORD, and there abide for ever." And Elkanah her husband said unto her, "Do what seemeth thee good; tarry until thou have weaned him; only the LORD establish his word." So the woman abode, and gave her son suck until she weaned him. And when she had weaned him, she took him up with her, with three bullocks, and one ephah* of flour, and a bottle of wine, and brought him unto the house of the LORD in Shiloh: and the child was young. And they slew a bullock, and brought the child to Eli. And she said, "Oh my lord, as thy soul liveth, my lord, I am the woman that stood by thee here, praying unto the LORD. For this child I prayed; and the LORD hath given me my petition which I asked of him: Therefore also I have lent him to the LORD; as long as he liveth he shall be lent to the LORD." And he worshipped the LORD there.

1 Samuel 1:19-28

307 And Mary arose in those days, and went into the hill country with haste, into a city of Juda; and entered into the house of Zacharias, and saluted Elisabeth. And it came to pass, that, when Elisabeth heard the salutation of Mary, the babe leaped in her womb; and Elisabeth was filled with the Holy Ghost: And she spake out with a loud voice, and said, "Blessed art thou among women, and blessed is the fruit of thy womb. And whence is this to me, that the mother of my Lord should come to me? For, lo, as soon as the voice of thy salutation sounded in mine ears, the babe leaped in my womb for joy. And blessed is she that believed: for there shall be a performance of those things which were told her from the Lord."

Luke 1:39-45

308 And Hannah prayed, and said,

"My heart rejoiceth in the LORD,
    Mine horn is exalted in the LORD:
My mouth is enlarged over mine enemies;
    Because I rejoice in thy salvation.
There is none holy as the LORD:
For there is none beside thee:
Neither is there any rock like our God.
Talk no more so exceeding proudly;
    Let not arrogancy come out of your mouth:
For the LORD is a God of knowledge,
    And by him actions are weighed.
The bows of the mighty men are broken,
    And they that stumbled are girded with strength.
They that were full have hired out themselves for bread;
    And they that were hungry ceased:
So that the barren hath born seven;
    And she that hath many children is waxed feeble.
The LORD killeth, and maketh alive:
    He bringeth down to the grave, and bringeth up.
The LORD maketh poor, and maketh rich:
    He bringeth low, and lifteth up.
He raiseth up the poor out of the dust,
    And lifteth up the beggar from the dunghill,
To set them among princes,
    And to make them inherit the throne of glory:
For the pillars of the earth are the LORD's,
    And he hath set the world upon them.
He will keep the feet of his saints,

And the wicked shall be silent in darkness;
    For by strength shall no man prevail.
The adversaries of the L ORD shall be broken to pieces;
    Out of heaven shall he thunder upon them:
The L ORD shall judge the ends of the earth;
    And he shall give strength unto his king,
    And exalt the horn of his anointed."

And Elkanah went to Ramah to his house. And the child did minister unto the L ORD before Eli the priest.

1 Samuel 2:1-11

309   And Mary said,

"My soul doth magnify the Lord,
And my spirit hath rejoiced in God my Saviour.
For he hath regarded the low estate of his handmaiden:
For, behold, from henceforth all generations shall call me blessed.
For he that is mighty hath done to me great things;
And holy is his name.
And his mercy is on them that fear him
From generation to generation.
He hath shewed strength with his arm;
He hath scattered the proud in the imagination of their hearts.
He hath put down the mighty from their seats,
And exalted them of low degree.
He hath filled the hungry with good things;
And the rich he hath sent empty away.
He hath holpen* his servant Israel,

In remembrance of his mercy;
As he spake to our fathers,
To Abraham, and to his seed for ever."

And Mary abode with her about three months, and returned to her own house.

Luke 1:46-56

310 O give thanks unto the LORD; for he is good:
　　For his mercy endureth for ever.
O give thanks unto the God of gods:
　　For his mercy endureth for ever.
O give thanks to the Lord of lords:
　　For his mercy endureth for ever.
To him who alone doeth great wonders:
　　For his mercy endureth for ever.
To him that by wisdom made the heavens:
　　For his mercy endureth for ever.
To him that stretched out the earth above the waters:
　　For his mercy endureth for ever.
To him that made great lights:
　　For his mercy endureth for ever:
The sun to rule by day:
　　For his mercy endureth for ever:
The moon and stars to rule by night:
　　For his mercy endureth for ever. . . .
Who remembered us in our low estate:
　　For his mercy endureth for ever:

And hath redeemed us from our enemies:

    For his mercy endureth for ever.

Who giveth food to all flesh:

    For his mercy endureth for ever.

O give thanks unto the God of heaven:

    For his mercy endureth for ever.

Psalm 136:1-9, 23-26

311   And the child Samuel grew on, and was in favour both with the LORD, and also with men.

1 Samuel 2:26

312   Now Elisabeth's full time came that she should be delivered; and she brought forth a son. And her neighbours and her cousins heard how the Lord had shewed great mercy upon her; and they rejoiced with her. And it came to pass, that on the eighth day they came to circumcise the child; and they called him Zacharias, after the name of his father. And his mother answered and said, "Not so; but he shall be called John." And they said unto her, "There is none of thy kindred that is called by this name." And they made signs to his father, how he would have him called. And he asked for a writing table, and wrote, saying, "His name is John." And they marvelled all. And his mouth was opened immediately, and his tongue loosed, and he spake, and praised God. And fear came on all that dwelt round about them: and all these sayings were noised abroad throughout all the hill country of Judaea. And all they that heard them laid them up in their hearts, saying, "What manner of child shall this be!" And the hand of the Lord was with him.

Luke 1:57-66

313   Now why dost thou cry out aloud?
      Is there no king in thee?
  Is thy counsellor perished?
      For pangs have taken thee as a woman in travail.
  Be in pain, and labour to bring forth, O daughter of Zion,
      Like a woman in travail:
  For now shalt thou go forth out of the city,
      And thou shalt dwell in the field,
      And thou shalt go even to Babylon;
  There shalt thou be delivered;
      There the LORD shall redeem thee
      From the hand of thine enemies.

Micah 4:9-10

314   And his father Zacharias was filled with the Holy Ghost, and prophesied, saying,

    "Blessed be the Lord God of Israel;
    For he hath visited and redeemed his people,
    And hath raised up an horn of salvation for us
    In the house of his servant David;
    As he spake by the mouth of his holy prophets,
    Which have been since the world began:
    That we should be saved from our enemies,
    And from the hand of all that hate us;
    To perform the mercy promised to our fathers,
    And to remember his holy covenant;
    The oath which he sware to our father Abraham,

That he would grant unto us,
That we being delivered out of the hand of our enemies
Might serve him without fear,
In holiness and righteousness before him,
All the days of our life.
And thou, child, shalt be called the prophet of the Highest:
For thou shalt go before the face of the Lord to prepare his ways;
To give knowledge of salvation unto his people
By the remission of their sins,
Through the tender mercy of our God;
Whereby the dayspring from on high hath visited us,
To give light to them that sit in darkness and in the shadow
    of death,
To guide our feet into the way of peace."

And the child grew, and waxed strong in spirit, and was in the deserts till the day of his shewing unto Israel.

Luke 1:67-80

315   The eternal God is thy refuge,
    And underneath are the everlasting arms:
And he shall thrust out the enemy from before thee;
    And shall say, "Destroy them."
Israel then shall dwell in safety alone:
    The fountain of Jacob shall be upon a land of corn* and wine;
    Also his heavens shall drop down dew.
Happy art thou, O Israel: Who is like unto thee,
    O people saved by the LORD,

The shield of thy help,
    And who is the sword of thy excellency!
And thine enemies shall be found liars unto thee;
    And thou shalt tread upon their high places.

Deuteronomy 33:27-29

316   And it came to pass in those days, that there went out a decree from Caesar Augustus, that all the world should be taxed. (And this taxing was first made when Cyrenius was governor of Syria.) And all went to be taxed, every one into his own city. And Joseph also went up from Galilee, out of the city of Nazareth, into Judaea, unto the city of David, which is called Bethlehem; (because he was of the house and lineage of David:) to be taxed with Mary his espoused wife, being great with child. And so it was, that, while they were there, the days were accomplished that she should be delivered. And she brought forth her firstborn son, and wrapped him in swaddling clothes, and laid him in a manger; because there was no room for them in the inn.

Luke 2:1-7

317   For unto us a child is born,
    Unto us a son is given:
And the government shall be upon his shoulder:
    And his name shall be called
Wonderful, Counsellor, The mighty God,
    The everlasting Father, The Prince of Peace.
Of the increase of his government and peace

There shall be no end,
Upon the throne of David, and upon his kingdom,
   To order it, and to establish it
With judgment and with justice from henceforth even for ever.
   The zeal of the LORD of hosts will perform this.

Isaiah 9:6-7

318 And there were in the same country shepherds abiding in the field, keeping watch over their flock by night. And, lo, the angel of the Lord came upon them, and the glory of the Lord shone round about them: and they were sore afraid. And the angel said unto them, "Fear not: for, behold, I bring you good tidings of great joy, which shall be to all people. For unto you is born this day in the city of David a Saviour, which is Christ the Lord. And this shall be a sign unto you; Ye shall find the babe wrapped in swaddling clothes, lying in a manger." And suddenly there was with the angel a multitude of the heavenly host praising God, and saying,

   "Glory to God in the highest,
   And on earth peace, good will toward men."

And it came to pass, as the angels were gone away from them into heaven, the shepherds said one to another, "Let us now go even unto Bethlehem, and see this thing which is come to pass, which the Lord hath made known unto us." And they came with haste, and found Mary, and Joseph, and the babe lying in a manger. And when they had seen it, they made known abroad the saying which was told them concerning this child. And all they that heard it wondered at those things which were told them by the shepherds. But Mary kept all these things, and pondered them in her heart. And the shepherds returned, glorifying and praising God for all the things that they had heard and seen, as it was told unto them.

Luke 2:8-20

319   Give the king thy judgments, O God,
        And thy righteousness unto the king's son.
      He shall judge thy people with righteousness,
        And thy poor with judgment.
      The mountains shall bring peace to the people,
        And the little hills, by righteousness.
      He shall judge the poor of the people,
        He shall save the children of the needy,
        And shall break in pieces the oppressor.
      They shall fear thee as long as the sun and moon endure,
        Throughout all generations.
      He shall come down like rain upon the mown grass:
        As showers that water the earth.
      In his days shall the righteous flourish;
        And abundance of peace so long as the moon endureth.

Psalm 72:1-7

320   And Simeon blessed them, and said unto Mary his mother,

        "Behold, this child is set for the fall and rising again of many
            in Israel;
        And for a sign which shall be spoken against;

(Yea, a sword shall pierce through thy own soul also,)
That the thoughts of many hearts may be revealed."

And there was one Anna, a prophetess, the daughter of Phanuel, of the tribe of Aser: she was of a great age, and had lived with an husband seven years from her virginity; and she was a widow of about fourscore and four years, which departed not from the temple, but served God with fastings and prayers night and day. And she coming in that instant gave thanks likewise unto the Lord, and spake of him to all them that looked for redemption in Jerusalem. And when they had performed all things according to the law of the Lord, they returned into Galilee, to their own city Nazareth. And the child grew, and waxed strong in spirit, filled with wisdom: and the grace of God was upon him.

Luke 2:34-40

321 "For from the rising of the sun even unto the going down of the same my name shall be great among the Gentiles; and in every place incense shall be offered unto my name, and a pure offering: for my name shall be great among the heathen," saith the LORD of hosts.

Malachi 1:11

322 Now his parents went to Jerusalem every year at the feast of the Passover. And when he was twelve years old, they went up to Jerusalem after the custom of the feast. And when they had fulfilled the days, as they returned, the child Jesus tarried behind in Jerusalem; and Joseph and his mother knew not of it. But they, supposing him to have been in the company, went a

day's journey; and they sought him among their kinsfolk and acquaintance. And when they found him not, they turned back again to Jerusalem, seeking him. And it came to pass, that after three days they found him in the temple, sitting in the midst of the doctors*, both hearing them, and asking them questions. And all that heard him were astonished at his understanding and answers. And when they saw him, they were amazed: and his mother said unto him, "Son, why hast thou thus dealt with us? Behold, thy father and I have sought thee sorrowing." And he said unto them, "How is it that ye sought me? Wist* ye not that I must be about my Father's business?" And they understood not the saying which he spake unto them. And he went down with them, and came to Nazareth, and was subject unto them: but his mother kept all these sayings in her heart. And Jesus increased in wisdom and stature, and in favour with God and man.

Luke 2:41-52

323 Moreover the Lord spake again unto Ahaz, saying, "Ask thee a sign of the Lord thy God; ask it either in the depth, or in the height above." But Ahaz said, "I will not ask, neither will I tempt the Lord." And he said, "Hear ye now, O house of David; Is it a small thing for you to weary men, but will ye weary my God also? Therefore the Lord himself shall give you a sign; Behold, a virgin shall conceive, and bear a son, and shall call his name Immanuel. Butter and honey shall he eat, that he may know to refuse the evil, and choose the good. For before the child shall know to refuse the evil, and choose the good, the land that thou abhorrest shall be forsaken of both her kings. The Lord shall bring upon thee, and upon thy people, and upon thy father's house, days that have not come, from the day that Ephraim departed from Judah; even the king of Assyria."

Isaiah 7:10-17

324 Now the birth of Jesus Christ was on this wise*: When as his mother
Mary was espoused to Joseph, before they came together, she was found
with child of the Holy Ghost. Then Joseph her husband, being a just
man, and not willing to make her a publick example, was minded to put
her away privily*. But while he thought on these things, behold, the angel
of the Lord appeared unto him in a dream, saying, "Joseph, thou son of
David, fear not to take unto thee Mary thy wife: for that which is conceived in her is of the Holy Ghost. And she shall bring forth a son, and
thou shalt call his name JESUS: for he shall save his people from their
sins." Now all this was done, that it might be fulfilled which was spoken
of the Lord by the prophet, saying,

> "Behold, a virgin shall be with child, and shall bring forth a son,
> And they shall call his name Emmanuel,"

which being interpreted is, God with us. Then Joseph being raised from
sleep did as the angel of the Lord had bidden him, and took unto him his
wife: And knew her not till she had brought forth her firstborn son: and
he called his name JESUS.

Matthew 1:18-25

325 And Joseph [son of Jacob] dreamed a dream, and he told it his brethren: and they hated him yet the more. And he said unto them, "Hear, I
pray you, this dream which I have dreamed: For, behold, we were bind-
ing sheaves in the field, and, lo, my sheaf arose, and also stood upright;
and, behold, your sheaves stood round about, and made obeisance to
my sheaf." And his brethren said to him, "Shalt thou indeed reign over
us? Or shalt thou indeed have dominion over us?" And they hated him
yet the more for his dreams, and for his words. And he dreamed yet an-

other dream, and told it his brethren, and said, "Behold, I have dreamed a dream more; and, behold, the sun and the moon and the eleven stars made obeisance to me." And he told it to his father, and to his brethren: and his father rebuked him, and said unto him, "What is this dream that thou hast dreamed? Shall I and thy mother and thy brethren indeed come to bow down ourselves to thee to the earth?" And his brethren envied him; but his father observed the saying.

Genesis 37:5-11

326   Now when Jesus was born in Bethlehem of Judaea in the days of Herod the king, behold, there came wise men from the east to Jerusalem, saying, "Where is he that is born King of the Jews? For we have seen his star in the east, and are come to worship him." When Herod the king had heard these things, he was troubled, and all Jerusalem with him. And when he had gathered all the chief priests and scribes of the people together, he demanded of them where Christ should be born. And they said unto him, "In Bethlehem of Judaea: for thus it is written by the prophet,

> 'And thou Bethlehem, in the land of Juda,
>   Art not the least among the princes of Juda:
> For out of thee shall come a Governor,
>   That shall rule my people Israel.'"

Matthew 2:1-6

327   And [Balaam] took up his parable, and said,

> "Balaam the son of Beor hath said,
>   And the man whose eyes are open hath said:

He hath said, which heard the words of God,
 And knew the knowledge of the most High,
Which saw the vision of the Almighty,
 Falling into a trance, but having his eyes open:
I shall see him, but not now:
 I shall behold him, but not nigh:
There shall come a Star out of Jacob,
 And a Sceptre shall rise out of Israel."

Numbers 24:15-17ab

328 Then Herod, when he had privily* called the wise men, enquired of them diligently what time the star appeared. And he sent them to Bethlehem, and said, "Go and search diligently for the young child; and when ye have found him, bring me word again, that I may come and worship him also." When they had heard the king, they departed; and, lo, the star, which they saw in the east, went before them, till it came and stood over where the young child was. When they saw the star, they rejoiced with exceeding great joy. And when they were come into the house, they saw the young child with Mary his mother, and fell down, and worshipped him: and when they had opened their treasures, they presented unto him gifts; gold, and frankincense, and myrrh. And being warned of God in a dream that they should not return to Herod, they departed into their own country another way.

Matthew 2:7-12

329 But thou, Bethlehem Ephratah,

Though thou be little among the thousands of Judah,

Yet out of thee shall he come forth unto me that is to be ruler in
Israel;

Whose goings forth have been from of old, from everlasting.

Therefore will he give them up, until the time

That she which travaileth hath brought forth:

Then the remnant of his brethren shall return

Unto the children of Israel.

And he shall stand and feed in the strength of the LORD,

In the majesty of the name of the LORD his God;

And they shall abide:

For now shall he be great unto the ends of the earth.

Micah 5:2-4

330 And when they saw him afar off, even before [Joseph] came near unto them, [his brothers] conspired against him to slay him. And they said one to another, "Behold, this dreamer cometh. Come now therefore, and let us slay him, and cast him into some pit, and we will say, 'Some evil beast hath devoured him': and we shall see what will become of his dreams." And Reuben heard it, and he delivered him out of their hands; and said, "Let us not kill him." And Reuben said unto them, "Shed no blood, but cast him into this pit that is in the wilderness, and lay no hand upon him"; that he might rid him out of their hands, to deliver him to his father again. And it came to pass, when Joseph was come unto his brethren, that they stript Joseph out of his coat, his coat of many colours that was on him; and they took him, and cast him into a pit: and the pit was empty, there was no water in it. And they sat down to eat bread: and they lifted up their eyes and looked, and, behold, a company of Ishmeelites came from Gilead with their camels bearing spicery and balm and myrrh, going to carry it down to Egypt. And Judah said unto his brethren, "What profit is it if we slay our brother, and conceal his blood? Come, and let us sell him to the Ishmeelites, and let not our hand be upon him; for he is our brother and our flesh." And his brethren were content. Then there passed by Midianites merchantmen; and they drew and lifted up Joseph out of the pit, and sold Joseph to the Ishmeelites for twenty pieces of silver: and they brought Joseph into Egypt.

Genesis 37:18-28

331 And when [the wise men] were departed, behold, the angel of the Lord appeareth to Joseph in a dream, saying, "Arise, and take the young child and his mother, and flee into Egypt, and be thou there until I bring thee word: for Herod will seek the young child to destroy him." When he arose, he took the young child and his mother by night, and departed into Egypt: And was there until the death of Herod: that it might be fulfilled which was spoken of the Lord by the prophet, saying, "Out of Egypt have I called my son."

Matthew 2:13-15

332 And Reuben returned unto the pit; and, behold, Joseph was not in the pit; and he rent his clothes. And he returned unto his brethren, and said, "The child is not; and I, whither shall I go?" And they took Joseph's coat, and killed a kid* of the goats, and dipped the coat in the blood; and they sent the coat of many colours, and they brought it to their father; and

said, "This have we found: know now whether it be thy son's coat or no."
And he knew it, and said, "It is my son's coat; an evil beast hath devoured
him; Joseph is without doubt rent in pieces." And Jacob rent his clothes,
and put sackcloth upon his loins, and mourned for his son many days.
And all his sons and all his daughters rose up to comfort him; but he refused to be comforted; and he said, "For I will go down into the grave
unto my son mourning." Thus his father wept for him. And the
Midianites sold him into Egypt unto Potiphar, an officer of Pharaoh's,
and captain of the guard.

Genesis 37:29-36

333 When Israel was a child, then I loved him,
     And called my son out of Egypt.
As they called them,
     So they went from them:
They sacrificed unto Baalim,
     And burned incense to graven images. . . .
How shall I give thee up, Ephraim?
     How shall I deliver thee, Israel?
How shall I make thee as Admah?
     How shall I set thee as Zeboim?
Mine heart is turned within me,
     My repentings are kindled together.
I will not execute the fierceness of mine anger,
     I will not return to destroy Ephraim:
For I am God, and not man;
     The Holy One in the midst of thee:
     And I will not enter into the city.

Hosea 11:1-2, 8-9

334　Now there arose up a new king over Egypt, which knew not Joseph. And he said unto his people, "Behold, the people of the children of Israel are more and mightier than we: Come on, let us deal wisely with them; lest they multiply, and it come to pass, that, when there falleth out any war, they join also unto our enemies, and fight against us, and so get them up out of the land." Therefore they did set over them taskmasters to afflict them with their burdens. And they built for Pharaoh treasure cities, Pithom and Raamses. But the more they afflicted them, the more they multiplied and grew. And they were grieved because of the children of Israel. . . . And Pharaoh charged all his people, saying, "Every [Hebrew] son that is born ye shall cast into the river, and every daughter ye shall save alive."

Exodus 1:8-12, 22

335　Thus saith the LORD;

　　"A voice was heard in Ramah,
　　　Lamentation, and bitter weeping;
　　Rahel* weeping for her children
　　　Refused to be comforted for her children,
　　　Because they were not."

Thus saith the LORD;

　　"Refrain thy voice from weeping,
　　　And thine eyes from tears:
　　For thy work shall be rewarded,"
　　　　saith the LORD;
　　　"And they shall come again from the land of the enemy.
　　And there is hope in thine end,"

saith the LORD,
"That thy children shall come again
To their own border."

Jeremiah 31:15-17

336   Then Herod, when he saw that he was mocked of the wise men, was exceeding wroth*, and sent forth, and slew all the children that were in Bethlehem, and in all the coasts thereof, from two years old and under, according to the time which he had diligently inquired of the wise men. Then was fulfilled that which was spoken by Jeremy* the prophet, saying,

"In Rama was there a voice heard,
Lamentation, and weeping, and great mourning,
Rachel weeping for her children,
And would not be comforted,
Because they are not."

But when Herod was dead, behold, an angel of the Lord appeareth in a dream to Joseph in Egypt, saying, "Arise, and take the young child and his mother, and go into the land of Israel: for they are dead which sought the young child's life." And he arose, and took the young child and his mother, and came into the land of Israel. But when he heard that Archelaus did reign in Judaea in the room of his father Herod, he was afraid to go thither: notwithstanding, being warned of God in a dream, he turned aside into the parts of Galilee: And he came and dwelt in a city called Nazareth: that it might be fulfilled which was spoken by the prophets, "He shall be called a Nazarene."

Matthew 2:16-23

337 And there went a man of the house of Levi, and took to wife a daughter of Levi. And the woman conceived, and bare a son: and when she saw him that he was a goodly child, she hid him three months. And when she could not longer hide him, she took for him an ark of bulrushes, and daubed it with slime and with pitch, and put the child therein; and she laid it in the flags by the river's brink. And his sister stood afar off, to wit* what would be done to him. And the daughter of Pharaoh came down to wash herself at the river; and her maidens walked along by the river's side; and when she saw the ark among the flags, she sent her maid to fetch it. And when she had opened it, she saw the child: and, behold, the babe wept. And she had compassion on him, and said, "This is one of the Hebrews' children." Then said his sister to Pharaoh's daughter, "Shall I go and call to thee a nurse of the Hebrew women, that she may nurse the child for thee?" And Pharaoh's daughter said to her, "Go." And the maid went and called the child's mother. And Pharaoh's daughter said unto her, "Take this child away, and nurse it for me, and I will give thee thy wages." And the woman took the child, and nursed it. And the child grew, and she brought him unto Pharaoh's daughter, and he became her son. And she called his name Moses: and she said, "Because I drew him out of the water."

Exodus 2:1-10

338 And it came to pass after these things, that his master [Potiphar]'s wife cast her eyes upon Joseph; and she said, "Lie with me." But he refused, and said unto his master's wife, "Behold, my master wotteth* not what is with me in the house, and he hath committed all that he hath to my hand; there is none greater in this house than I; neither hath he kept back any thing from me but thee, because thou art his wife: how then can I do this great wickedness, and sin against God?" And it came to pass, as she spake to Joseph day by day, that he hearkened not unto her, to lie by her, or to be with her. And it came to pass about this time, that Joseph went into the house to do his business; and there was none of the men of the house there within. And she caught him by his garment, saying, "Lie with me": and he left his garment in her hand, and fled, and got him out. . . . And she laid up his garment by her, until his lord came home. And she spake unto him according to these words, saying, "The Hebrew servant, which thou hast brought unto us, came in unto me to mock me: And it came to pass, as I lifted up my voice and cried, that he left his garment with me, and fled out." And it came to pass, when his master heard the words of his wife, which she spake unto him, saying, "After this manner did thy servant to me"; that his wrath was kindled. And Joseph's master took him, and put him into the prison, a place where the king's prisoners were bound: and he was there in the prison.

Genesis 39:7-12, 16-20

339 "Verily, verily, I say unto you, That ye shall weep and lament, but the world shall rejoice: and ye shall be sorrowful, but your sorrow shall be turned into joy. A woman when she is in travail hath sorrow, because her hour is come: but as soon as she is delivered of the child, she remembereth no more the anguish, for joy that a man is born into the world. And ye now therefore have sorrow: but I will see you again, and your heart shall rejoice, and your joy no man taketh from you. And in that day ye shall ask me nothing. Verily, verily, I say unto you, Whatsoever ye shall ask the Father in my name, he will give it you. Hitherto have ye asked nothing in my name: ask, and ye shall receive, that your joy may be full."

John 16:20-24

340 Then Pharaoh sent and called Joseph, and they brought him hastily out of the dungeon: and he shaved himself, and changed his raiment, and came in unto Pharaoh. And Pharaoh said unto Joseph, "I have dreamed a dream, and there is none that can interpret it: and I have heard say of thee, that thou canst understand a dream to interpret it." And Joseph answered Pharaoh, saying, "It is not in me: God shall give Pharaoh an answer of peace. . . . Behold, there come seven years of great plenty throughout all the land of Egypt: And there shall arise after them seven years of famine; and all the plenty shall be forgotten in the land of Egypt; and the famine shall consume the land; and the plenty shall not be known in the land by reason of that famine following; for it shall be very grievous. And for that the dream was doubled unto Pharaoh twice; it is because the thing is established by God, and God will shortly bring it to pass. Now therefore let Pharaoh look out a man discreet and wise, and set him over the land of Egypt. . . ."

And the thing was good in the eyes of Pharaoh, and in the eyes of all his servants. And Pharaoh said unto his servants, "Can we find such a one as this is, a man in whom the Spirit of God is?" And Pharaoh said unto Joseph, "Forasmuch as God hath shewed thee all this, there is none so discreet and wise as thou art: Thou shalt be over my house, and according unto thy word shall all my people be ruled: only in the throne will I be greater than thou." And Pharaoh said unto Joseph, "See, I have set thee over all the land of Egypt." And Pharaoh took off his ring from his hand, and put it upon Joseph's hand, and arrayed him in vestures of fine linen, and put a gold chain about his neck; and he made him to ride in the second chariot which he had; and they cried before him, "Bow the knee": and he made him ruler over all the land of Egypt.

Genesis 41:14-16, 29-33, 37-43

341 A man hath joy by the answer of his mouth:
      And a word spoken in due season, how good is it!

Proverbs 15:23

342 And [Joseph's brothers] went up out of Egypt, and came into the land of
      Canaan unto Jacob their father, and told him, saying, "Joseph is yet alive,
      and he is governor over all the land of Egypt." And Jacob's heart fainted,
      for he believed them not. And they told him all the words of Joseph,
      which he had said unto them: and when he saw the wagons which Joseph
      had sent to carry him, the spirit of Jacob their father revived: And Israel
      said, "It is enough; Joseph my son is yet alive: I will go and see him before
      I die."

Genesis 45:25-28

343 Praise ye the LORD:
      For it is good to sing praises unto our God;
        For it is pleasant; and praise is comely.
      The LORD doth build up Jerusalem:
        He gathereth together the outcasts of Israel.
      He healeth the broken in heart,
        And bindeth up their wounds.
      He telleth the number of the stars;
        He calleth them all by their names.
      Great is our Lord, and of great power:
        His understanding is infinite.
      The LORD lifteth up the meek:

He casteth the wicked down to the ground.
Sing unto the LORD with thanksgiving;
  Sing praise upon the harp unto our God.

Psalm 147:1-7

344 Blessed be the God and Father of our Lord Jesus Christ, which according to his abundant mercy hath begotten us again unto a lively hope by the resurrection of Jesus Christ from the dead, to an inheritance incorruptible, and undefiled, and that fadeth not away, reserved in heaven for you, who are kept by the power of God through faith unto salvation ready to be revealed in the last time. Wherein ye greatly rejoice, though now for a season, if need be, ye are in heaviness through manifold temptations: That the trial of your faith, being much more precious than of gold that perisheth, though it be tried with fire, might be found unto praise and honour and glory at the appearing of Jesus Christ: Whom having not seen, ye love; in whom, though now ye see him not, yet believing, ye rejoice with joy unspeakable and full of glory: Receiving the end of your faith, even the salvation of your souls. Of which salvation the prophets have inquired and searched diligently, who prophesied of the grace that should come unto you: Searching what, or what manner of time the Spirit of Christ which was in them did signify, when it testified beforehand the sufferings of Christ, and the glory that should follow.

1 Peter 1:3-11

345 Then spake Joshua to the LORD in the day when the LORD delivered up the Amorites before the children of Israel, and he said in the sight of Israel,

> "Sun, stand thou still upon Gibeon;
>> And thou, Moon, in the valley of Ajalon."
> And the sun stood still, and the moon stayed,
>> Until the people had avenged themselves upon their enemies.

Is not this written in the book of Jasher? So the sun stood still in the midst of heaven, and hasted not to go down about a whole day. And there was no day like that before it or after it, that the LORD hearkened unto the voice of a man: for the LORD fought for Israel.

Joshua 10:12-14

346 "But in those days, after that tribulation, the sun shall be darkened, and the moon shall not give her light, and the stars of heaven shall fall, and the powers that are in heaven shall be shaken. And then shall they see the Son of man coming in the clouds with great power and glory. And then shall he send his angels, and shall gather together his elect from the four winds, from the uttermost part of the earth to the uttermost part of heaven."

Mark 13:24-27

347 Behold, the day of the LORD cometh,
> Cruel both with wrath and fierce anger,
To lay the land desolate:

And he shall destroy the sinners thereof out of it.
For the stars of heaven and the constellations thereof
    Shall not give their light:
The sun shall be darkened in his going forth,
    And the moon shall not cause her light to shine.
And I will punish the world for their evil,
    And the wicked for their iniquity;
And I will cause the arrogancy of the proud to cease,
    And will lay low the haughtiness of the terrible.

Isaiah 13:9-11

348   Thus hath the Lord GOD shewed unto me: and behold a basket of summer fruit. And he said, "Amos, what seest thou?" And I said, "A basket of summer fruit." Then said the LORD unto me,

    "The end is come upon my people of Israel;
        I will not again pass by them any more.
    And the songs of the temple shall be howlings in that day,"
            saith the Lord GOD:
    "There shall be many dead bodies in every place;
        They shall cast them forth with silence."

Hear this, O ye that swallow up the needy,
    Even to make the poor of the land to fail,
Saying, "When will the new moon be gone,
    That we may sell corn*?
And the sabbath,
    That we may set forth wheat,
Making the ephah* small, and the shekel great,

And falsifying the balances by deceit?
That we may buy the poor for silver,
    And the needy for a pair of shoes;
    Yea, and sell the refuse of the wheat?"
The LORD hath sworn by the excellency of Jacob,
    "Surely I will never forget any of their works.
    Shall not the land tremble for this,
        And every one mourn that dwelleth therein?
    And it shall rise up wholly as a flood;
        And it shall be cast out and drowned, as by the flood
            of Egypt."

Amos 8:1-8

349 How art thou fallen from heaven,
        O Lucifer, son of the morning!
    How art thou cut down to the ground,
        Which didst weaken the nations!
    For thou hast said in thine heart,
        "I will ascend into heaven,
    I will exalt my throne
        Above the stars of God:
    I will sit also upon the mount of the congregation,
        In the sides of the north:
    I will ascend above the heights of the clouds;
        I will be like the most High."
    Yet thou shalt be brought down to hell,
        To the sides of the pit.
    They that see thee shall narrowly look upon thee,

And consider thee, saying,
"Is this the man that made the earth to tremble,
   That did shake kingdoms;
That made the world as a wilderness,
   And destroyed the cities thereof;
   That opened not the house of his prisoners?"

Isaiah 14:12-17

350   And I beheld when [the Lamb] had opened the sixth seal, and, lo, there was a great earthquake; and the sun became black as sackcloth of hair, and the moon became as blood; and the stars of heaven fell unto the earth, even as a fig tree casteth her untimely figs, when she is shaken of a mighty wind. And the heaven departed as a scroll when it is rolled together; and every mountain and island were moved out of their places. And the kings of the earth, and the great men, and the rich men, and the chief captains, and the mighty men, and every bondman, and every free man, hid themselves in the dens and in the rocks of the mountains; and said to the mountains and rocks, "Fall on us, and hide us from the face of him that sitteth on the throne, and from the wrath of the Lamb: For the great day of his wrath is come; and who shall be able to stand?"

Revelation 6:12-17

351   Remember now thy Creator in the days of thy youth, while the evil days come not, nor the years draw nigh, when thou shalt say, "I have no pleasure in them"; while the sun, or the light, or the moon, or the stars, be not darkened, nor the clouds return after the rain: In the day when the keep-

ers of the house shall tremble, and the strong men shall bow themselves, and the grinders cease because they are few, and those that look out of the windows be darkened, and the doors shall be shut in the streets, when the sound of the grinding is low, and he shall rise up at the voice of the bird, and all the daughters of musick shall be brought low; also when they shall be afraid of that which is high, and fears shall be in the way, and the almond tree shall flourish, and the grasshopper shall be a burden, and desire shall fail: because man goeth to his long home, and the mourners go about the streets: Or ever the silver cord be loosed, or the golden bowl be broken, or the pitcher be broken at the fountain, or the wheel broken at the cistern. Then shall the dust return to the earth as it was: and the spirit shall return unto God who gave it. Vanity of vanities, saith the preacher; all is vanity.

Ecclesiastes 12:1-8

352 But some man will say, "How are the dead raised up? And with what body do they come?" Thou fool, that which thou sowest is not quickened*, except it die: And that which thou sowest, thou sowest not that body that shall be, but bare grain, it may chance of wheat, or of some other grain: But God giveth it a body as it hath pleased him, and to every seed his own body. All flesh is not the same flesh: but there is one kind of flesh of men, another flesh of beasts, another of fishes, and another of birds. There are also celestial bodies, and bodies terrestrial: but the glory of the celestial is one, and the glory of the terrestrial is another. There is one glory of the sun, and another glory of the moon, and another glory of the stars: for one star differeth from another star in glory. So also is the resurrection of the dead. It is sown in corruption; it is raised in incorruption: It is sown in dishonour; it is raised in glory: It is sown in

weakness; it is raised in power: It is sown a natural body; it is raised a spiritual body. There is a natural body, and there is a spiritual body.

1 Corinthians 15:35-44

353 That which hath been is named already, and it is known that it is man: neither may he contend with him that is mightier than he. Seeing there be many things that increase vanity, what is man the better? . . . There is a vanity which is done upon the earth; that there be just men, unto whom it happeneth according to the work of the wicked; again, there be wicked men, to whom it happeneth according to the work of the righteous: I said that this also is vanity. Then I commended mirth, because a man hath no better thing under the sun, than to eat, and to drink, and to be merry: for that shall abide with him of his labour the days of his life, which God giveth him under the sun.

Ecclesiastes 6:10-11; 8:14-15

354 I charge thee therefore before God, and the Lord Jesus Christ, who shall judge the quick* and the dead at his appearing and his kingdom; Preach the word; be instant* in season, out of season; reprove, rebuke, exhort with all longsuffering and doctrine. For the time will come when they will not endure sound doctrine; but after their own lusts shall they heap to themselves teachers, having itching ears; And they shall turn away their ears from the truth, and shall be turned unto fables. But watch thou in all things, endure afflictions, do the work of an evangelist, make full proof of thy ministry. For I am now ready to be offered, and the time of my departure is at hand. I have fought a good fight, I have fin-

ished my course, I have kept the faith: Henceforth there is laid up for me a crown of righteousness, which the Lord, the righteous judge, shall give me at that day: and not to me only, but unto all them also that love his appearing.

2 Timothy 4:1-8

355   The day is thine, the night also is thine:
      Thou hast prepared the light and the sun.
  Thou hast set all the borders of the earth:
      Thou hast made summer and winter.

Psalm 74:16-17

356   Violence shall no more be heard in thy land,
      Wasting nor destruction within thy borders;
  But thou shalt call thy walls Salvation,
      And thy gates Praise.
  The sun shall be no more thy light by day;
      Neither for brightness shall the moon give light unto thee:
  But the LORD shall be unto thee an everlasting light,
      And thy God thy glory.
  Thy sun shall no more go down;
      Neither shall thy moon withdraw itself:
  For the LORD shall be thine everlasting light,
      And the days of thy mourning shall be ended.

Isaiah 60:18-20

357 "But of that day and that hour knoweth no man, no, not the angels which are in heaven, neither the Son, but the Father. Take ye heed, watch and pray: for ye know not when the time is."

Mark 13:32-33

358 To every thing there is a season,
   And a time to every purpose under the heaven:
A time to be born, and a time to die;
   A time to plant, and a time to pluck up that which is planted;
A time to kill, and a time to heal;
   A time to break down, and a time to build up;
A time to weep, and a time to laugh;
   A time to mourn, and a time to dance;
A time to cast away stones, and a time to gather stones together;
   A time to embrace, and a time to refrain from embracing;
A time to get, and a time to lose;
   A time to keep, and a time to cast away;
A time to rend, and a time to sew;
   A time to keep silence, and a time to speak;
A time to love, and a time to hate;
   A time of war, and a time of peace.
What profit hath he that worketh in that wherein he laboureth?

Ecclesiastes 3:1-9

The Fifth Day

Fish and Fowl

Abundance and Adequacy

The Dependable and the Unreliable

Law and Faith

The Character of Love

In four days of creation the stage is set for animate life. On the fifth Day again God speaks and moving creatures are made, beginning with fish of the sea and birds of the air. Move they do: teeming and multiplying. Life explodes from waves that had chaotically roiled. Where once nothing stirred, now swarm animals in incalculable abundance, fashioned by a God of boundless bounty.

The potential of abundance is realized in many forms: from humble acts of hospitality, social expressions of multiplication, to the uniquely divine bestowal of an everlasting covenant with humankind and the offering of its Savior. Life is created; it is nurtured as well. Tension arises when those blessed with such abundance regard themselves as their own benefactors. Confusion ensues when contingent and needy creatures fantasize themselves as their own creator, responsible for their own sustenance through self-righteousness or evanescent wealth. Scripture wrestles with these perdurable tensions and constant slippage. Its ultimate confession is that there is one alone whose glory bestrides heaven and earth, whose name alone is excellent and worthy of unmitigated praise. That one is the Lord God.

359 And God said, "Let the waters bring forth abundantly the moving creature that hath life, and fowl that may fly above the earth in the open firmament of heaven." And God created great whales, and every living creature that moveth, which the waters brought forth abundantly, after their
kind, and every winged fowl after his kind: And God saw that it was
good. And God blessed them, saying, "Be fruitful, and multiply, and fill
the waters in the seas, and let fowl multiply in the earth." And the evening and the morning were the fifth day.

Genesis 1:20-23

360 Blessed is the man that trusteth in the LORD,
     And whose hope the LORD is.
   For he shall be as a tree planted by the waters,
     And that spreadeth out her roots by the river,
   And shall not see when heat cometh,
     But her leaf shall be green;
   And shall not be careful* in the year of drought,
     Neither shall cease from yielding fruit.

Jeremiah 17:7-8

361 "Blessed are the poor in spirit: for theirs is the kingdom of heaven.
   Blessed are they that mourn: for they shall be comforted.
   Blessed are the meek: for they shall inherit the earth.
   Blessed are they which do hunger and thirst after righteousness:
         for they shall be filled.
   Blessed are the merciful: for they shall obtain mercy.

Blessed are the pure in heart: for they shall see God.

Blessed are the peacemakers: for they shall be called the children
of God.

Blessed are they which are persecuted for righteousness' sake:
for theirs is the kingdom of heaven.

Blessed are ye, when men shall revile you, and persecute you,
and shall say all manner of evil against you falsely, for
my sake. Rejoice, and be exceeding glad: for great is
your reward in heaven: for so persecuted they the
prophets which were before you."

Matthew 5:3-12

362   Righteous art thou, O LORD, when I plead with thee:
    Yet let me talk with thee of thy judgments:
  Wherefore* doth the way of the wicked prosper?
    Wherefore are all they happy that deal very treacherously?

Jeremiah 12:1

363   "But woe unto you that are rich! For ye have received
    your consolation.
  Woe unto you that are full! For ye shall hunger.
  Woe unto you that laugh now! For ye shall mourn and weep."

Luke 6:24-25

364 Teach me, O LORD, the way of thy statutes;
    And I shall keep it unto the end.
Give me understanding, and I shall keep thy law;
    Yea, I shall observe it with my whole heart.
Make me to go in the path of thy commandments;
    For therein do I delight.
Incline my heart unto thy testimonies,
    And not to covetousness.

Psalm 119:33-36

365 And when he was gone forth into the way, there came one running, and kneeled to him, and asked him, "Good Master, what shall I do that I may inherit eternal life?" And Jesus said unto him, "Why callest thou me good? There is none good but one, that is, God. Thou knowest the commandments, 'Do not commit adultery,' 'Do not kill,' 'Do not steal,' 'Do not bear false witness,' 'Defraud not,' 'Honour thy father and mother.'" And he answered and said unto him, "Master, all these have I observed from my youth." Then Jesus beholding him loved him, and said unto him, "One thing thou lackest: go thy way, sell whatsoever thou hast, and give to the poor, and thou shalt have treasure in heaven: and come, take up the cross, and follow me." And he was sad at that saying, and went away grieved: for he had great possessions.

Mark 10:17-22

366 Labour not to be rich:
    Cease from thine own wisdom.
Wilt thou set thine eyes upon that which is not?
    For riches certainly make themselves wings;
    They fly away as an eagle toward heaven. . . .
Apply thine heart unto instruction,
    And thine ears to the words of knowledge.

Proverbs 23:4-5, 12

367 And Jesus looked round about, and saith unto his disciples, "How hardly* shall they that have riches enter into the kingdom of God!" And the disciples were astonished at his words. But Jesus answereth again, and saith unto them, "Children, how hard is it for them that trust in riches to enter into the kingdom of God! It is easier for a camel to go through the eye of a needle, than for a rich man to enter into the kingdom of God." And they were astonished out of measure, saying among themselves, "Who then can be saved?" And Jesus looking upon them saith, "With men it is impossible, but not with God: for with God all things are possible." Then Peter began to say unto him, "Lo, we have left all, and have followed thee." And Jesus answered and said, "Verily I say unto you, There is no man that hath left house, or brethren, or sisters, or father, or mother, or wife, or children, or lands, for my sake, and the gospel's, but he shall receive an hundredfold now in this time, houses, and brethren, and sisters, and mothers, and children, and lands, with persecutions; and in the world to come eternal life. But many that are first shall be last; and the last first."

Mark 10:23-31

368 "Knowest thou not this of old,
    Since man was placed upon earth,
That the triumphing of the wicked is short,
    And the joy of the hypocrite but for a moment?
Though his excellency mount up to the heavens,
    And his head reach unto the clouds;
Yet he shall perish for ever like his own dung:
    They which have seen him shall say, 'Where is he?'
He shall fly away as a dream, and shall not be found:
    Yea, he shall be chased away as a vision of the night.
The eye also which saw him shall see him no more;
    Neither shall his place any more behold him.
His children shall seek to please the poor,
    And his hands shall restore their goods.
His bones are full of the sin of his youth,
    Which shall lie down with him in the dust."

Job 20:4-11

369 And I saw an angel standing in the sun; and he cried with a loud voice, saying to all the fowls that fly in the midst of heaven, "Come and gather yourselves together unto the supper of the great God; That ye may eat the flesh of kings, and the flesh of captains, and the flesh of mighty men, and the flesh of horses, and of them that sit on them, and the flesh of all men, both free and bond, both small and great." And I saw the beast, and the kings of the earth, and their armies, gathered together to make war against him that sat on the horse, and against his army. And the beast was taken, and with him the false prophet that wrought miracles before him, with which he deceived them that had received the mark of the beast, and them that worshipped his image. These both were cast alive into a lake of fire burning with brimstone. And the remnant were slain with the sword of him that sat upon the horse, which sword proceeded out of his mouth: and all the fowls were filled with their flesh.

Revelation 19:17-21

370 "And it shall come to pass in that day,
That the mountains shall drop down new wine,
    And the hills shall flow with milk,
And all the rivers of Judah shall flow with waters,
    And a fountain shall come forth of the house of the LORD,
        And shall water the valley of Shittim."

Joel 3:18

371 And [Jesus] said unto his disciples, "Therefore I say unto you, Take no thought for your life, what ye shall eat; neither for the body, what ye shall put on. The life is more than meat*, and the body is more than raiment. Consider the ravens: for they neither sow nor reap; which neither have storehouse nor barn; and God feedeth them: how much more are ye better than the fowls? And which of you with taking thought can add to his stature one cubit*? If ye then be not able to do that thing which is least, why take ye thought for the rest? Consider the lilies how they grow: they toil not, they spin not; and yet I say unto you, that Solomon in all his glory was not arrayed like one of these. If then God so clothe the grass, which is to day in the field, and to morrow is cast into the oven; how much more will he clothe you, O ye of little faith? And seek not ye

228

what ye shall eat, or what ye shall drink, neither be ye of doubtful mind. For all these things do the nations of the world seek after: and your Father knoweth that ye have need of these things. But rather seek ye the kingdom of God; and all these things shall be added unto you.

"Fear not, little flock; for it is your Father's good pleasure to give you the kingdom. Sell that ye have, and give alms; provide yourselves bags which wax not old, a treasure in the heavens that faileth not, where no thief approacheth, neither moth corrupteth. For where your treasure is, there will your heart be also."

Luke 12:22-34

372 If thine enemy be hungry, give him bread to eat;
    And if he be thirsty, give him water to drink:
For thou shalt heap coals of fire upon his head,
    And the LORD shall reward thee.

Proverbs 25:21-22

373 Bless them which persecute you: bless, and curse not. Rejoice with them that do rejoice, and weep with them that weep. Be of the same mind one toward another. Mind not high things, but condescend to men of low estate. Be not wise in your own conceits. Recompense to no man evil for evil. Provide things honest in the sight of all men. If it be possible, as much as lieth in you, live peaceably with all men. Dearly beloved, avenge not yourselves, but rather give place unto wrath: for it is written, "Vengeance is mine; I will repay," saith the Lord. Therefore "if thine enemy hunger, feed him; if he thirst, give him drink: for in so doing thou shalt

229

heap coals of fire on his head." Be not overcome of evil, but overcome evil with good.

Romans 12:14-21

374   By the rivers of Babylon, there we sat down,
     Yea, we wept, when we remembered Zion.
  We hanged our harps upon the willows
     In the midst thereof.
  For there they that carried us away captive required of us a song;
     And they that wasted* us required of us mirth,
  Saying, "Sing us one of the songs of Zion."
     How shall we sing the LORD's song in a strange land?
  If I forget thee, O Jerusalem,
     Let my right hand forget her cunning.
  If I do not remember thee,
     Let my tongue cleave* to the roof of my mouth;
  If I prefer not Jerusalem above my chief joy.
  Remember, O LORD, the children of Edom in the day of Jerusalem;
     Who said, "Rase it, rase it, even to the foundation thereof."
  O daughter of Babylon, who art to be destroyed;
     Happy shall he be, that rewardeth thee as thou hast served us.
  Happy shall he be, that taketh
     And dasheth thy little ones against the stones.

Psalm 137:1-9

375 Put on therefore, as the elect of God, holy and beloved, bowels* of mercies, kindness, humbleness of mind, meekness, longsuffering; forbearing one another, and forgiving one another, if any man have a quarrel against any: even as Christ forgave you, so also do ye. And above all these things put on charity*, which is the bond of perfectness. And let the peace of God rule in your hearts, to the which also ye are called in one body; and be ye thankful. Let the word of Christ dwell in you richly in all wisdom; teaching and admonishing one another in psalms and hymns and spiritual songs, singing with grace in your hearts to the Lord. And whatsoever ye do in word or deed, do all in the name of the Lord Jesus, giving thanks to God and the Father by him.

Colossians 3:12-17

376 He that sitteth in the heavens shall laugh:
    The Lord shall have them in derision.
Then shall he speak unto them in his wrath,
    And vex them in his sore displeasure.

Psalm 2:4-5

377 And the whole earth was of one language, and of one speech. And it came to pass, as they journeyed from the east, that they found a plain in the land of Shinar; and they dwelt there. And they said one to another, "Go to, let us make brick, and burn them thoroughly." And they had brick for stone, and slime had they for morter. And they said, "Go to, let us build us a city and a tower, whose top may reach unto heaven; and let us make us a name, lest we be scattered abroad upon the face of the whole earth." And the LORD came down to see the city and the tower, which the children of men builded. And the LORD said, "Behold, the people is one, and they have all one language; and this they begin to do: and now nothing will be restrained from them, which they have imagined to do. Go to, let us go down, and there confound their language, that they may not understand one another's speech." So the LORD scattered them abroad from thence upon the face of all the earth: and they left off to build the city. Therefore is the name of it called Babel; because the LORD did there confound the language of all the earth: and from thence did the LORD scatter them abroad upon the face of all the earth.

Genesis 11:1-9

378 Yet have I set my king
      Upon my holy hill of Zion.
  I will declare the decree:
  The LORD hath said unto me,
      "Thou art my Son;
      This day have I begotten thee.
  Ask of me, and I shall give thee the heathen for thine inheritance,
      And the uttermost parts of the earth for thy possession.
  Thou shalt break them with a rod of iron;
      Thou shalt dash them in pieces like a potter's vessel."

Psalm 2:6-9

379   Then Paul stood in the midst of Mars' Hill, and said, "Ye men of Athens, I perceive that in all things ye are too superstitious. For as I passed by, and beheld your devotions, I found an altar with this inscription, TO THE UNKNOWN GOD. Whom therefore ye ignorantly worship, him declare I unto you. God that made the world and all things therein, seeing that he is Lord of heaven and earth, dwelleth not in temples made with hands; Neither is worshipped with men's hands, as though he needed any thing, seeing he giveth to all life, and breath, and all things; And hath made of one blood all nations of men for to dwell on all the face of the earth, and hath determined the times before appointed, and the bounds of their habitation; That they should seek the Lord, if haply* they might feel after him, and find him, though he be not far from every one of us: For in him we live, and move, and have our being; as certain also of your own poets have said, 'For we are also his offspring.' Forasmuch then as we are the offspring of God, we ought not to think that the Godhead is like unto gold, or silver, or stone, graven by art and man's device. And the times of this ignorance God winked at; but now commandeth all men every where to repent: Because he hath appointed a day, in the which he will judge the world in righteousness by that man whom he hath ordained; whereof he hath given assurance unto all men, in that he hath raised him from the dead."

Acts 17:22-31

380   At that time when David saw that the LORD had answered him in the threshingfloor of Ornan the Jebusite, then he sacrificed there. . . . Then David said, "This is the house of the LORD God, and this is the altar of the burnt offering for Israel." And David commanded to gather together the strangers that were in the land of Israel; and he set masons to hew wrought stones to build the house of God. And David prepared iron in abundance for the nails for the doors of the gates, and for the joinings; and brass in abundance without weight; also cedar trees in abundance: for the Zidonians and they of Tyre brought much cedar wood to David. And David said, "Solomon my son is young and tender, and the house that is to be builded for the LORD must be exceeding magnifical, of fame and of glory throughout all countries: I will therefore now make preparation for it." So David prepared abundantly before his death.

1 Chronicles 21:28; 22:1-5

381 And one of the company said unto [Jesus], "Master, speak to my brother, that he divide the inheritance with me." And he said unto him, "Man, who made me a judge or a divider over you?" And he said unto them, "Take heed, and beware of covetousness: for a man's life consisteth not in the abundance of the things which he possesseth." And he spake a parable unto them, saying, "The ground of a certain rich man brought forth plentifully: And he thought within himself, saying, 'What shall I do, because I have no room where to bestow my fruits?' And he said, 'This will I do: I will pull down my barns, and build greater; and there will I bestow all my fruits and my goods. And I will say to my soul, "Soul, thou hast much goods laid up for many years; take thine ease, eat, drink, and be merry."' But God said unto him, 'Thou fool, this night thy soul shall be required of thee: then whose shall those things be, which thou hast provided?' So is he that layeth up treasure for himself, and is not rich toward God."

Luke 12:13-21

382   Then he called for Solomon his son, and charged him to build an house for the LORD God of Israel. . . . "Now, behold, in my trouble I have prepared for the house of the LORD an hundred thousand talents of gold, and a thousand thousand talents of silver; and of brass and iron without weight; for it is in abundance: timber also and stone have I prepared; and thou mayest add thereto." . . .

So when David was old and full of days, he made Solomon his son king over Israel. And he gathered together all the princes of Israel, with the priests and the Levites. Now the Levites were numbered from the age of thirty years and upward: and their number by their polls, man by man, was thirty and eight thousand. Of which, twenty and four thousand were to set forward the work of the house of the LORD; and six thousand were officers and judges: Moreover four thousand were porters; and four thousand praised the LORD with the instruments which I made, said David, to praise therewith.

1 Chronicles 22:6, 14; 23:1-5

383   "I hate, I despise your feast days,
    And I will not smell in your solemn assemblies.
Though ye offer me burnt offerings and your meat* offerings,
    I will not accept them:
Neither will I regard
    The peace offerings of your fat beasts.
Take thou away from me the noise of thy songs;
    For I will not hear the melody of thy viols.
But let judgment run down as waters,
    And righteousness as a mighty stream."

Amos 5:21-24

384 I thank my God, making mention of thee always in my prayers, hearing
     of thy love and faith, which thou hast toward the Lord Jesus, and toward
     all saints; that the communication of thy faith may become effectual by
     the acknowledging of every good thing which is in you in Christ Jesus.
     For we have great joy and consolation in thy love, because the bowels* of
     the saints are refreshed by thee, brother.

Philemon 4-7

385 Wherewith shall I come before the LORD,
         And bow myself before the high God?
     Shall I come before him with burnt offerings,
         With calves of a year old?
     Will the LORD be pleased with thousands of rams,
         Or with ten thousands of rivers of oil?
     Shall I give my firstborn for my transgression,
         The fruit of my body for the sin of my soul?
     He hath shewed thee, O man, what is good;
         And what doth the LORD require of thee,
     But to do justly, and to love mercy,
         And to walk humbly with thy God?

Micah 6:6-8

386 And, behold, a certain lawyer stood up, and tempted [Jesus], saying,
     "Master, what shall I do to inherit eternal life?" He said unto him, "What
     is written in the law? How readest thou?" And he answering said, "Thou
     shalt love the Lord thy God with all thy heart, and with all thy soul, and

with all thy strength, and with all thy mind; and thy neighbour as thy-self." And he said unto him, "Thou hast answered right: this do, and thou shalt live." But he, willing to justify himself, said unto Jesus, "And who is my neighbour?"

And Jesus answering said, "A certain man went down from Jerusalem to Jericho, and fell among thieves, which stripped him of his raiment, and wounded him, and departed, leaving him half dead. And by chance there came down a certain priest that way: and when he saw him, he passed by on the other side. And likewise a Levite, when he was at the place, came and looked on him, and passed by on the other side. But a certain Samaritan, as he journeyed, came where he was: and when he saw him, he had compassion on him, and went to him, and bound up his wounds, pouring in oil and wine, and set him on his own beast, and brought him to an inn, and took care of him. And on the morrow when he departed, he took out two pence, and gave them to the host, and said unto him, 'Take care of him; and whatsoever thou spendest more, when I come again, I will repay thee.'

"Which now of these three, thinkest thou, was neighbour unto him that fell among the thieves?" And he said, "He that shewed mercy on him." Then said Jesus unto him, "Go, and do thou likewise."

Luke 10:25-37

387 And when the Queen of Sheba heard of the fame of Solomon, she came to prove* Solomon with hard questions at Jerusalem, with a very great company, and camels that bare spices, and gold in abundance, and precious stones: and when she was come to Solomon, she communed with him of all that was in her heart. And Solomon told her all her questions: and there was nothing hid from Solomon which he

told her not. . . . And King Solomon gave to the Queen of Sheba all her desire, whatsoever she asked, beside that which she had brought unto the king. So she turned, and went away to her own land, she and her servants.

2 Chronicles 9:1-2, 12

388   Drink waters out of thine own cistern,
      And running waters out of thine own well.
   Let thy fountains be dispersed abroad,
      And rivers of waters in the streets.
   Let them be only thine own,
      And not strangers' with thee.
   Let thy fountain be blessed:
      And rejoice with the wife of thy youth.
   Let her be as the loving hind and pleasant roe;
      Let her breasts satisfy thee at all times;
      And be thou ravished always with her love.
   And why wilt thou, my son, be ravished with a strange woman,
      And embrace the bosom of a stranger?

Proverbs 5:15-20

389   But King Solomon loved many strange women . . . of the nations concerning which the LORD said unto the children of Israel, "Ye shall not go in to them, neither shall they come in unto you: for surely they will turn away your heart after their gods": Solomon clave unto these in love. . . . Wherefore the LORD said unto Solomon, "Forasmuch as this

is done of thee, and thou hast not kept my covenant and my statutes, which I have commanded thee, I will surely rend the kingdom from thee, and will give it to thy servant. Notwithstanding in thy days I will not do it for David thy father's sake: but I will rend it out of the hand of thy son. Howbeit* I will not rend away all the kingdom; but will give one tribe to thy son for David my servant's sake, and for Jerusalem's sake which I have chosen."

1 Kings 11:1a, 2, 11-13

390   Then certain of the scribes and of the Pharisees answered, saying, "Master, we would see a sign from thee." But he answered and said unto them, "An evil and adulterous generation seeketh after a sign; and there shall no sign be given to it, but the sign of the prophet Jonas*: For as Jonas was three days and three nights in the whale's belly; so shall the Son of man be three days and three nights in the heart of the earth. The men of Nineveh shall rise in judgment with this generation, and shall condemn it: because they repented at the preaching of Jonas; and, behold, a greater than Jonas is here. The queen of the south shall rise up in the judgment with this generation, and shall condemn it: for she came from the uttermost parts of the earth to hear the wisdom of Solomon; and, behold, a greater than Solomon is here."

Matthew 12:38-42

391 Now the word of the LORD came unto Jonah the son of Amittai, saying, "Arise, go to Nineveh, that great city, and cry against it; for their wickedness is come up before me." But Jonah rose up to flee unto Tarshish from the presence of the LORD, and went down to Joppa; and he found a ship going to Tarshish: so he paid the fare thereof, and went down into it, to go with them unto Tarshish from the presence of the LORD.

But the LORD sent out a great wind into the sea, and there was a mighty tempest in the sea, so that the ship was like to be broken. Then the mariners were afraid, and cried every man unto his god, and cast forth the wares that were in the ship into the sea, to lighten it of them. But Jonah was gone down into the sides of the ship; and he lay, and was fast asleep. So the shipmaster came to him, and said unto him, "What meanest thou, O sleeper? Arise, call upon thy God, if so be that God will think upon us, that we perish not." And they said every one to his fellow, "Come, and let us cast lots, that we may know for whose cause this evil is upon us." So they cast lots, and the lot fell upon Jonah. . . . And he said unto them, "Take me up, and cast me forth into the sea; so shall the sea be calm unto you: for I know that for my sake this great tempest is upon you." Nevertheless the men rowed hard to bring it to the land; but they could not: for the sea wrought, and was tempestuous against them. Wherefore they cried unto the LORD, and said, "We beseech thee, O LORD, we beseech thee, let us not perish for this man's life, and lay not upon us innocent blood: for thou, O LORD, hast done as it pleased thee." So they took up Jonah, and cast him forth into the sea: and the sea ceased from her raging. Then the men feared the LORD exceedingly, and offered a sacrifice unto the LORD, and made vows.

Jonah 1:1-7, 12-16

392   Go to now, ye that say, "Today or tomorrow we will go into such a city, and continue there a year, and buy and sell, and get gain": Whereas ye know not what shall be on the morrow. For what is your life? It is even a vapour, that appeareth for a little time, and then vanisheth away. For that ye ought to say, "If the Lord will, we shall live, and do this, or that." But now ye rejoice in your boastings: all such rejoicing is evil. Therefore to him that knoweth to do good, and doeth it not, to him it is sin.

James 4:13-17

393   Now the LORD had prepared a great fish to swallow up Jonah. And Jonah was in the belly of the fish three days and three nights.

Jonah 1:17

394   "For wrath killeth the foolish man,
          And envy slayeth the silly one. . . .
    Although affliction cometh not forth of the dust,
          Neither doth trouble spring out of the ground;
    Yet man is born unto trouble,
          As the sparks fly upward."

Job 5:2, 6-7

395 Then Jonah prayed unto the LORD his God out of the fish's belly, and
said,

> "I cried by reason of mine affliction unto the LORD,
>   And he heard me;
> Out of the belly of hell cried I,
>   And thou heardest my voice.
> For thou hadst cast me into the deep,
>   In the midst of the seas;
> And the floods compassed me about:
>   All thy billows and thy waves passed over me.
> Then I said, 'I am cast out of thy sight;
>   Yet I will look again toward thy holy temple.'
> The waters compassed me about,
>   Even to the soul:
> The depth closed me round about,
>   The weeds were wrapped about my head.
> I went down to the bottoms of the mountains;
>   The earth with her bars was about me for ever:
> Yet hast thou brought up my life from corruption,
>   O LORD my God.
>
> When my soul fainted within me I remembered the LORD:
>   And my prayer came in unto thee, into thine holy temple.
> They that observe lying vanities
>   Forsake their own mercy.
> But I will sacrifice unto thee
>   With the voice of thanksgiving;
> I will pay that that I have vowed.
>   Salvation is of the LORD."

And the L ORD spake unto the fish, and it vomited out Jonah upon the dry land.

Jonah 2:1-10

396 He sent from above, he took me,
    He drew me out of many waters.
He delivered me from my strong enemy,
    And from them which hated me:
    For they were too strong for me.
They prevented* me in the day of my calamity:
    But the L ORD was my stay.
He brought me forth also into a large place;
    He delivered me, because he delighted in me.

Psalm 18:16-19

397 Finally, brethren, pray for us, that the word of the Lord may have free course, and be glorified, even as it is with you: And that we may be delivered from unreasonable and wicked men: for all men have not faith. But the Lord is faithful, who shall stablish you, and keep you from evil. And we have confidence in the Lord touching* you, that ye both do and will do the things which we command you. And the Lord direct your hearts into the love of God, and into the patient waiting for Christ.

2 Thessalonians 3:1-5

398   "And all thy children shall be taught of the LORD;
          And great shall be the peace of thy children.
      In righteousness shalt thou be established:
          Thou shalt be far from oppression;
      For thou shalt not fear: and from terror;
          For it shall not come near thee."

Isaiah 54:13-14

399   For I rejoiced greatly, when the brethren came and testified of the truth that is in thee, even as thou walkest in the truth. I have no greater joy than to hear that my children walk in truth. Beloved, thou doest faithfully whatsoever thou doest to the brethren, and to strangers; which have borne witness of thy charity* before the church: whom if thou bring forward on their journey after a godly sort, thou shalt do well: Because that for his name's sake they went forth, taking nothing of the Gentiles. We therefore ought to receive such, that we might be fellowhelpers to the truth.

3 John 3-8

400   "Yet now hear, O Jacob my servant;
          And Israel, whom I have chosen: . . .
      For I will pour water upon him that is thirsty,
          And floods upon the dry ground:
      I will pour my spirit upon thy seed,
          And my blessing upon thine offspring:
      And they shall spring up as among the grass,
          As willows by the water courses. . . .

244

Thus saith the LORD the King of Israel,
    And his redeemer the LORD of hosts;
I am the first, and I am the last;
    And beside me there is no God."

Isaiah 44:1, 3-4, 6

401   And one of the multitude answered and said, "Master, I have brought unto thee my son, which hath a dumb spirit; and wheresoever he taketh him, he teareth him: and he foameth, and gnasheth with his teeth, and pineth away: and I spake to thy disciples that they should cast him out; and they could not." [Jesus] answereth him, and saith, "O faithless generation, how long shall I be with you? How long shall I suffer* you? Bring him unto me." And they brought him unto him: and when he saw him, straightway the spirit tare him; and he fell on the ground, and wallowed foaming. And he asked his father, "How long is it ago since this came unto him?" And he said, "Of a child. And ofttimes it hath cast him into the fire, and into the waters, to destroy him: but if thou canst do any thing, have compassion on us, and help us." Jesus said unto him, "If thou canst believe, all things are possible to him that believeth." And straightway the father of the child cried out, and said with tears, "Lord, I believe; help thou mine unbelief." When Jesus saw that the people came running together, he rebuked the foul spirit, saying unto him, "Thou dumb and deaf spirit, I charge thee, come out of him, and enter no more into him." And the spirit cried, and rent him sore, and came out of him: and he was as one dead; insomuch that many said, "He is dead." But Jesus took him by the hand, and lifted him up; and he arose. And when he was come into the house, his disciples asked him privately, "Why could not we cast him out?" And he said unto them, "This kind can come forth by nothing, but by prayer and fasting."

Mark 9:17-29

402 And the word of the LORD came unto me, saying, "Son of man, put forth a riddle, and speak a parable unto the house of Israel; And say, 'Thus saith the Lord GOD; A great eagle with great wings, longwinged, full of feathers, which had divers colours, came unto Lebanon, and took the highest branch of the cedar: He cropped off the top of his young twigs, and carried it into a land of traffick; he set it in a city of merchants. He took also of the seed of the land, and planted it in a fruitful field; he placed it by great waters, and set it as a willow tree. And it grew, and became a spreading vine of low stature, whose branches turned toward him, and the roots thereof were under him: so it became a vine, and brought forth branches, and shot forth sprigs.'"

Ezekiel 17:1-6

403 "I am the true vine, and my Father is the husbandman. Every branch in me that beareth not fruit he taketh away: and every branch that beareth fruit, he purgeth it, that it may bring forth more fruit. Now ye are clean through the word which I have spoken unto you. Abide in me, and I in you. As the branch cannot bear fruit of itself, except it abide in the vine; no more can ye, except ye abide in me. I am the vine, ye are the branches: He that abideth in me, and I in him, the same bringeth forth much fruit: for without me ye can do nothing. If a man abide not in me, he is cast forth as a branch, and is withered; and men gather them, and cast them into the fire, and they are burned. If ye abide in me, and my words abide in you, ye shall ask what ye will, and it shall be done unto you. Herein is my Father glorified, that ye bear much fruit; so shall ye be my disciples. As the Father hath loved me, so have I loved you: continue ye in my love. If ye keep my commandments, ye shall abide in my love; even as I have kept my Father's commandments, and abide in his love. These things

have I spoken unto you, that my joy might remain in you, and that your joy might be full."

John 15:1-11

404   Cease from anger, and forsake wrath:
     Fret not thyself in any wise* to do evil.
  For evildoers shall be cut off:
     But those that wait upon the LORD,
     They shall inherit the earth.
  For yet a little while, and the wicked shall not be:
     Yea, thou shalt diligently consider his place, and it shall not be.
  But the meek shall inherit the earth;
     And shall delight themselves in the abundance of peace.

Psalm 37:8-11

405   Put [the church] in mind to be subject to principalities and powers, to obey magistrates, to be ready to every good work, to speak evil of no man, to be no brawlers, but gentle, shewing all meekness unto all men. For we ourselves also were sometimes foolish, disobedient, deceived, serving divers lusts and pleasures, living in malice and envy, hateful, and hating one another. But after that the kindness and love of God our Saviour toward man appeared, not by works of righteousness which we have done, but according to his mercy he saved us, by the washing of regeneration, and renewing of the Holy Ghost; Which he shed on us abundantly through Jesus Christ our Saviour; that being justified by his grace, we should be made heirs according to the hope of eternal life. This is a faith-

ful saying, and these things I will that thou affirm constantly, that they which have believed in God might be careful to maintain good works. These things are good and profitable unto men. But avoid foolish questions, and genealogies, and contentions, and strivings about the law; for they are unprofitable and vain. A man that is an heretick after the first and second admonition reject; knowing that he that is such is subverted, and sinneth, being condemned of himself.

Titus 3:1-11

406　Make a joyful noise unto the LORD,
　　　All ye lands.
　　Serve the LORD with gladness:
　　　Come before his presence with singing.
　　Know ye that the LORD he is God:
　　　It is he that hath made us, and not we ourselves;
　　We are his people,
　　　And the sheep of his pasture.
　　Enter into his gates with thanksgiving,
　　　And into his courts with praise:
　　　Be thankful unto him,
　　　And bless his name.
　　For the LORD is good;
　　　His mercy is everlasting;
　　　And his truth endureth to all generations.

Psalm 100:1-5

407 And they departed into a desert place by ship privately. And the people saw them departing, and many knew him, and ran afoot thither out of all cities, and outwent them, and came together unto him. And Jesus, when he came out, saw much people, and was moved with compassion toward them, because they were as sheep not having a shepherd: and he began to teach them many things. And when the day was now far spent, his disciples came unto him, and said, "This is a desert place, and now the time is far passed: Send them away, that they may go into the country round about, and into the villages, and buy themselves bread: for they have nothing to eat." He answered and said unto them, "Give ye them to eat." And they say unto him, "Shall we go and buy two hundred pennyworth* of bread, and give them to eat?" He saith unto them, "How many loaves have ye? Go and see." And when they knew, they say, "Five, and two fishes." And he commanded them to make all sit down by companies upon the green grass. And they sat down in ranks, by hundreds, and by fifties. And when he had taken the five loaves and the two fishes, he looked up to heaven, and blessed, and brake the loaves, and gave them to his disciples to set before them; and the two fishes divided he among them all. And they did all eat, and were filled. And they took up twelve baskets full of the fragments, and of the fishes. And they that did eat of the loaves were about five thousand men.

Mark 6:32-44

408 And the whole congregation of the children of Israel murmured against Moses and Aaron in the wilderness: And the children of Israel said unto them, "Would to God we had died by the hand of the LORD in the land of Egypt, when we sat by the flesh pots, and when we did eat bread to the full; for ye have brought us forth into this wilderness, to kill this whole assembly with hunger." Then said the LORD unto Moses, "Behold, I will rain bread from heaven for you; and the people shall go out and gather a certain rate every day, that I may prove* them, whether they will walk in my law, or no." ... And it came to pass, that at even* the quails came up, and covered the camp: and in the morning the dew lay round about the host. And when the dew that lay was gone up, behold, upon the face of the wilderness there lay a small round thing, as small as the hoar frost on the ground. And when the children of Israel saw it, they said one to another, "It is manna": for they wist* not what it was. And Moses said unto them, "This is the bread which the LORD hath given you to eat."

Exodus 16:2-4, 13-15

409 And Jesus said unto them, "I am the bread of life: he that cometh to me shall never hunger; and he that believeth on me shall never thirst." ... The Jews then murmured at him, because he said, "I am the bread which came down from heaven." And they said, "Is not this Jesus, the son of Joseph, whose father and mother we know? How is it then that he saith, 'I came down from heaven?'" Jesus therefore answered and said unto them, "Murmur not among yourselves. No man can come to me, except the Father which hath sent me draw him: and I will raise him up at the last day.... Verily, verily, I say unto you, He that believeth on me hath everlasting life. I am that bread of life. Your fathers did eat manna in the wilderness, and are dead. This is the bread which cometh down from heaven, that a man may eat thereof, and not die. I am the living bread which came down from heaven: if any man eat of this bread, he shall live for ever: and the bread that I will give is my flesh, which I will give for the life of the world."

John 6:35, 41-44, 47-51

410 O how love I thy law!

    It is my meditation all the day.

Thou through thy commandments hast made me wiser than
      mine enemies:

    For they are ever with me.

I have more understanding than all my teachers:

    For thy testimonies are my meditation.

I understand more than the ancients,

    Because I keep thy precepts.

I have refrained my feet from every evil way,

    That I might keep thy word.

I have not departed from thy judgments:

    For thou hast taught me.

How sweet are thy words unto my taste!

    Yea, sweeter than honey to my mouth!

Through thy precepts I get understanding:

    Therefore I hate every false way.

Psalm 119:97-104

411 We who are Jews by nature, and not sinners of the Gentiles, knowing that a man is not justified by the works of the law, but by the faith of Jesus Christ, even we have believed in Jesus Christ, that we might be justified by the faith of Christ, and not by the works of the law: for by the works of the law shall no flesh be justified. . . . I am crucified with Christ: nevertheless I live; yet not I, but Christ liveth in me: and the life which I now live in the flesh I live by the faith of the Son of God, who loved me, and gave himself for me. I do not frustrate the grace of God: for if righteousness come by the law, then Christ is dead in vain.

Galatians 2:15-16, 20-21

412 Yea, a man may say, "Thou hast faith, and I have works": shew me thy faith without thy works, and I will shew thee my faith by my works. Thou believest that there is one God; thou doest well: the devils also believe, and tremble. But wilt thou know, O vain man, that faith without works is dead? Was not Abraham our father justified by works, when he had offered Isaac his son upon the altar? Seest thou how faith wrought with his works, and by works was faith made perfect? And the scripture was fulfilled which saith, "Abraham believed God, and it was imputed unto him for righteousness": and he was called the Friend of God. Ye see then how that by works a man is justified, and not by faith only.... For as the body without the spirit is dead, so faith without works is dead also.

James 2:18-24, 26

413 After these things the word of the LORD came unto Abram in a vision, saying, "Fear not, Abram: I am thy shield, and thy exceeding great reward." ... And Abram said, "Behold, to me thou hast given no seed: and, lo, one born in my house is mine heir." And, behold, the word of the LORD came unto him, saying, "This shall not be thine heir; but he that shall come forth out of thine own bowels shall be thine heir." And he brought him forth abroad, and said, "Look now toward heaven, and tell the stars, if thou be able to number them": and he said unto him, "So shall thy seed be." And he believed in the LORD; and he counted it to him for righteousness.

Genesis 15:1, 3-6

414 What shall we say then that Abraham our father, as pertaining to the flesh, hath found? For if Abraham were justified by works, he hath whereof to glory; but not before God. For what saith the scripture? "Abraham believed God, and it was counted unto him for righteousness." Now to him that worketh is the reward not reckoned of grace, but of debt. But to him that worketh not, but believeth on him that justifieth the ungodly, his faith is counted for righteousness. . . . Therefore it is of faith, that it might be by grace; to the end the promise might be sure to all the seed; not to that only which is of the law, but to that also which is of the faith of Abraham; who is the father of us all.

Romans 4:1-5, 16

415 What doth it profit, my brethren, though a man say he hath faith, and have not works? Can faith save him? If a brother or sister be naked, and destitute of daily food, and one of you say unto them, "Depart in peace, be ye warmed and filled"; notwithstanding ye give them not those things which are needful to the body; what doth it profit? Even so faith, if it hath not works, is dead, being alone.

James 2:14-17

416 Then said Jesus to those Jews which believed on him, "If ye continue in my word, then are ye my disciples indeed; and ye shall know the truth, and the truth shall make you free." They answered him, "We be Abraham's seed, and were never in bondage to any man: How sayest thou, 'Ye shall be made free?'" Jesus answered them, "Verily, verily, I say unto you, Whosoever committeth sin is the servant of sin. And the servant abideth not in the house for ever: but the Son abideth ever. If the Son therefore shall make you free, ye shall be free indeed. I know that ye are Abraham's seed; but ye seek to kill me, because my word hath no place in you. I speak that which I have seen with my Father: and ye do that which ye have seen with your father."

John 8:31-38

417   And at the evening sacrifice I arose up from my heaviness; and having rent my garment and my mantle, I fell upon my knees, and spread out my hands unto the LORD my God, and said, "O my God, I am ashamed and blush to lift up my face to thee, my God: for our iniquities are increased over our head, and our trespass is grown up unto the heavens. Since the days of our fathers have we been in a great trespass unto this day; and for our iniquities have we, our kings, and our priests, been delivered into the hand of the kings of the lands, to the sword, to captivity, and to a spoil, and to confusion of face, as it is this day. And now for a little space grace hath been shewed from the LORD our God, to leave us a remnant to escape, and to give us a nail in his holy place, that our God may lighten our eyes, and give us a little reviving in our bondage."

Ezra 9:5-8

418   What shall we say then? Is the law sin? God forbid. Nay, I had not known sin, but by the law: for I had not known lust, except the law had said, "Thou shalt not covet." But sin, taking occasion by the commandment, wrought in me all manner of concupiscence. . . . For we know that the law is spiritual: but I am carnal, sold under sin. For that which I do I al-

254

low not: for what I would, that do I not; but what I hate, that do I. If then I do that which I would not, I consent unto the law that it is good. . . . I find then a law, that, when I would do good, evil is present with me. For I delight in the law of God after the inward man: But I see another law in my members, warring against the law of my mind, and bringing me into captivity to the law of sin which is in my members. O wretched man that I am! Who shall deliver me from the body of this death? I thank God through Jesus Christ our Lord. So then with the mind I myself serve the law of God; but with the flesh the law of sin.

Romans 7:7-8a, 14-16, 21-25

419 Now faith is the substance of things hoped for, the evidence of things not seen. For by it the elders obtained a good report. Through faith we understand that the worlds were framed by the word of God, so that things which are seen were not made of things which do appear. . . . By faith the walls of Jericho fell down, after they were compassed about seven days. By faith the harlot Rahab perished not with them that believed not, when she had received the spies with peace.

Hebrews 11:1-3, 30-31

420 And it came to pass on the seventh day, that [Joshua and the people] rose early about the dawning of the day, and compassed the city after the same manner seven times: only on that day they compassed the city seven times. And it came to pass at the seventh time, when the priests blew with the trumpets, Joshua said unto the people, "Shout; for the LORD hath given you the city. And the city shall be accursed, even it, and all that are therein, to the LORD: only Rahab the harlot shall live, she and all that are with her in the house, because she hid the messengers that we sent." . . . So the people shouted when the priests blew with the trumpets: and it came to pass, when the people heard the sound of the trumpet, and the people shouted with a great shout, that the wall fell down flat, so that the people went up into the city, every man straight before him, and they took the city. And they utterly destroyed all that was in the city, both man and woman, young and old, and ox, and sheep, and ass, with the edge of the sword. . . . And Joshua saved Rahab the harlot alive, and her father's household, and all that she had; and she dwelleth in Israel even unto this day; because she hid the messengers, which Joshua sent to spy out Jericho.

Joshua 6:15-17, 20-21, 25

421   I rejoiced greatly that I found of thy children walking in truth, as we have received a commandment from the Father. And now I beseech thee, lady, not as though I wrote a new commandment unto thee, but that which we had from the beginning, that we love one another. And this is love, that we walk after his commandments. This is the commandment, that, as ye have heard from the beginning, ye should walk in it.

2 John 4-6

422   Now it came to pass, as they went, that he entered into a certain village: and a certain woman named Martha received him into her house. And she had a sister called Mary, which also sat at Jesus' feet, and heard his word. But Martha was cumbered about much serving, and came to him,

and said, "Lord, dost thou not care that my sister hath left me to serve alone? Bid her therefore that she help me." And Jesus answered and said unto her, "Martha, Martha, thou art careful* and troubled about many things: But one thing is needful: and Mary hath chosen that good part, which shall not be taken away from her."

Luke 10:38-42

423 Now before the feast of the Passover, when Jesus knew that his hour was come that he should depart out of this world unto the Father, having loved his own which were in the world, he loved them unto the end. And supper being ended, the devil having now put into the heart of Judas Iscariot, Simon's son, to betray him; Jesus knowing that the Father had given all things into his hands, and that he was come from God, and went to God; he riseth from supper, and laid aside his garments; and took a towel, and girded himself. After that he poureth water into a bason, and began to wash the disciples' feet, and to wipe them with the towel wherewith he was girded. Then cometh he to Simon Peter: and Peter saith unto him, "Lord, dost thou wash my feet?" Jesus answered and said unto him, "What I do thou knowest not now; but thou shalt know hereafter." Peter saith unto him, "Thou shalt never wash my feet." Jesus answered him, "If I wash thee not, thou hast no part with me." Simon Peter saith unto him, "Lord, not my feet only, but also my hands and my head." . . .

So after he had washed their feet, and had taken his garments, and was set down again, he said unto them, "Know ye what I have done to you? Ye call me Master and Lord: and ye say well; for so I am. If I then, your Lord and Master, have washed your feet; ye also ought to wash one another's feet. For I have given you an example, that ye should do as I have done to you. Verily, verily, I say unto you, The servant is not greater than his lord; neither he that is sent greater than he that sent him. If ye know these things, happy are ye if ye do them."

John 13:1-9, 12-17

424   And one of the elders answered, saying unto me, "What are these which are arrayed in white robes? And whence came they?" And I said unto him, "Sir, thou knowest." And he said to me, "These are they which came out of great tribulation, and have washed their robes, and made them white in the blood of the Lamb."
Therefore are they before the throne of God,
   And serve him day and night in his temple:
And he that sitteth on the throne
   Shall dwell among them.
They shall hunger no more, neither thirst any more;
   Neither shall the sun light on them, nor any heat.
For the Lamb which is in the midst of the throne shall feed them,
   And shall lead them unto living fountains of waters:
   And God shall wipe away all tears from their eyes."

Revelation 7:13-17

425   "This is my commandment, That ye love one another, as I have loved you. Greater love hath no man than this, that a man lay down his life for his friends. Ye are my friends, if ye do whatsoever I command you. Henceforth I call you not servants; for the servant knoweth not what his lord doeth: but I have called you friends; for all things that I have heard

of my Father I have made known unto you. Ye have not chosen me, but I have chosen you, and ordained you, that ye should go and bring forth fruit, and that your fruit should remain: that whatsoever ye shall ask of the Father in my name, he may give it you. These things I command you, that ye love one another."

John 15:12-17

426 And it came to pass, that, as they went in the way, a certain man said unto him, "Lord, I will follow thee whithersoever thou goest." And Jesus said unto him, "Foxes have holes, and birds of the air have nests; but the Son of man hath not where to lay his head." And he said unto another, "Follow me." But he said, "Lord, suffer* me first to go and bury my father." Jesus said unto him, "Let the dead bury their dead: but go thou and preach the kingdom of God." And another also said, "Lord, I will follow thee; but let me first go bid them farewell, which are at home at my house." And Jesus said unto him, "No man, having put his hand to the plough, and looking back, is fit for the kingdom of God."

Luke 9:57-62

427 Beloved, let us love one another: for love is of God; and every one that loveth is born of God, and knoweth God. He that loveth not knoweth not God; for God is love. In this was manifested the love of God toward us, because that God sent his only begotten Son into the world, that we might live through him. Herein is love, not that we loved God, but that he loved us, and sent his Son to be the propitiation for our sins. Beloved, if God so loved us, we ought also to love one another. . . . God is love; and

he that dwelleth in love dwelleth in God, and God in him. Herein is our love made perfect, that we may have boldness in the day of judgment: because as he is, so are we in this world. There is no fear in love; but perfect love casteth out fear: because fear hath torment. He that feareth is not made perfect in love. We love him, because he first loved us. If a man say, "I love God," and hateth his brother, he is a liar: for he that loveth not his brother whom he hath seen, how can he love God whom he hath not seen? And this commandment have we from him, that he who loveth God love his brother also.

1 John 4:7-11, 16b-21

428 Praise ye the LORD.
Praise ye the LORD from the heavens:
     Praise him in the heights.
Praise ye him, all his angels:
     Praise ye him, all his hosts.
Praise ye him, sun and moon:
     Praise him, all ye stars of light.
Praise him, ye heavens of heavens,
     And ye waters that be above the heavens.
Let them praise the name of the LORD:
     For he commanded, and they were created.
He hath also stablished them for ever and ever:
     He hath made a decree which shall not pass.
Praise the LORD from the earth,
     Ye dragons, and all deeps:
Fire, and hail; snow, and vapours;
     Stormy wind fulfilling his word:

Mountains, and all hills;
    Fruitful trees, and all cedars:
Beasts, and all cattle;
    Creeping things, and flying fowl:
Kings of the earth, and all people;
    Princes, and all judges of the earth:
Both young men, and maidens;
    Old men, and children:
Let them praise the name of the LORD:
    For his name alone is excellent;
    His glory is above the earth and heaven.
He also exalteth the horn of his people,
    The praise of all his saints;
    Even of the children of Israel, a people near unto him.
Praise ye the LORD.

Psalm 148:1-14

The Sixth Day

God's Economy

Men and Women and Children

Stewardship Gracious and Abusive

Greed and Trust

The Promise of New Life

SEX, POWER, AND MONEY: The familiar troika, as fresh as the morning's headlines and as ancient as Scripture itself. Creation's sixth Day opens the door to them all, posing persistent questions about how, for good and ill, we govern our life and the lives of others. That God's economy contradicts those of our own construction is no surprise — yet ever astounding.

429 And God said, "Let the earth bring forth the living creature after his kind, cattle, and creeping thing, and beast of the earth after his kind": and it was so. And God made the beast of the earth after his kind, and cattle after their kind, and every thing that creepeth upon the earth after his kind: and God saw that it was good. And God said, "Let us make man in our image, after our likeness: and let them have dominion over the fish of the sea, and over the fowl of the air, and over the cattle, and over all the earth, and over every creeping thing that creepeth upon the earth." So God created man in his own image, in the image of God created he him; male and female created he them. And God blessed them, and God said unto them, "Be fruitful, and multiply, and replenish the earth, and subdue it: and have dominion over the fish of the sea, and over the fowl of the air, and over every living thing that moveth upon the earth." And God said, "Behold, I have given you every herb bearing seed, which is upon the face of all the earth, and every tree, in the which is the fruit of a tree yielding seed; to you it shall be for meat*. And to every beast of the earth, and to every fowl of the air, and to every thing that creepeth upon the earth, wherein there is life, I have given every green herb for meat": and it was so. And God saw every thing that he had made, and, behold, it was very good. And the evening and the morning were the sixth day.

Genesis 1:24-31

430 And the third day there was a marriage in Cana of Galilee; and the mother of Jesus was there: And both Jesus was called, and his disciples, to the marriage. And when they wanted wine, the mother of Jesus saith unto him, "They have no wine." Jesus saith unto her, "Woman, what have I to do with thee? Mine hour is not yet come." His mother saith unto the servants, "Whatsoever he saith unto you, do it." And there were set there six waterpots of stone, after the manner of the purifying of the Jews, containing two or three firkins* apiece. Jesus saith unto them, "Fill the waterpots with water." And they filled them up to the brim. And he saith unto them, "Draw out now, and bear unto the governor of the feast." And they bare it. When the ruler of the feast had tasted the water that was made wine, and knew not whence it was: (but the servants which drew the water knew;) the governor of the feast called the bridegroom, and saith unto him, "Every man at the beginning doth set forth good wine; and when men have well drunk, then that which is worse: but thou hast kept the good wine until now." This beginning of miracles did Jesus in Cana of Galilee, and manifested forth his glory; and his disciples believed on him.

John 2:1-11

431   If a bird's nest chance to be before thee in the way in any tree, or on the ground, whether they be young ones, or eggs, and the dam* sitting upon the young, or upon the eggs, thou shalt not take the dam with the young: But thou shalt in any wise* let the dam go, and take the young to thee; that it may be well with thee, and that thou mayest prolong thy days.

Deuteronomy 22:6-7

432   Let a man so account of us, as of the ministers of Christ, and stewards of the mysteries of God. Moreover it is required in stewards, that a man be found faithful. But with me it is a very small thing that I should be judged of you, or of man's judgment: yea, I judge not mine own self. For I know nothing by myself; yet am I not hereby justified: but he that

judgeth me is the Lord. Therefore judge nothing before the time, until the Lord come, who both will bring to light the hidden things of darkness, and will make manifest the counsels of the hearts: and then shall every man have praise of God.

1 Corinthians 4:1-5

433 And [Jesus] said also unto his disciples, "There was a certain rich man, which had a steward; and the same was accused unto him that he had wasted his goods. And he called him, and said unto him, 'How is it that I hear this of thee? Give an account of thy stewardship; for thou mayest be no longer steward.' Then the steward said within himself, 'What shall I do? For my lord taketh away from me the stewardship: I cannot dig; to beg I am ashamed. I am resolved what to do, that, when I am put out of the stewardship, they may receive me into their houses.' So he called every one of his lord's debtors unto him, and said unto the first, 'How much owest thou unto my lord?' And he said, 'An hundred measures of oil.' And he said unto him, 'Take thy bill, and sit down quickly, and write fifty.' Then said he to another, 'And how much owest thou?' And he said, 'An hundred measures of wheat.' And he said unto him, 'Take thy bill, and write fourscore.' And the lord commended the unjust steward, because he had done wisely: for the children of this world are in their generation wiser than the children of light. And I say unto you, Make to yourselves friends of the mammon of unrighteousness; that, when ye fail, they may receive you into everlasting habitations. He that is faithful in that which is least is faithful also in much: and he that is unjust in the least is unjust also in much. If therefore ye have not been faithful in the unrighteous mammon, who will commit to your trust the true riches? And if ye have not been faithful in that which is another man's, who shall

give you that which is your own? No servant can serve two masters: for either he will hate the one, and love the other; or else he will hold to the one, and despise the other. Ye cannot serve God and mammon."

Luke 16:1-13

434   And the LORD spake unto Moses in Mount Sinai, saying, "Speak unto the children of Israel, and say unto them, 'When ye come into the land which I give you, then shall the land keep a sabbath unto the LORD. Six years thou shalt sow thy field, and six years thou shalt prune thy vineyard, and gather in the fruit thereof; but in the seventh year shall be a sabbath of rest unto the land, a sabbath for the LORD: thou shalt neither sow thy field, nor prune thy vineyard. . . . And ye shall hallow the fiftieth year, and proclaim liberty throughout all the land unto all the inhabitants thereof: it shall be a jubilee unto you; and ye shall return every man unto his possession, and ye shall return every man unto his family.'"

Leviticus 25:1-4, 10

435   Then they that gladly received [Peter's] word were baptized: and the same day there were added unto them about three thousand souls. And they continued stedfastly in the apostles' doctrine and fellowship, and in breaking of bread, and in prayers. And fear came upon every soul: and many wonders and signs were done by the apostles. And all that believed were together, and had all things common; and sold their possessions and goods, and parted them to all men, as every man had need. And they, continuing daily with one accord in the temple, and breaking bread from house to house, did eat their meat* with gladness and singleness of heart, praising

God, and having favour with all the people. And the Lord added to the church daily such as should be saved.

Acts 2:41-47

436   But there remained two of the men in the camp, the name of the one was Eldad, and the name of the other Medad: and the spirit rested upon them; and they were of them that were written, but went not out unto the tabernacle*: and they prophesied in the camp. And there ran a young man, and told Moses, and said, "Eldad and Medad do prophesy in the camp." And Joshua the son of Nun, the servant of Moses, one of his young men, answered and said, "My lord Moses, forbid them." And Moses said unto him, "Enviest thou for my sake? Would God that all the LORD's people were prophets, and that the LORD would put his spirit upon them!" And Moses gat* him into the camp, he and the elders of Israel.

Numbers 11:26-30

437   And John answered him, saying, "Master, we saw one casting out devils in thy name, and he followeth not us: and we forbad him, because he followeth not us." But Jesus said, "Forbid him not: for there is no man which shall do a miracle in my name, that can lightly speak evil of me. For he that is not against us is on our part. For whosoever shall give you a cup of water to drink in my name, because ye belong to Christ, verily I say unto you, he shall not lose his reward."

Mark 9:38-41

438   Except the L ORD build the house,
     They labour in vain that build it:
   Except the L ORD keep the city,
     The watchman waketh but in vain.
   It is vain for you to rise up early,
     To sit up late,
   To eat the bread of sorrows:
     For so he giveth his beloved sleep.
   Lo, children are an heritage of the L ORD:
     And the fruit of the womb is his reward.
   As arrows are in the hand of a mighty man;
     So are children of the youth.
   Happy is the man
     That hath his quiver full of them:
   They shall not be ashamed,
     But they shall speak with the enemies in the gate.

Psalm 127:1-5

439   And they brought young children to him, that he should touch them: and his disciples rebuked those that brought them. But when Jesus saw it, he was much displeased, and said unto them, "Suffer* the little children to come unto me, and forbid them not: for of such is the kingdom of God. Verily I say unto you, Whosoever shall not receive the kingdom of God as a little child, he shall not enter therein." And he took them up in his arms, put his hands upon them, and blessed them.

Mark 10:13-16

440 And Adam knew Eve his wife; and she conceived, and bare Cain, and said, "I have gotten a man from the LORD." And she again bare his brother Abel. And Abel was a keeper of sheep, but Cain was a tiller of the ground. And in process of time it came to pass, that Cain brought of the fruit of the ground an offering unto the LORD. And Abel, he also brought of the firstlings of his flock and of the fat thereof. And the LORD had respect unto Abel and to his offering: But unto Cain and to his offering he had not respect. And Cain was very wroth*, and his countenance fell. And the LORD said unto Cain, "Why art thou wroth? And why is thy countenance fallen? If thou doest well, shalt thou not be accepted? And if thou doest not well, sin lieth at the door. And unto thee shall be his desire, and thou shalt rule over him." And Cain talked with Abel his brother: and it came to pass, when they were in the field, that Cain rose up against Abel his brother, and slew him.

Genesis 4:1-8

441 From whence come wars and fightings among you? Come they not hence, even of your lusts that war in your members? Ye lust, and have not: ye kill, and desire to have, and cannot obtain: ye fight and war, yet ye have not, because ye ask not. Ye ask, and receive not, because ye ask amiss, that ye may consume it upon your lusts. Ye adulterers and adulteresses, know ye not that the friendship of the world is enmity with God? Whosoever therefore will be a friend of the world is the enemy of God.

James 4:1-4

442 And the LORD said unto Cain, "Where is Abel thy brother?" And he said, "I know not: Am I my brother's keeper?" And he said, "What hast thou done? The voice of thy brother's blood crieth unto me from the ground. And now art thou cursed from the earth, which hath opened her mouth to receive thy brother's blood from thy hand; when thou tillest the ground, it shall not henceforth yield unto thee her strength; a fugitive and a vagabond shalt thou be in the earth." And Cain said unto the LORD, "My punishment is greater than I can bear. Behold, thou hast driven me out this day from the face of the earth; and from thy face shall I be hid; and I shall be a fugitive and a vagabond in the earth; and it shall come to pass, that every one that findeth me shall slay me." And the LORD said unto him, "Therefore whosoever slayeth Cain, vengeance shall be taken on him sevenfold." And the LORD set a mark upon Cain, lest any finding him should kill him. And Cain went out from the presence of the LORD, and dwelt in the land of Nod, on the east of Eden.

Genesis 4:9-16

443 In this the children of God are manifest, and the children of the devil: whosoever doeth not righteousness is not of God, neither he that loveth not his brother. For this is the message that ye heard from the beginning, that we should love one another. Not as Cain, who was of that wicked one, and slew his brother. And wherefore* slew he him? Because his own works were evil, and his brother's righteous. Marvel not, my brethren, if the world hate you. We know that we have passed from death unto life, because we love the brethren. He that loveth not his brother abideth in death. Whosoever hateth his brother is a murderer: and ye know that no murderer hath eternal life abiding in him. Hereby perceive we the love of God, because he laid down his life for us: and we ought to lay down our lives for

the brethren. But whoso hath this world's good, and seeth his brother have need, and shutteth up his bowels* of compassion from him, how dwelleth the love of God in him? My little children, let us not love in word, neither in tongue; but in deed and in truth.

1 John 3:10-18

444   How fair and how pleasant art thou,
     O love, for delights!
This thy stature is like to a palm tree,
     And thy breasts to clusters of grapes.
I said, "I will go up to the palm tree,
     I will take hold of the boughs thereof":
Now also thy breasts shall be as clusters of the vine,
     And the smell of thy nose like apples;
And the roof of thy mouth like the best wine for my beloved,
     That goeth down sweetly,
     Causing the lips of those that are asleep to speak.
I am my beloved's,
     And his desire is toward me.
Come, my beloved,
     Let us go forth into the field;
     Let us lodge in the villages.
Let us get up early to the vineyards;
     Let us see if the vine flourish,
Whether the tender grape appear,
     And the pomegranates bud forth:
There will I give thee my loves.

Song of Songs 7:6-12

445 Now concerning the things whereof ye wrote unto me [Paul]: It is good for a man not to touch a woman. Nevertheless, to avoid fornication, let every man have his own wife, and let every woman have her own husband. Let the husband render unto the wife due benevolence: and likewise also the wife unto the husband. The wife hath not power of her own body, but the husband: and likewise also the husband hath not power of his own body, but the wife. Defraud ye not one the other, except it be with consent for a time, that ye may give yourselves to fasting and prayer; and come together again, that Satan tempt you not for your incontinency. But I speak this by permission, and not of commandment. For I would that all men were even as I myself. But every man hath his proper gift of God, one after this manner, and another after that. . . . Let every man abide, wherein he was called, therein abide with God.

1 Corinthians 7:1-7, 24

446 And when [Samson] came unto Lehi, the Philistines shouted against him: and the Spirit of the LORD came mightily upon him, and the cords that were upon his arms became as flax that was burnt with fire, and his bands loosed from off his hands. And he found a new jawbone of an ass, and put forth his hand, and took it, and slew a thousand men therewith. And Samson said,

> "With the jawbone of an ass,
>   Heaps upon heaps,
> With the jaw of an ass have
>   I slain a thousand men."

Judges 15:14-16

447   There be three things which are too wonderful for me,
        Yea, four which I know not:
  The way of an eagle in the air;
        The way of a serpent upon a rock;
  The way of a ship in the midst of the sea;
        And the way of a man with a maid.

Proverbs 30:18-19

448   And it came to pass afterward, that [Samson] loved a woman in the valley of Sorek, whose name was Delilah. . . . And she said unto him, "How
  canst thou say, 'I love thee,' when thine heart is not with me? Thou hast
  mocked me these three times, and hast not told me wherein thy great
  strength lieth." And it came to pass, when she pressed him daily with her
  words, and urged him, so that his soul was vexed unto death; that he told
  her all his heart, and said unto her, "There hath not come a razor upon
  mine head; for I have been a Nazarite unto God from my mother's
  womb: if I be shaven, then my strength will go from me, and I shall become weak, and be like any other man."

Judges 16:4, 15-17

449   Let him kiss me with the kisses of his mouth:
  For thy love is better than wine.
        Because of the savour of thy good ointments
  Thy name is as ointment poured forth,
        Therefore do the virgins love thee.
  Draw me, we will run after thee:

The king hath brought me into his chambers:
We will be glad and rejoice in thee,
    We will remember thy love more than wine:
    The upright love thee.
I am black, but comely, O ye daughters of Jerusalem,
    As the tents of Kedar, as the curtains of Solomon.

Song of Songs 1:2-5

450   And when Delilah saw that he had told her all his heart, she sent and
called for the lords of the Philistines, saying, "Come up this once, for he
hath shewed me all his heart." Then the lords of the Philistines came up
unto her, and brought money in their hand. And she made him sleep
upon her knees; and she called for a man, and she caused him to shave off
the seven locks of his head; and she began to afflict him, and his strength
went from him. And she said, "The Philistines be upon thee, Samson."
And he awoke out of his sleep, and said, "I will go out as at other times
before, and shake myself." And he wist* not that the LORD was departed
from him. But the Philistines took him, and put out his eyes, and
brought him down to Gaza, and bound him with fetters of brass; and he
did grind in the prison house. Howbeit* the hair of his head began to
grow again after he was shaven.

Judges 16:18-22

451   "And I say unto you my friends, Be not afraid of them that kill the body,
and after that have no more that they can do. But I will forewarn you
whom ye shall fear: Fear him, which after he hath killed hath power to

cast into hell; yea, I say unto you, Fear him. Are not five sparrows sold for two farthings, and not one of them is forgotten before God? But even the very hairs of your head are all numbered. Fear not therefore: ye are of more value than many sparrows."

Luke 12:4-7

452 Now the house was full of men and women; and all the lords of the Philistines were there; and there were upon the roof about three thousand men and women, that beheld while Samson made sport. And Samson called unto the LORD, and said, "O Lord God, remember me, I pray thee, and strengthen me, I pray thee, only this once, O God, that I may be at once avenged of the Philistines for my two eyes." And Samson took hold of the two middle pillars upon which the house stood, and on which it was borne up, of the one with his right hand, and of the other with his left. And Samson said, "Let me die with the Philistines." And he bowed himself with all his might; and the house fell upon the lords, and upon all the people that were therein. So the dead which he slew at his death were more than they which he slew in his life.

Judges 16:27-30

453 And being in Bethany in the house of Simon the leper, as he sat at meat*, there came a woman having an alabaster box of ointment of spikenard very precious*; and she brake the box, and poured it on his head. And there were some that had indignation within themselves, and said, "Why was this waste of the ointment made? For it might have been sold for more than three hundred pence, and have been given to the poor." And

they murmured against her. And Jesus said, "Let her alone; why trouble ye her? She hath wrought a good work on me. For ye have the poor with you always, and whensoever ye will ye may do them good: but me ye have not always. She hath done what she could: she is come aforehand to anoint my body to the burying. Verily I say unto you, Wheresoever this gospel shall be preached throughout the whole world, this also that she hath done shall be spoken of for a memorial of her."

Mark 14:3-9

454 And when the words were heard which David spake, they rehearsed them before Saul: and he sent for him. And David said to Saul, "Let no man's heart fail because of him; thy servant will go and fight with this Philistine [Goliath]." And Saul said to David, "Thou art not able to go against this Philistine to fight with him: for thou art but a youth, and he a man of war from his youth." And David said unto Saul, "Thy servant kept his father's sheep, and there came a lion, and a bear, and took a lamb out of the flock: And I went out after him, and smote him, and delivered it out of his mouth: and when he arose against me, I caught him by his beard, and smote him, and slew him. Thy servant slew both the lion and the bear: and this uncircumcised Philistine shall be as one of them, seeing he hath defied the armies of the living God." David said moreover, "The LORD that delivered me out of the paw of the lion, and out of the paw of the bear, he will deliver me out of the hand of this Philistine." And Saul said unto David, "Go, and the LORD be with thee."

1 Samuel 17:31-37

455　For though we walk in the flesh, we do not war after the flesh: (For the weapons of our warfare are not carnal, but mighty through God to the pulling down of strong holds;) Casting down imaginations, and every high thing that exalteth itself against the knowledge of God, and bringing into captivity every thought to the obedience of Christ; and having in a readiness to revenge all disobedience, when your obedience is fulfilled.

2 Corinthians 10:3-6

456　And the Philistine came on and drew near unto David; and the man that bare the shield went before him. And when the Philistine looked about, and saw David, he disdained him: for he was but a youth, and ruddy, and of a fair countenance. And the Philistine said unto David, "Am I a dog, that thou comest to me with staves?" And the Philistine cursed David by his gods. And the Philistine said to David, "Come to me, and I will give thy flesh unto the fowls of the air, and to the beasts of the field." Then said David to the Philistine, "Thou comest to me with a sword, and with a spear, and with a shield: but I come to thee in the name of the LORD of hosts, the God of the armies of Israel, whom thou hast defied."

1 Samuel 17:41-45

457　The elders which are among you I exhort, who am also an elder, and a witness of the sufferings of Christ, and also a partaker of the glory that shall be revealed: Feed the flock of God which is among you, taking the oversight thereof, not by constraint, but willingly; not for filthy lucre, but of a ready mind; neither as being lords over God's heritage, but being ensamples* to the flock. And when the chief Shepherd shall appear, ye shall receive a crown of glory that fadeth not away. Likewise, ye younger, submit yourselves unto the elder. Yea, all of you be subject one to another, and be clothed with humility: for God resisteth the proud, and giveth grace to the humble. Humble yourselves therefore under the mighty hand of God, that he may exalt you in due time: Casting all your care upon him; for he careth for you.

1 Peter 5:1-7

458 And it came to pass, when the Philistine arose, and came and drew nigh to meet David, that David hastened, and ran toward the army to meet the Philistine. And David put his hand in his bag, and took thence a stone, and slang it, and smote the Philistine in his forehead, that the stone sunk into his forehead; and he fell upon his face to the earth. So David prevailed over the Philistine with a sling and with a stone, and smote the Philistine, and slew him; but there was no sword in the hand of David. Therefore David ran, and stood upon the Philistine, and took his sword, and drew it out of the sheath thereof, and slew him, and cut off his head therewith. And when the Philistines saw their champion was dead, they fled.

1 Samuel 17:48-51

459 Then said [Jesus] also to him that bade him, "When thou makest a dinner or a supper, call not thy friends, nor thy brethren, neither thy kinsmen, nor thy rich neighbours; lest they also bid thee again, and a recompence be made thee. But when thou makest a feast, call the poor, the maimed, the

lame, the blind: And thou shalt be blessed; for they cannot recompense thee: for thou shalt be recompensed at the resurrection of the just."

Luke 14:12-14

460 And the word of the LORD came unto me, saying, "Son of man, prophesy against the shepherds of Israel, prophesy, and say unto them, 'Thus saith the Lord GOD unto the shepherds; Woe be to the shepherds of Israel that do feed themselves! Should not the shepherds feed the flocks? Ye eat the fat, and ye clothe you with the wool, ye kill them that are fed: but ye feed not the flock. The diseased have ye not strengthened, neither have ye healed that which was sick, neither have ye bound up that which was broken, neither have ye brought again that which was driven away, neither have ye sought that which was lost; but with force and with cruelty have ye ruled them. And they were scattered, because there is no shepherd: and they became meat* to all the beasts of the field, when they were scattered. My sheep wandered through all the mountains, and upon every high hill: yea, my flock was scattered upon all the face of the earth, and none did search or seek after them. Therefore, ye shepherds, hear the word of the LORD; As I live, saith the Lord GOD, Surely because my flock became a prey, and my flock became meat to every beast of the field, because there was no shepherd, neither did my shepherds search for my flock, but the shepherds fed themselves, and fed not my flock; Therefore, O ye shepherds, hear the word of the LORD; Thus saith the Lord GOD; Behold, I am against the shepherds; and I will require my flock at their hand, and cause them to cease from feeding the flock; neither shall the shepherds feed themselves any more; for I will deliver my flock from their mouth, that they may not be meat for them.'"

Ezekiel 34:1-10

461 "I am the good shepherd, and know my sheep, and am known of mine. As the Father knoweth me, even so know I the Father: and I lay down my life for the sheep. And other sheep I have, which are not of this fold: them also I must bring, and they shall hear my voice; and there shall be one fold, and one shepherd. Therefore doth my Father love me, because I lay down my life, that I might take it again. No man taketh it from me, but I lay it down of myself. I have power to lay it down, and I have power to take it again. This commandment have I received of my Father."

John 10:14-18

462 "For thus saith the Lord GOD; Behold, I, even I, will both search my sheep, and seek them out. As a shepherd seeketh out his flock in the day that he is among his sheep that are scattered; so will I seek out my sheep, and will deliver them out of all places where they have been scattered in the cloudy and dark day. And I will bring them out from the people, and gather them from the countries, and will bring them to their own land, and feed them upon the mountains of Israel by the rivers, and in all the inhabited places of the country. I will feed them in a good pasture, and upon the high mountains of Israel shall their fold be: there shall they lie in a good fold, and in a fat pasture shall they feed upon the mountains of Israel. I will feed my flock, and I will cause them to lie down, saith the Lord GOD. I will seek that which was lost, and bring again that which was driven away, and will bind up that which was broken, and will strengthen that which was sick: but I will destroy the fat and the strong; I will feed them with judgment."

Ezekiel 34:11-16

463 Then took they [Jesus], and led him, and brought him into the high priest's house. And Peter followed afar off. And when they had kindled a fire in the midst of the hall, and were set down together, Peter sat down among them. But a certain maid beheld him as he sat by the fire, and earnestly looked upon him, and said, "This man was also with him." And he denied him, saying, "Woman, I know him not." And after a little while another saw him, and said, "Thou art also of them." And Peter said, "Man, I am not." And about the space of one hour after another confidently affirmed, saying, "Of a truth this fellow also was with him: for he is a Galilaean." And Peter said, "Man, I know not what thou sayest." And immediately, while he yet spake, the cock crew. And the Lord turned, and looked upon Peter. And Peter remembered the word of the Lord, how he had said unto him, "Before the cock crow, thou shalt deny me thrice." And Peter went out, and wept bitterly.

Luke 22:54-62

464 Let your conversation be without covetousness; and be content with such things as ye have: for he hath said, "I will never leave thee, nor forsake thee." So that we may boldly say,

"The Lord is my helper,
And I will not fear what man shall do unto me."

Hebrews 13:5-6

465 Then Judas, which had betrayed [Jesus], when he saw that he was condemned, repented himself, and brought again the thirty pieces of silver to the chief priests and elders, saying, "I have sinned in that I have betrayed the innocent blood." And they said, "What is that to us? See thou to that." And he cast down the pieces of silver in the temple, and departed, and went and hanged himself. And the chief priests took the silver pieces, and said, "It is not lawful for to put them into the treasury, because it is the price of blood." And they took counsel, and bought with them the potter's field, to bury strangers in. Wherefore that field was called, "The field of blood," unto this day.

Matthew 27:3-8

466 But godliness with contentment is great gain. For we brought nothing into this world, and it is certain we can carry nothing out. And having food and raiment let us be therewith content. But they that will be rich fall into temptation and a snare, and into many foolish and hurtful lusts, which drown men in destruction and perdition. For the love of money is the root of all evil: which while some coveted after, they have erred from the faith, and pierced themselves through with many sorrows.

1 Timothy 6:6-10

467 But Mary stood without at the sepulchre weeping: and as she wept, she stooped down, and looked into the sepulchre, and seeth two angels in white sitting, the one at the head, and the other at the feet, where the body of Jesus had lain. And they say unto her, "Woman, why weepest thou?" She saith unto them, "Because they have taken away my LORD, and I know not where they have laid him." And when she had thus said, she turned herself back, and saw Jesus standing, and knew not that it was Jesus. Jesus saith unto her, "Woman, why weepest thou? Whom seekest thou?" She, supposing him to be the gardener, saith unto him, "Sir, if

thou have borne him hence, tell me where thou hast laid him, and I will take him away." Jesus saith unto her, "Mary." She turned herself, and saith unto him, "Rabboni"; which is to say, "Master." Jesus saith unto her, "Touch me not; for I am not yet ascended to my Father: but go to my brethren, and say unto them, 'I ascend unto my Father, and your Father; and to my God, and your God.'" Mary Magdalene came and told the disciples that she had seen the Lord, and that he had spoken these things unto her.

John 20:11-18

468 The LORD is my shepherd;
 I shall not want.
He maketh me to lie down in green pastures:
 He leadeth me beside the still waters.
He restoreth my soul:
 He leadeth me in the paths of righteousness for his name's sake.
Yea, though I walk through the valley of the shadow of death,
 I will fear no evil:
For thou art with me;
 Thy rod and thy staff they comfort me.
Thou preparest a table before me
 In the presence of mine enemies:
Thou anointest my head with oil;
 My cup runneth over.
Surely goodness and mercy shall follow me
 All the days of my life:
And I will dwell in the house of the LORD for ever.

Psalm 23:1-6

469 So when they had dined, Jesus saith to Simon Peter, "Simon, son of Jonas, lovest thou me more than these?" He saith unto him, "Yea, Lord; thou knowest that I love thee." He saith unto him, "Feed my lambs." He saith to him again the second time, "Simon, son of Jonas, lovest thou me?" He saith unto him, "Yea, Lord; thou knowest that I love thee." He saith unto him, "Feed my sheep." He saith unto him the third time, "Simon, son of Jonas, lovest thou me?" Peter was grieved because he said unto him the third time, "Lovest thou me?" And he said unto him, "Lord, thou knowest all things; thou knowest that I love thee." Jesus saith unto him, "Feed my sheep. Verily, verily, I say unto thee, When thou wast young, thou girdest thyself, and walkedst whither thou wouldest: but when thou shalt be old, thou shalt stretch forth thy hands, and another shall gird thee, and carry thee whither thou wouldest not." This spake he, signifying by what death he should glorify God. And when he had spoken this, he saith unto him, "Follow me."

John 21:15-19

470 Moreover thou shalt not lie carnally with thy neighbour's wife, to defile thyself with her.

Leviticus 18:20

471 And it came to pass in an eveningtide, that David arose from off his bed, and walked upon the roof of the king's house: and from the roof he saw a woman washing herself; and the woman was very beautiful to look upon. And David sent and inquired after the woman. And one said, "Is not this Bathsheba, the daughter of Eliam, the wife of Uriah the Hittite?" And David sent messengers, and took her; and she came in unto him, and he

lay with her; for she was purified from her uncleanness: and she returned unto her house. And the woman conceived, and sent and told David, and said, "I am with child."

2 Samuel 11:2-5

472   Better is the end of a thing than the beginning thereof: and the patient in spirit is better than the proud in spirit. Be not hasty in thy spirit to be angry: for anger resteth in the bosom of fools. Say not thou, "What is the cause that the former days were better than these?" For thou dost not inquire wisely concerning this.

Ecclesiastes 7:8-10

473   And David sent to Joab, saying, "Send me Uriah the Hittite." And Joab sent Uriah to David. And when Uriah was come unto him, David demanded of him how Joab did, and how the people did, and how the war prospered. And David said to Uriah, "Go down to thy house, and wash thy feet." And Uriah departed out of the king's house, and there followed him a mess of meat* from the king. But Uriah slept at the door of the king's house with all the servants of his lord, and went not down to his house. And when they had told David, saying, "Uriah went not down unto his house," David said unto Uriah, "Camest thou not from thy journey? Why then didst thou not go down unto thine house?" And Uriah said unto David, "The ark, and Israel, and Judah, abide in tents; and my lord Joab, and the servants of my lord, are encamped in the open fields; shall I then go into mine house, to eat and to drink, and to lie with my wife? As thou livest, and as thy soul liveth, I will not do this thing." And David said to

Uriah, "Tarry here to day also, and to morrow I will let thee depart." So Uriah abode in Jerusalem that day, and the morrow. And when David had called him, he did eat and drink before him; and he made him drunk: and at even* he went out to lie on his bed with the servants of his lord, but went not down to his house.

2 Samuel 11:6-13

474   Understand, ye brutish among the people:
      And ye fools, when will ye be wise?
  He that planted the ear, shall he not hear?
      He that formed the eye, shall he not see?
  He that chastiseth the heathen, shall not he correct?
      He that teacheth man knowledge, shall not he know?
  The LORD knoweth the thoughts of man,
      That they are vanity.

Psalm 94:8-11

475   And it came to pass in the morning, that David wrote a letter to Joab, and sent it by the hand of Uriah. And he wrote in the letter, saying, "Set ye Uriah in the forefront of the hottest battle, and retire ye from him, that he may be smitten, and die." And it came to pass, when Joab observed the city, that he assigned Uriah unto a place where he knew that valiant men were. And the men of the city went out, and fought with Joab: and there fell some of the people of the servants of David; and Uriah the Hittite died also. . . . And when the wife of Uriah heard that Uriah her husband was dead, she mourned for her husband. And when the mourning was past,

David sent and fetched her to his house, and she became his wife, and bare him a son. But the thing that David had done displeased the LORD.

2 Samuel 11:14-17, 26-27

476   "The first of the firstfruits of thy land thou shalt bring unto the house of the LORD thy God. Thou shalt not seethe a kid* in his mother's milk." And the LORD said unto Moses, "Write thou these words: for after the tenor of these words I have made a covenant with thee and with Israel."

Exodus 34:26-27

477   And the LORD sent Nathan unto David. And he came unto him, and said unto him, "There were two men in one city; the one rich, and the other poor. The rich man had exceeding many flocks and herds: But the poor man had nothing, save one little ewe lamb, which he had bought and nourished up: and it grew up together with him, and with his children; it did eat of his own meat*, and drank of his own cup, and lay in his bosom, and was unto him as a daughter. And there came a traveller unto the rich man, and he spared to take of his own flock and of his own herd, to dress for the wayfaring man that was come unto him; but took the poor man's lamb, and dressed it for the man that was come to him." And David's anger was greatly kindled against the man; and he said to Nathan, "As the LORD liveth, the man that hath done this thing shall surely die: And he shall restore the lamb fourfold, because he did this thing, and because he had no pity."

And Nathan said to David, "Thou art the man."

2 Samuel 12:1-7a

478 Having eyes full of adultery, and that cannot cease from sin; beguiling unstable souls: an heart they have exercised with covetous practices; cursed children: . . . For it had been better for them not to have known the way of righteousness, than, after they have known it, to turn from the holy commandment delivered unto them. But it is happened unto them according to the true proverb, "The dog is turned to his own vomit again; and the sow that was washed to her wallowing in the mire."

2 Peter 2:14, 21-22

479 "Thus saith the LORD God of Israel [to David], 'I anointed thee king over Israel, and I delivered thee out of the hand of Saul; and I gave thee thy master's house, and thy master's wives into thy bosom, and gave thee the house of Israel and of Judah; and if that had been too little, I would moreover have given unto thee such and such things. Wherefore* hast thou despised the commandment of the LORD, to do evil in his sight? Thou hast killed Uriah the Hittite with the sword, and hast taken his wife to be thy wife, and hast slain him with the sword of the children of Ammon. Now therefore the sword shall never depart from thine house; because thou hast despised me, and hast taken the wife of Uriah the Hittite to be thy wife.' Thus saith the LORD, 'Behold, I will raise up evil against thee out of thine own house, and I will take thy wives before thine eyes, and give them unto thy neighbour, and he shall lie with thy wives in the sight of this sun. For thou didst it secretly: but I will do this thing before all Israel, and before the sun.'" And David said unto Nathan, "I have sinned against the LORD." And Nathan said unto David, "The LORD also hath put away thy sin; thou shalt not die. Howbeit*, because by this deed thou hast given great occasion to the enemies of the LORD

to blaspheme, the child also that is born unto thee shall surely die." And
Nathan departed unto his house.

2 Samuel 12:7b-15a

480   Have mercy upon me, O God,
     According to thy lovingkindness:
According unto the multitude of thy tender mercies
     Blot out my transgressions.
Wash me throughly from mine iniquity,
     And cleanse me from my sin.
For I acknowledge my transgressions:
     And my sin is ever before me.
Against thee, thee only, have I sinned,
     And done this evil in thy sight:
That thou mightest be justified when thou speakest,
     And be clear when thou judgest.
Behold, I was shapen in iniquity;
     And in sin did my mother conceive me.
Behold, thou desirest truth in the inward parts:
     And in the hidden part thou shalt make me to know wisdom.
Purge me with hyssop, and I shall be clean:
     Wash me, and I shall be whiter than snow.
Make me to hear joy and gladness;
     That the bones which thou hast broken may rejoice.
Hide thy face from my sins,
     And blot out all mine iniquities.
Create in me a clean heart, O God;
     And renew a right spirit within me.

Cast me not away from thy presence;
  And take not thy holy spirit from me.
Restore unto me the joy of thy salvation;
  And uphold me with thy free spirit.
Then will I teach transgressors thy ways;
  And sinners shall be converted unto thee.
Deliver me from bloodguiltiness, O God, thou God of
    my salvation:
  And my tongue shall sing aloud of thy righteousness.
O Lord, open thou my lips;
  And my mouth shall shew forth thy praise.
For thou desirest not sacrifice;
  Else would I give it:
  Thou delightest not in burnt offering.
The sacrifices of God are a broken spirit:
  A broken and a contrite heart, O God, thou wilt not despise.

Psalm 51:1-17

481　And the LORD struck the child that Uriah's wife bare unto David, and it was very sick. David therefore besought God for the child; and David fasted, and went in, and lay all night upon the earth. And the elders of his house arose, and went to him, to raise him up from the earth: but he would not, neither did he eat bread with them. And it came to pass on the seventh day, that the child died. And the servants of David feared to tell him that the child was dead: for they said, "Behold, while the child was yet alive, we spake unto him, and he would not hearken unto our voice: how will he then vex himself, if we tell him that the child is dead?" But when David saw that his servants whispered, David perceived that the child was dead: therefore David said unto his servants, "Is the child dead?" And they said, "He is dead."

2 Samuel 12:15b-19

482   "I would seek unto God,
           And unto God would I commit my cause:
      Which doeth great things and unsearchable;
           Marvellous things without number:
      Who giveth rain upon the earth,
           And sendeth waters upon the fields:
      To set up on high those that be low;
           That those which mourn may be exalted to safety.
      He disappointeth the devices of the crafty,
           So that their hands cannot perform their enterprise.
      He taketh the wise in their own craftiness:
           And the counsel of the froward* is carried headlong.
      They meet with darkness in the day time,
           And grope in the noonday as in the night."

Job 5:8-14

483   Then David arose from the earth, and washed, and anointed himself, and changed his apparel, and came into the house of the LORD, and worshipped: then he came to his own house; and when he required, they set bread before him, and he did eat. Then said his servants unto him, "What thing is this that thou hast done? Thou didst fast and weep for the child, while it was alive; but when the child was dead, thou didst rise

and eat bread." And he said, "While the child was yet alive, I fasted and wept: for I said, 'Who can tell whether GOD will be gracious to me, that the child may live?' But now he is dead, wherefore* should I fast? Can I bring him back again? I shall go to him, but he shall not return to me." And David comforted Bathsheba his wife, and went in unto her, and lay with her: and she bare a son, and he called his name Solomon: and the LORD loved him.

2 Samuel 12:20-24a

484   Whoredom and wine and new wine
       Take away the heart.
My people ask counsel at their stocks,
       And their staff declareth unto them:
For the spirit of whoredoms hath caused them to err,
       And they have gone a whoring from under their God. . . .
For Israel slideth back as a backsliding heifer:
       Now the LORD will feed them as a lamb in a large place.

Hosea 4:11-12, 16

485   This is a true saying, "If a man desire the office of a bishop, he desireth a good work." A bishop then must be blameless, the husband of one wife, vigilant, sober, of good behaviour, given to hospitality, apt to teach; Not given to wine, no striker, not greedy of filthy lucre; but patient, not a brawler, not covetous; One that ruleth well his own house, having his children in subjection with all gravity; (For if a man know not how to rule his own house, how shall he take care of the church of God?)

1 Timothy 3:1-5

486   If we have forgotten the name of our God,
        Or stretched out our hands to a strange god;
Shall not God search this out?
        For he knoweth the secrets of the heart.
Yea, for thy sake are we killed all the day long;
        We are counted as sheep for the slaughter.

Psalm 44:20-22

487   Now when the turn of Esther, the daughter of Abihail the uncle of Mordecai, who had taken her for his daughter, was come to go in unto the [Persian] king, she required nothing but what Hegai the king's chamberlain, the keeper of the women, appointed. And Esther obtained favour in the sight of all them that looked upon her. So Esther was taken unto king Ahasuerus into his house royal in the tenth month, which is the month Tebeth, in the seventh year of his reign. And the king loved Esther above all the women, and she obtained grace and favour in his sight more than all the virgins; so that he set the royal crown upon her head, and made her queen instead of Vashti.

Esther 2:15-17

488   What shall we then say to these things? If God be for us, who can be against us? He that spared not his own Son, but delivered him up for us all, how shall he not with him also freely give us all things? Who shall lay any thing to the charge of God's elect? It is God that justifieth. Who is he that condemneth? It is Christ that died, yea rather, that is risen again, who is even at the right hand of God, who also maketh intercession for

us. Who shall separate us from the love of Christ? Shall tribulation, or distress, or persecution, or famine, or nakedness, or peril, or sword? As it is written,

> "For thy sake we are killed all the day long;
> We are accounted as sheep for the slaughter."

Nay, in all these things we are more than conquerors through him that loved us. For I am persuaded, that neither death, nor life, nor angels, nor principalities, nor powers, nor things present, nor things to come, nor height, nor depth, nor any other creature, shall be able to separate us from the love of God, which is in Christ Jesus our Lord.

Romans 8:31-39

489 And the king said again unto Esther on the second day at the banquet of wine, "What is thy petition, Queen Esther? And it shall be granted thee: and what is thy request? And it shall be performed, even to the half of the kingdom." Then Esther the queen answered and said, "If I have found favour in thy sight, O king, and if it please the king, let my life be given me at my petition, and my people at my request: For we are sold, I and my people, to be destroyed, to be slain, and to perish. But if we had been sold for bondmen and bondwomen, I had held my tongue, although the enemy could not countervail the king's damage." . . .

Then the king Ahasuerus said unto Esther the queen and to Mordecai the Jew, "Behold, I have given Esther the house of Haman, and him they have hanged upon the gallows, because he laid his hand upon the Jews. Write ye also for the Jews, as it liketh you, in the king's name, and seal it with the king's ring: For the writing which is written in the king's name, and sealed with the king's ring, may no man reverse."

Esther 7:2-4; 8:7-8

490   "For the kingdom of heaven is like unto a man that is an householder, which went out early in the morning to hire labourers into his vineyard. And when he had agreed with the labourers for a penny a day, he sent them into his vineyard. And he went out about the third hour, and saw others standing idle in the marketplace, and said unto them; 'Go ye also into the vineyard, and whatsoever is right I will give you.' And they went their way. Again he went out about the sixth and ninth hour, and did likewise. And about the eleventh hour he went out, and found others standing idle, and saith unto them, 'Why stand ye here all the day idle?' They say unto him, 'Because no man hath hired us.' He saith unto them, 'Go ye also into the vineyard; and whatsoever is right, that shall ye receive.' So when even* was come, the lord of the vineyard saith unto his steward, 'Call the labourers, and give them their hire, beginning from the last unto the first.' And when they came that were hired about the eleventh hour, they received every man a penny. But when the first came, they supposed that they should have received more; and they likewise received every man a penny. And when they had received it, they murmured against the goodman* of the house, saying, 'These last have wrought but one hour, and thou hast made them equal unto us, which have borne the burden and heat of the day.' But he answered one of them, and said, 'Friend, I do thee no wrong: didst not thou agree with me for a penny? Take that thine is, and go thy way: I will give unto this last, even as unto thee. Is it not lawful for me to do what I will with mine own? Is thine eye evil, because I am good?' So the last shall be first, and the first last: for many be called, but few chosen."

Matthew 20:1-16

491 The hand of the LORD was upon me, and carried me out in the spirit of the LORD, and set me down in the midst of the valley which was full of bones, and caused me to pass by them round about: and, behold, there were very many in the open valley; and, lo, they were very dry. And he said unto me, "Son of man, can these bones live?" And I answered, "O Lord GOD, thou knowest." Again he said unto me, "Prophesy upon these bones, and say unto them, 'O ye dry bones, hear the word of the LORD. Thus saith the Lord GOD unto these bones; Behold, I will cause breath to enter into you, and ye shall live: And I will lay sinews upon you, and will bring up flesh upon you, and cover you with skin, and put breath in you, and ye shall live; and ye shall know that I am the LORD.'"

Ezekiel 37:1-6

492 There was a man of the Pharisees, named Nicodemus, a ruler of the Jews: The same came to Jesus by night, and said unto him, "Rabbi, we know that thou art a teacher come from God: for no man can do these miracles that thou doest, except God be with him." Jesus answered and said unto him, "Verily, verily, I say unto thee, Except a man be born again, he cannot see the kingdom of God." Nicodemus saith unto him, "How can a man be born when he is old? Can he enter the second time into his mother's womb, and be born?" Jesus answered, "Verily, verily, I say unto thee, Except a man be born of water and of the Spirit, he cannot enter into the kingdom of God. That which is born of the flesh is flesh; and that which is born of the Spirit is spirit. Marvel not that I said unto thee, 'Ye must be born again.' The wind bloweth where it listeth, and thou hearest the sound thereof, but canst not tell whence it cometh, and whither it goeth: so is every one that is born of the Spirit." Nicodemus answered and said unto him, "How can these things be?" Jesus answered

and said unto him, "Art thou a master of Israel, and knowest not these things? Verily, verily, I say unto thee, We speak that we do know, and testify that we have seen; and ye receive not our witness. If I have told you earthly things, and ye believe not, how shall ye believe, if I tell you of heavenly things?"

John 3:1-12

493 So I prophesied as I was commanded: and as I prophesied, there was a noise, and behold a shaking, and the bones came together, bone to his bone. And when I beheld, lo, the sinews and the flesh came up upon them, and the skin covered them above: but there was no breath in them. Then said he unto me, "Prophesy unto the wind, prophesy, son of man, and say to the wind, 'Thus saith the Lord GOD: Come from the four winds, O breath, and breathe upon these slain, that they may live.'" So I prophesied as he commanded me, and the breath came into them, and they lived, and stood up upon their feet, an exceeding great army. Then he said unto me, "Son of man, these bones are the whole house of Israel: behold, they say, 'Our bones are dried, and our hope is lost: we are cut off for our parts.' Therefore prophesy and say unto them, 'Thus saith the Lord GOD; Behold, O my people, I will open your graves, and cause you to come up out of your graves, and bring you into the land of Israel. And ye shall know that I am the LORD, when I have opened your graves, O my people, and brought you up out of your graves, and shall put my spirit in you, and ye shall live, and I shall place you in your own land: then shall ye know that I the LORD have spoken it, and performed it, saith the LORD.'"

Ezekiel 37:7-14

494 "Verily, verily, I say unto you, The hour is coming, and now is, when the dead shall hear the voice of the Son of God: and they that hear shall live. For as the Father hath life in himself; so hath he given to the Son to have life in himself; and hath given him authority to execute judgment also, because he is the Son of man. Marvel not at this: for the hour is coming, in the which all that are in the graves shall hear his voice, and shall come forth; they that have done good, unto the resurrection of life; and they that have done evil, unto the resurrection of damnation."

John 5:25-29

495 And I heard as it were the voice of a great multitude, and as the voice of many waters, and as the voice of mighty thunderings, saying,

> "Alleluia: for the Lord God omnipotent reigneth.
> Let us be glad and rejoice, and give honour to him:
> For the marriage of the Lamb is come,
> And his wife hath made herself ready.
> And to her was granted that she should be arrayed in fine linen,
>   clean and white":

for the fine linen is the righteousness of saints. And he saith unto me, "Write, 'Blessed are they which are called unto the marriage supper of the Lamb.'" And he saith unto me, "These are the true sayings of God." And I fell at his feet to worship him. And he said unto me, "See thou do it not: I am thy fellowservant, and of thy brethren that have the testimony of Jesus: worship God: for the testimony of Jesus is the spirit of prophecy."

Revelation 19:6-10

496 O LORD our Lord,
    How excellent is thy name in all the earth!
  Who hast set thy glory above the heavens.
    Out of the mouth of babes and sucklings
  Hast thou ordained strength because of thine enemies,
    That thou mightest still the enemy and the avenger.
  When I consider thy heavens, the work of thy fingers,
    The moon and the stars, which thou hast ordained;
  What is man, that thou art mindful of him?
    And the son of man, that thou visitest him?
  For thou hast made him a little lower than the angels,
    And hast crowned him with glory and honour.
  Thou madest him to have dominion over the works of thy hands;
    Thou hast put all things under his feet:
  All sheep and oxen, yea, and the beasts of the field;
    The fowl of the air, and the fish of the sea,
    And whatsoever passeth through the paths of the seas.
  O LORD our Lord,
    How excellent is thy name in all the earth!

Psalm 8:1-9

The Seventh Day

Sabbath

Sanctuary

Death and Restoration

Rest and Peace

THE CREATOR'S *pièce de résistance* is quitting labor and honoring rest. So important is Sabbath that God sanctifies it — sets its apart — as a complete Day unto itself. Genesis thus administers a final jolt to a 24/7 world, whose relentless technology balloons in proportion inverse to its healthy civilization.

Like their Creator, nevertheless, creatures rest. When they haven't gotten enough, they seek more. Scripture speaks at length about Sabbath and sanctuary, time and place set apart for renewal by God. It speaks also of their abrogation, with justifications as varied as their circumstances. Death, activity's ultimate cessation, evokes a panorama of biblical responses: acquiescence and terror, fury and dedication, desolation and nobility. With allowance for alternative narrations, the same biblical figure — a Job or a Jesus — confronts pain-ridden mortality in very different ways. Both Testaments contemplate the hope and character of life beyond the grave. Such reflections extend the Sabbath principle: God's creatures recognize, not only creation's ultimate dissolution, but also its divine transfiguration by eternal peace, rest, and renewal.

497   Thus the heavens and the earth were finished, and all the host of them. And on the seventh day God ended his work which he had made; and he rested on the seventh day from all his work which he had made. And God blessed the seventh day, and sanctified it: because that in it he had rested from all his work which God created and made.

Genesis 2:1-3

498   And the LORD spake unto Moses, saying, "Speak thou also unto the children of Israel, saying, 'Verily my sabbaths ye shall keep: for it is a sign between me and you throughout your generations; that ye may know that I am the LORD that doth sanctify you. Ye shall keep the sabbath therefore; for it is holy unto you: every one that defileth it shall surely be put to death: for whosoever doeth any work therein, that soul shall be cut off from among his people. Six days may work be done; but in the seventh is the sabbath of rest, holy to the LORD: whosoever doeth any work in the sabbath day, he shall surely be put to death. Wherefore the children of Israel shall keep the sabbath, to observe the sabbath throughout their generations, for a perpetual covenant. It is a sign between me and the children of Israel for ever: for in six days the LORD made heaven and earth, and on the seventh day he rested, and was refreshed.'"

Exodus 31:12-17

499   And [Jesus] was teaching in one of the synagogues on the sabbath. And, behold, there was a woman which had a spirit of infirmity eighteen years, and was bowed together, and could in no wise* lift up herself. And when Jesus saw her, he called her to him, and said unto her, "Woman, thou art

loosed from thine infirmity." And he laid his hands on her: and immediately she was made straight, and glorified God. And the ruler of the synagogue answered with indignation, because that Jesus had healed on the sabbath day, and said unto the people, "There are six days in which men ought to work: in them therefore come and be healed, and not on the sabbath day." The Lord then answered him, and said, "Thou hypocrite, doth not each one of you on the sabbath loose his ox or his ass from the stall, and lead him away to watering? And ought not this woman, being a daughter of Abraham, whom Satan hath bound, lo, these eighteen years, be loosed from this bond on the sabbath day?" And when he had said these things, all his adversaries were ashamed: and all the people rejoiced for all the glorious things that were done by him.

Luke 13:10-17

500   "Thus saith the LORD: Take heed to yourselves, and bear no burden on the sabbath day, nor bring it in by the gates of Jerusalem; neither carry forth a burden out of your houses on the sabbath day, neither do ye any work, but hallow ye the sabbath day, as I commanded your fathers."

Jeremiah 17:21-22

501   And them that had escaped from the sword carried [the Chaldean king] away to Babylon; where they were servants to him and his sons until the reign of the kingdom of Persia: To fulfil the word of the LORD by the mouth of Jeremiah, until the land had enjoyed her sabbaths: for as long as she lay desolate she kept sabbath, to fulfil threescore and ten years.

2 Chronicles 36:20-21

502 And it came to pass, that he went through the corn fields on the sabbath day; and his disciples began, as they went, to pluck the ears of corn. And the Pharisees said unto [Jesus], "Behold, why do they on the sabbath day that which is not lawful?" And he said unto them, "Have ye never read what David did, when he had need, and was an hungred, he, and they that were with him? How he went into the house of God in the days of Abiathar the high priest, and did eat the shewbread, which is not lawful to eat but for the priests, and gave also to them which were with him?" And he said unto them, "The sabbath was made for man, and not man for the sabbath: Therefore the Son of man is Lord also of the sabbath."

Mark 2:23-28

503 In those days saw I [Nehemiah] in Judah some treading wine presses on the sabbath, and bringing in sheaves, and lading asses; as also wine, grapes, and figs, and all manner of burdens, which they brought into Jerusalem on the sabbath day. . . . Then I contended with the nobles of Judah, and said unto them, "What evil thing is this that ye do, and profane the sabbath day? Did not your fathers thus, and did not our God bring all this evil upon us, and upon this city? Yet ye bring more wrath upon Israel by profaning the sabbath." And it came to pass, that when the gates of Jerusalem began to be dark before the sabbath, I commanded that the gates should be shut, and charged that they should not be opened till after the sabbath: and some of my servants set I at the gates, that there should no burden be brought in on the sabbath day. . . . And I commanded the Levites that they should cleanse themselves, and that they should come and keep the gates, to sanctify the sabbath day. Remember me, O my God, concerning this also, and spare me according to the greatness of thy mercy.

Nehemiah 13:15, 17-19, 22

504 The Jews therefore said unto him that was cured, "It is the sabbath day: it is not lawful for thee to carry thy bed." He answered them, "He that made me whole, the same said unto me, 'Take up thy bed, and walk.'" Then asked they him, "What man is that which said unto thee, 'Take up thy bed, and walk?'" And he that was healed wist* not who it was: for Jesus had conveyed himself away, a multitude being in that place. Afterward Jesus findeth him in the temple, and said unto him, "Behold, thou art made whole: sin no more, lest a worse thing come unto thee." The man departed, and told the Jews that it was Jesus, which had made him whole. And therefore did the Jews persecute Jesus, and sought to slay him, because he had done these things on the sabbath day. But Jesus answered them, "My Father worketh hitherto, and I work." Therefore the Jews sought the more to kill him, because he not only had broken the sabbath, but said also that God was his Father, making himself equal with God.

John 5:10-18

505 Where there is no vision, the people perish:
But he that keepeth the law, happy is he.

Proverbs 29:18

506 Prove* all things; hold fast that which is good. Abstain from all appearance of evil. And the very God of peace sanctify you wholly; and I pray God your whole spirit and soul and body be preserved blameless unto the coming of our Lord Jesus Christ. Faithful is he that calleth you, who also will do it.

1 Thessalonians 5:21-24

507 "Remember the word which Moses the servant of the LORD commanded you, saying, 'The LORD your God hath given you rest, and hath given you this land.' . . . Until the LORD have given your brethren rest, as he hath given you, and they also have possessed the land which the LORD your God giveth them: then ye shall return unto the land of your possession, and enjoy it, which Moses the LORD's servant gave you on this side Jordan toward the sunrising."

Joshua 1:13, 15

508 For if Jesus* had given them rest, then would he not afterward have spoken of another day. There remaineth therefore a rest to the people of God. For he that is entered into his rest, he also hath ceased from his own works, as God did from his. Let us labour therefore to enter into that rest, lest any man fall after the same example of unbelief. For the word of God is quick*, and powerful, and sharper than any two-edged sword, piercing even to the dividing asunder of soul and spirit, and of the joints and marrow, and is a discerner of the thoughts and intents of the heart. Neither is there any creature that is not manifest in his sight: but all things are naked and opened unto the eyes of him with whom we have to do. Seeing then that we have a great high priest, that is passed into the heavens, Jesus the Son of God, let us hold fast our profession. For we have not an high priest which cannot be touched with the feeling of our infirmities; but was in all points tempted like as we are, yet without sin. Let us therefore come boldly unto the throne of grace, that we may obtain mercy, and find grace to help in time of need.

Hebrews 4:8-16

509   "Come unto me, all ye that labour and are heavy laden, and I will give you rest. Take my yoke upon you, and learn of me; for I am meek and lowly in heart: and ye shall find rest unto your souls. For my yoke is easy, and my burden is light."

Matthew 11:28-30

510   "Behold, a son shall be born to thee, who shall be a man of rest; and I will give him rest from all his enemies round about: for his name shall be Solomon, and I will give peace and quietness unto Israel in his days. He shall build an house for my name; and he shall be my son, and I will be his father; and I will establish the throne of his kingdom over Israel for ever."

1 Chronicles 22:9-10

511   And [Jesus] said, "A certain man had two sons: And the younger of them said to his father, 'Father, give me the portion of goods that falleth to me.' And he divided unto them his living. And not many days after the younger son gathered all together, and took his journey into a far country, and there wasted his substance with riotous living. And when he had spent all, there arose a mighty famine in that land; and he began to be in want. And he went and joined himself to a citizen of that country; and he sent him into his fields to feed swine. And he would fain have filled his belly with the husks that the swine did eat: and no man gave unto him. And when he came to himself, he said, 'How many hired servants of my father's have bread enough and to spare, and I perish with hunger! I will arise and go to my father, and will say unto him, Father, I have sinned against heaven, and before thee, and am no more worthy to be called thy son: make me as one of thy hired servants.' And he arose, and came to his father. But when he was yet a great way off, his father saw him, and had compassion, and ran, and fell on his neck, and kissed him. And the son said unto him, 'Father, I have sinned against heaven, and in thy sight, and am no more worthy to be called thy son.' But the father said to his servants, 'Bring forth the best robe, and put it on him; and put a ring on his hand, and shoes on his feet: And bring hither the fatted calf, and kill it; and let us eat, and be merry: For this my son was dead, and is alive again; he was lost, and is found.' And they began to be merry.

"Now his elder son was in the field: and as he came and drew nigh to the house, he heard musick and dancing. And he called one of the servants, and asked what these things meant. And he said unto him, 'Thy brother is come; and thy father hath killed the fatted calf, because he hath received him safe and sound.' And he was angry, and would not go in: therefore came his father out, and intreated him. And he answering said to his father, 'Lo, these many years do I serve thee, neither transgressed I at any time thy commandment: and yet thou never gavest me a kid*, that I might make merry with my friends: But as soon as this thy son was come, which hath devoured thy living with harlots, thou hast killed for him the fatted calf.' And he said unto him, 'Son, thou art ever with me, and all that I have is thine. It was meet* that we should make merry, and be glad: for this thy brother was dead, and is alive again; and was lost, and is found.'"

Luke 15:11-32

512 I was glad when they said unto me,
     "Let us go into the house of the LORD."
Our feet shall stand

Within thy gates, O Jerusalem.
Jerusalem is builded as a city
    That is compact together:
Whither the tribes go up,
    The tribes of the LORD,
Unto the testimony of Israel,
    To give thanks unto the name of the LORD.
For there are set thrones of judgment,
    The thrones of the house of David.
Pray for the peace of Jerusalem:
    They shall prosper that love thee.
Peace be within thy walls,
    And prosperity within thy palaces.
For my brethren and companions' sakes,
    I will now say, "Peace be within thee."
Because of the house of the LORD our God
    I will seek thy good.

Psalm 122:1-9

513   For from the least of them even unto the greatest of them
        Every one is given to covetousness;
    And from the prophet even unto the priest
        Every one dealeth falsely.
    They have healed also the hurt of the daughter of my people slightly,
        Saying, "Peace, peace";
        When there is no peace.

Jeremiah 6:13-14

514 And the Jews' Passover was at hand, and Jesus went up to Jerusalem, and found in the temple those that sold oxen and sheep and doves, and the changers of money sitting: And when he had made a scourge of small cords, he drove them all out of the temple, and the sheep, and the oxen; and poured out the changers' money, and overthrew the tables; and said unto them that sold doves, "Take these things hence; make not my Father's house an house of merchandise." And his disciples remembered that it was written, "The zeal of thine house hath eaten me up." Then answered the Jews and said unto him, "What sign shewest thou unto us, seeing that thou doest these things?" Jesus answered and said unto them, "Destroy this temple, and in three days I will raise it up." Then said the Jews, "Forty and six years was this temple in building, and wilt thou rear it up in three days?" But he spake of the temple of his body. When therefore he was risen from the dead, his disciples remembered that he had said this unto them; and they believed the scripture, and the word which Jesus had said. Now when he was in Jerusalem at the Passover, in the feast day, many believed in his name, when they saw the miracles which he did. But Jesus did not commit himself unto them, because he knew all men, and needed not that any should testify of man: for he knew what was in man.

John 2:13-25

515 Thus saith the LORD of hosts; "Consider your ways. Go up to the mountain, and bring wood, and build the house; and I will take pleasure in it, and I will be glorified," saith the LORD. "Ye looked for much, and, lo, it came to little; and when ye brought it home, I did blow upon it. Why?" saith the LORD of hosts. "Because of mine house that is waste, and ye run every man unto his own house. Therefore the heaven over you is stayed from dew, and the earth is stayed from her fruit."

Haggai 1:7-10

516 "Howbeit* [preached Stephen] the most High dwelleth not in temples made with hands; as saith the prophet,

> 'Heaven is my throne,
> And earth is my footstool:
> What house will ye build me?' saith the Lord:
> 'Or what is the place of my rest?
> Hath not my hand made all these things?'

Ye stiffnecked and uncircumcised in heart and ears, ye do always resist the Holy Ghost: as your fathers did, so do ye. Which of the prophets have not your fathers persecuted? And they have slain them which shewed before of the coming of the Just One; of whom ye have been now the betrayers and murderers: Who have received the law by the disposition of angels, and have not kept it."

Acts 7:48-53

517 Know ye not that your body is the temple of the Holy Ghost which is in you, which ye have of God, and ye are not your own? For ye are bought with a price: therefore glorify God in your body, and in your spirit, which are God's.

1 Corinthians 6:19-20

518 "Sanctify them through thy truth: thy word is truth. As thou hast sent me into the world, even so have I also sent them into the world. And for their sakes I sanctify myself, that they also might be sanctified through the truth. Neither pray I for these alone, but for them also which shall believe on me through their word; that they all may be one; as thou, Father, art in me, and I in thee, that they also may be one in us: that the world may believe that thou hast sent me."

John 17:17-21

519 Then Job arose, and rent his mantle, and shaved his head, and fell down upon the ground, and worshipped, and said, "Naked came I out of my mother's womb, and naked shall I return thither: the LORD gave, and the LORD hath taken away; blessed be the name of the LORD."

Job 1:20-21

520 All these are the twelve tribes of [Jacob]: and this is it that their father spake unto them, and blessed them; every one according to his blessing he blessed them. And he charged them, and said unto them, "I am to be gathered unto my people: bury me with my fathers in the cave that is in the field of Ephron the Hittite, in the cave that is in the field of Machpelah, which is before Mamre, in the land of Canaan, which Abraham bought with the field of Ephron the Hittite for a possession of a buryingplace. There they buried Abraham and Sarah his wife; there they buried Isaac and Rebekah his wife; and there I buried Leah. The purchase of the field and of the cave that is therein was from the children of Heth." And when Jacob had made an end of commanding his sons, he gathered up his feet into the bed, and yielded up the ghost, and was gathered unto his people. And Joseph fell upon his father's face, and wept upon him, and kissed him. And Joseph commanded his servants the physicians to embalm his father: and the physicians embalmed Israel. And forty days were fulfilled for him; for so are fulfilled the days of those which are embalmed: and the Egyptians mourned for him threescore and ten days.

Genesis 49:28–50:3

521 My heart is sore pained within me:
     And the terrors of death are fallen upon me.
Fearfulness and trembling are come upon me,
     And horror hath overwhelmed me.
And I said, "Oh that I had wings like a dove!
     For then would I fly away, and be at rest.
Lo, then would I wander far off,
     And remain in the wilderness. *Selah**.
I would hasten my escape
     From the windy storm and tempest."

Psalm 55:4-8

522 And when Joseph's brethren saw that their father was dead, they said, "Joseph will peradventure* hate us, and will certainly requite us all the evil which we did unto him." And they sent a messenger unto Joseph, saying, "Thy father did command before he died, saying, 'So shall ye say unto Joseph, Forgive, I pray thee now, the trespass of thy brethren, and their sin; for they did unto thee evil': and now, we pray thee, forgive the trespass of the servants of the God of thy father." And Joseph wept when they spake unto him. And his brethren also went and fell down before his face; and they said, "Behold, we be thy servants." And Joseph said

unto them, "Fear not: for am I in the place of God? But as for you, ye thought evil against me; but God meant it unto good, to bring to pass, as it is this day, to save much people alive. Now therefore fear ye not: I will nourish you, and your little ones." And he comforted them, and spake kindly unto them.

Genesis 50:15-21

523 When Jesus came into the coasts of Caesarea Philippi, he asked his disciples, saying, "Whom do men say that I the Son of man am?" And they said, "Some say that thou art John the Baptist: some, Elias*; and others, Jeremias*, or one of the prophets." He saith unto them, "But whom say ye that I am?" And Simon Peter answered and said, "Thou art the Christ, the Son of the living God." And Jesus answered and said unto him, "Blessed art thou, Simon Barjona: for flesh and blood hath not revealed it unto thee, but my Father which is in heaven. And I say also unto thee, That thou art Peter, and upon this rock I will build my church; and the gates of hell shall not prevail against it. And I will give unto thee the keys of the kingdom of heaven: and whatsoever thou shalt bind on earth shall be bound in heaven: and whatsoever thou shalt loose on earth shall be loosed in heaven." Then charged he his disciples that they should tell no man that he was Jesus the Christ.

From that time forth began Jesus to shew unto his disciples, how that he must go unto Jerusalem, and suffer many things of the elders and chief priests and scribes, and be killed, and be raised again the third day. Then Peter took him, and began to rebuke him, saying, "Be it far from thee, Lord: this shall not be unto thee." But he turned, and said unto Peter, "Get thee behind me, Satan: thou art an offence unto me: for thou savourest not the things that be of God, but those that be of men." Then said Jesus unto his disciples, "If any man will come after me, let him deny himself, and take up his cross, and follow me. For whosoever will save his life shall lose it: and whosoever will lose his life for my sake shall find it. For what is a man profited, if he shall gain the whole world, and lose his own soul? Or what shall a man give in exchange for his soul? For the Son of man shall come in the glory of his Father with his angels; and then he shall reward every man according to his works. Verily I say unto you, There be some standing here, which shall not taste of death, till they see the Son of man coming in his kingdom."

Matthew 16:13-28

524 And Joseph dwelt in Egypt, he, and his father's house: and Joseph lived an hundred and ten years. And Joseph saw Ephraim's children of the third generation: the children also of Machir the son Manasseh were brought up upon Joseph's knees. And Joseph said unto his brethren, "I die: and God will surely visit you, and bring you out of this land unto the land which he sware to Abraham, to Isaac, and to Jacob." And Joseph took an oath of the children of Israel, saying, "God will surely visit you, and ye shall carry up my bones from hence." So Joseph died, being an hundred and ten years old: and they embalmed him, and he was put in a coffin in Egypt.

Genesis 50:22-26

525 For thus saith the Lord GOD, the Holy One of Israel;
　　"In returning and rest shall ye be saved;
　　In quietness and in confidence shall be your strength:

And ye would not." . . .
And therefore will the LORD wait, that he may be gracious unto you,
   And therefore will he be exalted, that he may have mercy upon you:
For the LORD is a God of judgment:
   Blessed are all they that wait for him.

Isaiah 30:15, 18

526 And Moses went up from the plains of Moab unto the mountain of Nebo, to the top of Pisgah, that is over against Jericho. And the LORD shewed him all the land of Gilead, unto Dan, and all Naphtali, and the land of Ephraim, and Manasseh, and all the land of Judah, unto the utmost sea, and the south, and the plain of the valley of Jericho, the city of palm trees, unto Zoar. And the LORD said unto him, "This is the land which I sware unto Abraham, unto Isaac, and unto Jacob, saying, 'I will give it unto thy seed': I have caused thee to see it with thine eyes, but thou shalt not go over thither." So Moses the servant of the LORD died there in the land of Moab, according to the word of the LORD. And he buried him in a valley in the land of Moab, over against Bethpeor: but no man knoweth of his sepulchre unto this day. And Moses was an hundred and twenty years old when he died: his eye was not dim, nor his natural force abated. And the children of Israel wept for Moses in the plains of Moab thirty days: so the days of weeping and mourning for Moses were ended. And Joshua the son of Nun was full of the spirit of wisdom; for Moses had laid his hands upon him: and the children of Israel hearkened unto him, and did as the LORD commanded Moses. And there arose not a prophet since in Israel like unto Moses, whom the LORD knew face to face, in all the signs and the wonders, which the LORD sent him to do in the land of Egypt to Pharaoh, and to all his servants, and to all his land,

and in all that mighty hand, and in all the great terror which Moses shewed in the sight of all Israel.

Deuteronomy 34:1-12

527   Therefore being justified by faith, we have peace with God through our Lord Jesus Christ: By whom also we have access by faith into this grace wherein we stand, and rejoice in hope of the glory of God. And not only so, but we glory in tribulations also: knowing that tribulation worketh patience; and patience, experience; and experience, hope: And hope maketh not ashamed; because the love of God is shed abroad in our hearts by the Holy Ghost which is given unto us.

Romans 5:1-5

528   And Joshua wrote these words in the book of the law of God, and took a great stone, and set it up there under an oak, that was by the sanctuary of the LORD. And Joshua said unto all the people, "Behold, this stone shall be a witness unto us; for it hath heard all the words of the LORD which he spake unto us: it shall be therefore a witness unto you, lest ye deny your God." So Joshua let the people depart, every man unto his inheritance.

And it came to pass after these things, that Joshua the son of Nun, the servant of the LORD, died, being an hundred and ten years old. And they buried him in the border of his inheritance in Timnath-serah, which is in mount Ephraim, on the north side of the hill of Gaash. And Israel served the LORD all the days of Joshua, and all the days of the elders that overlived* Joshua, and which had known all the works of the LORD, that he had done for Israel.

Joshua 24:26-31

529   How beautiful upon the mountains
      Are the feet of him that bringeth good tidings,
  That publisheth peace; that bringeth good tidings of good,
      That publisheth salvation;
      That saith unto Zion, "Thy God reigneth!"
  Thy watchmen shall lift up the voice;
      With the voice together shall they sing:
  For they shall see eye to eye,
      When the LORD shall bring again Zion.
  Break forth into joy, sing together,
      Ye waste places of Jerusalem:
  For the LORD hath comforted his people,
      He hath redeemed Jerusalem.

Isaiah 52:7-9

530   Now the Philistines fought against Israel: and the men of Israel fled from before the Philistines, and fell down slain in Mount Gilboa. And the Philistines followed hard upon Saul and upon his sons; and the Philistines slew Jonathan, and Abinadab, and Malchi-shua, Saul's sons. And the battle went sore against Saul, and the archers hit him; and he was sore wounded of the archers. Then said Saul unto his armourbearer, "Draw thy sword, and thrust me through therewith; lest these uncircumcised come and thrust me through, and abuse me." But his armourbearer would not; for he was sore afraid. Therefore Saul took a sword, and fell upon it. And when his armourbearer saw that Saul was dead, he fell likewise upon his sword, and died with him. . . . And it came to pass on the morrow, when the Philistines came to strip the slain, that they found Saul and his three sons fallen in mount Gilboa. And they cut

off his head, and stripped off his armour, and sent into the land of the Philistines round about, to publish it in the house of their idols, and among the people. And they put his armour in the house of Ashtaroth: and they fastened his body to the wall of Beth-shan. And when the inhabitants of Jabesh-gilead heard of that which the Philistines had done to Saul; All the valiant men arose, and went all night, and took the body of Saul and the bodies of his sons from the wall of Beth-shan, and came to Jabesh, and burnt them there. And they took their bones, and buried them under a tree at Jabesh, and fasted seven days.

1 Samuel 31:1-5, 8-13

531 Be patient therefore, brethren, unto the coming of the Lord. . . . Be ye also patient; stablish your hearts: for the coming of the Lord draweth nigh. . . . Behold, we count them happy which endure. Ye have heard of the patience of Job, and have seen the end of the Lord; that the Lord is very pitiful, and of tender mercy.

James 5:7a, 8, 11

532 After this opened Job his mouth, and cursed his day. . . .
"Why died I not from the womb?
    Why did I not give up the ghost when I came out of the belly? . . .
Wherefore* is light given to him that is in misery,
    And life unto the bitter in soul;
Which long for death, but it cometh not;
    And dig for it more than for hid treasures;
Which rejoice exceedingly,

322

And are glad, when they can find the grave?
Why is light given to a man whose way is hid,
    And whom God hath hedged in?
For my sighing cometh before I eat,
    And my roarings are poured out like the waters.
For the thing which I greatly feared is come upon me,
    And that which I was afraid of is come unto me.
I was not in safety, neither had I rest, neither was I quiet;
        yet trouble came."

Job 3:1, 11, 20-26

533   Now King David was old and stricken in years; and they covered him with
clothes, but he gat* no heat. Wherefore his servants said unto him, "Let
there be sought for my lord the king a young virgin: and let her stand before
the king, and let her cherish him, and let her lie in thy bosom, that my lord
the king may get heat." So they sought for a fair damsel throughout all the
coasts of Israel, and found Abishag a Shunammite, and brought her to the
king. And the damsel was very fair, and cherished the king, and ministered
to him: but the king knew her not. . . .

Now the days of David drew nigh that he should die; and he
charged Solomon his son, saying, "I go the way of all the earth: be thou
strong therefore, and shew thyself a man; and keep the charge of the
LORD thy God, to walk in his ways, to keep his statutes, and his commandments, and his judgments, and his testimonies, as it is written in
the law of Moses. . . .

So David slept with his fathers, and was buried in the city of David.
And the days that David reigned over Israel were forty years: seven years
reigned he in Hebron, and thirty and three years reigned he in Jerusalem.

Then sat Solomon upon the throne of David his father; and his kingdom was established greatly.

1 Kings 1:1-4; 2:1-3, 10-12

534 For all this I considered in my heart even to declare all this, that the righteous, and the wise, and their works, are in the hand of God: no man knoweth either love or hatred by all that is before them. All things come alike to all: there is one event to the righteous, and to the wicked; to the good and to the clean, and to the unclean; to him that sacrificeth, and to him that sacrificeth not: as is the good, so is the sinner; and he that sweareth, as he that feareth an oath. This is an evil among all things that are done under the sun, that there is one event unto all: yea, also the heart of the sons of men is full of evil, and madness is in their heart while they live, and after that they go to the dead. For to him that is joined to all the living there is hope: for a living dog is better than a dead lion. For the living know that they shall die: but the dead know not any thing, neither have they any more a reward; for the memory of them is forgotten. Also their love, and their hatred, and their envy, is now perished; neither have they any more a portion for ever in any thing that is done under the sun.

Ecclesiastes 9:1-6

535 And it came to pass, when they were gone over, that Elijah said unto Elisha, "Ask what I shall do for thee, before I be taken away from thee." And Elisha said, "I pray thee, let a double portion of thy spirit be upon me." And he said, "Thou hast asked a hard thing: nevertheless, if thou see me when I am taken from thee, it shall be so unto thee; but if not, it

shall not be so." And it came to pass, as they still went on, and talked, that, behold, there appeared a chariot of fire, and horses of fire, and parted them both asunder; and Elijah went up by a whirlwind into heaven. And Elisha saw it, and he cried, "My father, my father, the chariot of Israel, and the horsemen thereof." And he saw him no more: and he took hold of his own clothes, and rent them in two pieces.

2 Kings 2:9-12

536 How doth the city sit solitary,
     That was full of people.
   How is she become as a widow,
     She that was great among the nations,
   And princess among the provinces,
     How is she become tributary.
   She weepeth sore in the night,
     And her tears are on her cheeks:
   Among all her lovers
     She hath none to comfort her:
   All her friends have dealt treacherously with her,
     They are become her enemies. . . .
   See, O LORD, and consider;
     For I am become vile.
   Is it nothing to you, all ye that pass by?
     Behold, and see
   If there be any sorrow
     Like unto my sorrow,
   Which is done unto me, wherewith the LORD hath afflicted me
     In the day of his fierce anger. . . .

Thou, O LORD, remainest for ever;
    Thy throne from generation to generation.
Wherefore* dost thou forget us for ever,
    And forsake us so long time?
Turn thou us unto thee, O LORD, and we shall be turned;
    Renew our days as of old.
But thou hast utterly rejected us;
    Thou art very wroth* against us.

Lamentations 1:1-2, 11c-12; 5:19-22

537   And God saw [Nineveh's] works, that they turned from their evil way; and
God repented of the evil, that he had said that he would do unto them; and
he did it not. But it displeased Jonah exceedingly, and he was very angry.
And he prayed unto the LORD, and said, "I pray thee, O LORD, was not
this my saying, when I was yet in my country? Therefore I fled before unto
Tarshish: for I knew that thou art a gracious God, and merciful, slow to anger, and of great kindness, and repentest thee of the evil. Therefore now, O
LORD, take, I beseech thee, my life from me; for it is better for me to die
than to live." Then said the LORD, "Doest thou well to be angry?" So Jonah went out of the city, and sat on the east side of the city, and there made
him a booth, and sat under it in the shadow, till he might see what would
become of the city.

Jonah 3:10–4:5

538   Go thy way, eat thy bread with joy, and drink thy wine with a merry heart;
for God now accepteth thy works. Let thy garments be always white; and let

thy head lack no ointment. Live joyfully with the wife whom thou lovest all the days of the life of thy vanity, which he hath given thee under the sun, all the days of thy vanity: for that is thy portion in this life, and in thy labour which thou takest under the sun. Whatsoever thy hand findeth to do, do it with thy might; for there is no work, nor device, nor knowledge, nor wisdom, in the grave, whither thou goest.

Ecclesiastes 9:7-10

539   And the LORD God prepared a gourd, and made it to come up over Jonah, that it might be a shadow over his head, to deliver him from his grief. So Jonah was exceeding glad of the gourd. But God prepared a worm when the morning rose the next day, and it smote the gourd that it withered. And it came to pass, when the sun did arise, that God prepared a vehement east wind; and the sun beat upon the head of Jonah, that he fainted, and wished in himself to die, and said, "It is better for me to die than to live." And God said to Jonah, "Doest thou well to be angry for the gourd?" And he said, "I do well to be angry, even unto death." Then said the LORD, "Thou hast had pity on the gourd, for the which thou hast not laboured, neither madest it grow; which came up in a night, and perished in a night: And should not I spare Nineveh, that great city, wherein are more than sixscore thousand persons that cannot discern between their right hand and their left hand; and also much cattle?"

Jonah 4:6-11

540   Then when Jesus came, he found that [Lazarus] had lain in the grave four days already. Now Bethany was nigh unto Jerusalem, about fifteen furlongs off: And many of the Jews came to Martha and Mary, to comfort them concerning their brother. Then Martha, as soon as she heard that Jesus was coming, went and met him: but Mary sat still in the house. Then said Martha unto Jesus, "Lord, if thou hadst been here, my brother had not died. But I know, that even now, whatsoever thou wilt ask of God, God will give it thee." Jesus saith unto her, "Thy brother shall rise again." Martha saith unto him, "I know that he shall rise again in the resurrection at the last day." Jesus said unto her, "I am the resurrection, and the life: he that believeth in me, though he were dead, yet shall he live: And whosoever liveth and believeth in me shall never die. Believest thou this?" She saith unto him, "Yea, Lord: I believe that thou art the Christ, the Son of God, which should come into the world."

John 11:17-27

541   "There was a certain rich man, which was clothed in purple and fine linen, and fared sumptuously every day: And there was a certain beggar named Lazarus, which was laid at his gate, full of sores, and desiring to be fed with the crumbs which fell from the rich man's table: moreover the dogs came and licked his sores. And it came to pass, that the beggar died, and was carried by the angels into Abraham's bosom: the rich man also died, and was buried; and in hell he lift up his eyes, being in torments, and seeth Abraham afar off, and Lazarus in his bosom. And he cried and said, 'Father Abraham, have mercy on me, and send Lazarus, that he may dip the tip of his finger in water, and cool my tongue; for I am tormented in this flame.' But Abraham said, 'Son, remember that thou in thy lifetime receivedst thy good things, and likewise Lazarus evil things: but

now he is comforted, and thou art tormented. And beside all this, between us and you there is a great gulf fixed: so that they which would pass
from hence to you cannot; neither can they pass to us, that would come
from thence.' Then he said, 'I pray thee therefore, father, that thou
wouldest send him to my father's house: For I have five brethren; that he
may testify unto them, lest they also come into this place of torment.'
Abraham saith unto him, 'They have Moses and the prophets; let them
hear them.' And he said, 'Nay, father Abraham: but if one went unto
them from the dead, they will repent.' And he said unto him, 'If they hear
not Moses and the prophets, neither will they be persuaded, though one
rose from the dead.'"

Luke 16:19-31

542 When Jesus therefore saw [Mary] weeping, and the Jews also weeping
which came with her, he groaned in the spirit, and was troubled, and
said, "Where have ye laid him?" They said unto him, "Lord, come and
see." Jesus wept. Then said the Jews, "Behold how he loved him!" And
some of them said, "Could not this man, which opened the eyes of the
blind, have caused that even this man should not have died?" Jesus therefore again groaning in himself cometh to the grave. It was a cave, and a
stone lay upon it. Jesus said, "Take ye away the stone." Martha, the sister
of him that was dead, saith unto him, "Lord, by this time he stinketh: for
he hath been dead four days." Jesus saith unto her, "Said I not unto thee,
that, if thou wouldest believe, thou shouldest see the glory of God?"
Then they took away the stone from the place where the dead was laid.
And Jesus lifted up his eyes, and said, "Father, I thank thee that thou hast
heard me. And I knew that thou hearest me always: but because of the
people which stand by I said it, that they may believe that thou hast sent

me." And when he thus had spoken, he cried with a loud voice, "Lazarus, come forth." And he that was dead came forth, bound hand and foot with graveclothes: and his face was bound about with a napkin. Jesus saith unto them, "Loose him, and let him go." Then many of the Jews which came to Mary, and had seen the things which Jesus did, believed on him.

John 11:33-45

543 I returned, and saw under the sun, that the race is not to the swift, nor the battle to the strong, neither yet bread to the wise, nor yet riches to men of understanding, nor yet favour to men of skill; but time and chance happeneth to them all. For man also knoweth not his time: as the fishes that are taken in an evil net, and as the birds that are caught in the snare; so are the sons of men snared in an evil time, when it falleth suddenly upon them.

Ecclesiastes 9:11-12

544 And when they were come to the place, which is called Calvary, there they crucified [Jesus], and the malefactors, one on the right hand, and the other on the left. Then said Jesus, "Father, forgive them; for they know not what they do." And they parted his raiment, and cast lots. And the people stood beholding. And the rulers also with them derided him, saying, "He saved others; let him save himself, if he be Christ, the chosen of God." And the soldiers also mocked him, coming to him, and offering him vinegar, and saying, "If thou be the king of the Jews, save thyself." And a superscription also was written over him in letters of Greek, and

Latin, and Hebrew, THIS IS THE KING OF THE JEWS. And one of the malefactors which were hanged railed on him, saying, "If thou be Christ, save thyself and us." But the other answering rebuked him, saying, "Dost not thou fear God, seeing thou art in the same condemnation? And we indeed justly; for we receive the due reward of our deeds: but this man hath done nothing amiss." And he said unto Jesus, "Lord, remember me when thou comest into thy kingdom." And Jesus said unto him, "Verily I say unto thee, Today shalt thou be with me in paradise."

Luke 23:33-43

545 When [Stephen's audience] heard these things [against the temple], they were cut to the heart, and they gnashed on him with their teeth. But he, being full of the Holy Ghost, looked up stedfastly into heaven, and saw the glory of God, and Jesus standing on the right hand of God, and said, "Behold, I see the heavens opened, and the Son of man standing on the right hand of God." Then they cried out with a loud voice, and stopped their ears, and ran upon him with one accord, and cast him out of the city, and stoned him: and the witnesses laid down their clothes at a young man's feet, whose name was Saul. And they stoned Stephen, calling upon God, and saying, "Lord Jesus, receive my spirit." And he kneeled down, and cried with a loud voice, "Lord, lay not this sin to their charge." And when he had said this, he fell asleep.

Acts 7:54-60

546   In thee, O Lᴏʀᴅ, do I put my trust;
      Let me never be ashamed: . . .
    Into thine hand I commit my spirit:
      Thou hast redeemed me, O Lᴏʀᴅ God of truth.

Psalm 31:1, 5

547   And it was about the sixth hour, and there was a darkness over all the earth until the ninth hour. And the sun was darkened, and the veil of the temple was rent in the midst. And when Jesus had cried with a loud voice, he said, "Father, into thy hands I commend my spirit": and having said thus, he gave up the ghost. Now when the centurion saw what was done, he glorified God, saying, "Certainly this was a righteous man." And all the people that came together to that sight, beholding the things which were done, smote their breasts, and returned. And all his acquaintance, and the women that followed him from Galilee, stood afar off, beholding these things.

Luke 23:44-49

548   My God, my God, why hast thou forsaken me?
      Why art thou so far from helping me, and from the words of
        my roaring?
   O my God, I cry in the daytime, but thou hearest not;
      And in the night season, and am not silent. . . .
   All they that see me laugh me to scorn:
      They shoot out the lip, they shake the head saying,

If a Man Die, Shall He Live Again?

"He trusted on the LORD that he would deliver him:
Let him deliver him, seeing he delighted in him."

Psalm 22:1-2, 7-8

549   And when the sixth hour was come, there was darkness over the whole land until the ninth hour. And at the ninth hour Jesus cried with a loud voice, saying, *Eloi, Eloi, lama sabachthani?* which is, being interpreted, "My God, my God, why hast thou forsaken me?" And some of them that stood by, when they heard it, said, "Behold, he calleth Elias*." And one ran and filled a spunge full of vinegar, and put it on a reed, and gave him to drink, saying, "Let alone; let us see whether Elias will come to take him down." And Jesus cried with a loud voice, and gave up the ghost. And the veil of the temple was rent in twain* from the top to the bottom. And when the centurion, which stood over against him, saw that he so cried out, and gave up the ghost, he said, "Truly this man was the Son of God." There were also women looking on afar off: among whom was Mary Magdalene, and Mary the mother of James the less and of Joses, and Salome; (who also, when he was in Galilee, followed him, and ministered unto him;) and many other women which came up with him unto Jerusalem.

Mark 15:33-41

550   Man that is born of a woman is of few days and full of trouble.
He cometh forth like a flower, and is cut down:
    He fleeth also as a shadow, and continueth not. . . .
If a man die, shall he live again?

All the days of my appointed time will I wait,
   Till my change come.
Thou shalt call, and I will answer thee:
   Thou wilt have a desire to the work of thine hands.
For now thou numberest my steps:
   Dost thou not watch over my sin?
My transgression is sealed up in a bag,
   And thou sewest up mine iniquity.

Job 14:1-2, 14-17

551   And, behold, two of them went that same day to a village called Emmaus, which was from Jerusalem about threescore furlongs. And they talked together of all these things which had happened. And it came to pass, that, while they communed together and reasoned, Jesus himself drew near, and went with them. But their eyes were holden* that they should not know him. And he said unto them, "What manner of communications are these that ye have one to another, as ye walk, and are sad?" And the one of them, whose name was Cleopas, answering said unto him, "Art thou only a stranger in Jerusalem, and hast not known the things which are come to pass therein these days?" And he said unto them, "What things?" And they said unto him, "Concerning Jesus of Nazareth, which was a prophet mighty in deed and word before God and all the people: and how the chief priests and our rulers delivered him to be condemned to death, and have crucified him. But we trusted that it had been he which should have redeemed Israel: and beside all this, to day is the third day since these things were done. Yea, and certain women also of our company made us astonished, which were early at the sepulchre; and when they found not his body, they came, saying, that they had also

334

seen a vision of angels, which said that he was alive. And certain of them which were with us went to the sepulchre, and found it even so as the women had said: but him they saw not." Then he said unto them, "O fools, and slow of heart to believe all that the prophets have spoken: Ought not Christ to have suffered these things, and to enter into his glory?" And beginning at Moses and all the prophets, he expounded unto them in all the scriptures the things concerning himself.

Luke 24:13-27

552 Sing, O daughter of Zion;
   Shout, O Israel;
  Be glad and rejoice with all the heart,
   O daughter of Jerusalem.

  The LORD hath taken away thy judgments,
   He hath cast out thine enemy:
  The king of Israel, even the LORD, is in the midst of thee:
   Thou shalt not see evil any more.

Zephaniah 3:14-15

553 And they drew nigh unto the village, whither they went: and [Jesus] made as though he would have gone further. But they constrained him, saying, "Abide with us: for it is toward evening, and the day is far spent." And he went in to tarry with them. And it came to pass, as he sat at meat* with them, he took bread, and blessed it, and brake, and gave to them. And their eyes were opened, and they knew him; and he vanished out of

their sight. And they said one to another, "Did not our heart burn within us, while he talked with us by the way, and while he opened to us the scriptures?" And they rose up the same hour, and returned to Jerusalem, and found the eleven gathered together, and them that were with them, saying, "The Lord is risen indeed, and hath appeared to Simon." And they told what things were done in the way, and how he was known of them in breaking of bread.

Luke 24:28-35

554   That which was from the beginning, which we have heard, which we have seen with our eyes, which we have looked upon, and our hands have handled, of the Word of life; (for the life was manifested, and we have seen it, and bear witness, and shew unto you that eternal life, which was with the Father, and was manifested unto us;) that which we have seen and heard declare we unto you, that ye also may have fellowship with us: and truly our fellowship is with the Father, and with his Son Jesus Christ. And these things write we unto you, that your joy may be full.

1 John 1:1-4

555   But Thomas, one of the twelve, called Didymus, was not with them when Jesus came. The other disciples therefore said unto him, "We have seen the Lord." But he said unto them, "Except I shall see in his hands the print of the nails, and put my finger into the print of the nails, and thrust my hand into his side, I will not believe." And after eight days again his disciples were within, and Thomas with them: then came Jesus, the doors being shut, and stood in the midst, and said, "Peace be unto you."

Then saith he to Thomas, "Reach hither thy finger, and behold my hands; and reach hither thy hand, and thrust it into my side: and be not faithless, but believing." And Thomas answered and said unto him, "My Lord and my God." Jesus saith unto him, "Thomas, because thou hast seen me, thou hast believed: blessed are they that have not seen, and yet have believed."

John 20:24-29

556 I will ransom them from the power of the grave;
  I will redeem them from death:
O death, I will be thy plagues;
  O grave, I will be thy destruction:
  Repentance shall be hid from mine eyes.

Hosea 13:14

557 "Ye men of Israel, hear these words; Jesus of Nazareth, a man approved of God among you by miracles and wonders and signs, which God did by him in the midst of you, as ye yourselves also know: Him, being delivered by the determinate counsel and foreknowledge of God, ye have taken, and by wicked hands have crucified and slain: Whom God hath raised up, having loosed the pains of death: because it was not possible that he should be holden* of it. For David speaketh concerning him,

 'I foresaw the Lord always before my face,
 For he is on my right hand, that I should not be moved:
 Therefore did my heart rejoice, and my tongue was glad;

Moreover also my flesh shall rest in hope:
Because thou wilt not leave my soul in hell,
Neither wilt thou suffer* thine Holy One to see corruption.
Thou hast made known to me the ways of life;
Thou shalt make me full of joy with thy countenance.'

Men and brethren, let me freely speak unto you of the patriarch David, that he is both dead and buried, and his sepulchre is with us unto this day. Therefore being a prophet, and knowing that God had sworn with an oath to him, that of the fruit of his loins, according to the flesh, he would raise up Christ to sit on his throne; He seeing this before spake of the resurrection of Christ, that his soul was not left in hell, neither his flesh did see corruption. This Jesus hath God raised up, whereof we all are witnesses. Therefore being by the right hand of God exalted, and having received of the Father the promise of the Holy Ghost, he hath shed forth this, which ye now see and hear. For David is not ascended into the heavens: but he saith himself,

'The Lord said unto my Lord, Sit thou on my right hand,
Until I make thy foes thy footstool.'

Therefore let all the house of Israel know assuredly, that God hath made that same Jesus, whom ye have crucified, both Lord and Christ."

Acts 2:22-36

558 I love the LORD, because he hath heard
    My voice and my supplications.
Because he hath inclined his ear unto me,
    Therefore will I call upon him as long as I live.

The sorrows of death compassed me,
    And the pains of hell gat* hold upon me:
    I found trouble and sorrow.
Then called I upon the name of the LORD;
    "O LORD, I beseech thee, deliver my soul."
Gracious is the LORD, and righteous;
    Yea, our God is merciful.
The LORD preserveth the simple:
    I was brought low, and he helped me.
Return unto thy rest, O my soul;
    For the LORD hath dealt bountifully with thee.
For thou hast delivered my soul from death,
    Mine eyes from tears, and my feet from falling.
I will walk before the LORD
    In the land of the living.

Psalm 116:1-9

559   And Herod [Agrippa] was highly displeased with them of Tyre and Sidon: but they came with one accord to him, and, having made Blastus the king's chamberlain their friend, desired peace; because their country was nourished by the king's country. And upon a set day Herod, arrayed in royal apparel, sat upon his throne, and made an oration unto them. And the people gave a shout, saying, "It is the voice of a god, and not of a man." And immediately the angel of the Lord smote him, because he gave not God the glory: and he was eaten of worms, and gave up the ghost. But the word of God grew and multiplied.

Acts 12:20-24

560 And there shall come forth a rod out of the stem of Jesse,
  And a Branch shall grow out of his roots:
And the spirit of the LORD shall rest upon him,
  The spirit of wisdom and understanding,
  The spirit of counsel and might,
  The spirit of knowledge and of the fear of the LORD;
And shall make him of quick understanding in the fear of the LORD:
And he shall not judge after the sight of his eyes,
  Neither reprove after the hearing of his ears:
But with righteousness shall he judge the poor,
  And reprove with equity for the meek of the earth:
  And he shall smite the earth with the rod of his mouth,
  And with the breath of his lips shall he slay the wicked.
And righteousness shall be the girdle* of his loins,
  And faithfulness the girdle* of his reins.
The wolf also shall dwell with the lamb,
  And the leopard shall lie down with the kid*;
  And the calf and the young lion and the fatling together;
  And a little child shall lead them.
And the cow and the bear shall feed;
  Their young ones shall lie down together:
  And the lion shall eat straw like the ox.
And the sucking child shall play on the hole of the asp,
  And the weaned child shall put his hand on the cockatrice'* den.
They shall not hurt nor destroy
  In all my holy mountain:
For the earth shall be full of the knowledge of the LORD,
  As the waters cover the sea.
And in that day there shall be a root of Jesse,
  Which shall stand for an ensign of the people;

To it shall the Gentiles seek:
    And his rest shall be glorious.

Isaiah 11:1-10

561   Behold, I shew you a mystery; We shall not all sleep, but we shall all be changed, in a moment, in the twinkling of an eye, at the last trump: for the trumpet shall sound, and the dead shall be raised incorruptible, and we shall be changed. For this corruptible must put on incorruption, and this mortal must put on immortality. So when this corruptible shall have put on incorruption, and this mortal shall have put on immortality, then shall be brought to pass the saying that is written,

> "Death is swallowed up in victory.
> O death, where is thy sting?
> O grave, where is thy victory?"

The sting of death is sin; and the strength of sin is the law. But thanks be to God, which giveth us the victory through our Lord Jesus Christ. Therefore, my beloved brethren, be ye stedfast, unmoveable, always abounding in the work of the Lord, forasmuch as ye know that your labour is not in vain in the Lord.

1 Corinthians 15:51-58

562   And in this mountain shall the LORD of hosts make unto all people a feast of fat things, a feast of wines on the lees*, of fat things full of marrow, of wines on the lees well refined. And he will destroy in this mountain the face of the covering cast over all people, and the vail* that is

spread over all nations. He will swallow up death in victory; and the Lord GOD will wipe away tears from off all faces; and the rebuke of his people shall he take away from off all the earth: for the LORD hath spoken it. And it shall be said in that day, "Lo, this is our God; we have waited for him, and he will save us: this is the LORD; we have waited for him, we will be glad and rejoice in his salvation."

Isaiah 25:6-9

563 And I saw a new heaven and a new earth: for the first heaven and the first earth were passed away; and there was no more sea. And I John saw the holy city, new Jerusalem, coming down from God out of heaven, prepared as a bride adorned for her husband. And I heard a great voice out of heaven saying, "Behold, the tabernacle* of God is with men, and he will dwell with them, and they shall be his people, and God himself shall be with them, and be their God. And God shall wipe away all tears from their eyes; and there shall be no more death, neither sorrow, nor crying, neither shall there be any more pain: for the former things are passed away."

Revelation 21:1-4

564 But in the last days it shall come to pass,
  That the mountain of the house of the LORD
Shall be established in the top of the mountains,
  And it shall be exalted above the hills;
And people shall flow unto it.
  And many nations shall come, and say,

"Come, and let us go up to the mountain of the LORD,
    And to the house of the God of Jacob;
And he will teach us of his ways,
    And we will walk in his paths":
For the law shall go forth of Zion,
    And the word of the LORD from Jerusalem.
And he shall judge among many people,
    And rebuke strong nations afar off;
And they shall beat their swords into plowshares,
    And their spears into pruning-hooks:
Nation shall not lift up a sword against nation,
    Neither shall they learn war any more.
But they shall sit every man under his vine and under his fig tree;
    And none shall make them afraid:
    For the mouth of the LORD of hosts hath spoken it.
For all people will walk
    Every one in the name of his god,
And we will walk in the name of the LORD our God
    For ever and ever.

Micah 4:1-5

565   And from Miletus [Paul] sent to Ephesus, and called the elders of the church. And when they were come to him, he said unto them, "Ye know, from the first day that I came into Asia, after what manner I have been with you at all seasons, serving the Lord with all humility of mind, and with many tears, and temptations, which befell me by the lying in wait of the Jews: And how I kept back nothing that was profitable unto you, but have shewed you, and have taught you publickly, and from house to house, testifying both to the Jews, and also to the Greeks, repentance toward God, and faith toward our Lord Jesus Christ. And now, behold, I go bound in the spirit unto Jerusalem, not knowing the things that shall befall me there: Save that the Holy Ghost witnesseth in every city, saying that bonds and afflictions abide me. But none of these things move me, neither count I my life dear unto myself, so that I might finish my course with joy, and the ministry, which I have received of the Lord Jesus, to testify the gospel of the grace of God. And now, behold, I know that ye all, among whom I have gone preaching the kingdom of God, shall see my face no more. Wherefore I take you to record this day, that I am pure from the blood of all men. For I have not shunned to declare unto you all the counsel of God. Take heed therefore unto yourselves, and to all the flock, over the which the Holy Ghost hath made you overseers, to feed the church of God, which he hath purchased with his own blood. For I know this, that after my departing shall grievous wolves enter in among you, not sparing the flock. Also of your own selves shall men arise, speaking perverse things, to draw away disciples after them. Therefore watch, and remember, that by the space of three years I ceased not to warn every one night and day with tears. And now, brethren, I commend you to God, and to the word of his grace, which is able to build you up, and to give you an inheritance among all them which are sanctified. I have coveted no man's silver, or gold, or apparel. Yea, ye yourselves know, that these hands have ministered unto my necessities, and to them that were with me. I have shewed you all things, how that so labouring ye ought to support the weak, and to remember the words of the Lord Jesus, how he said, 'It is more blessed to give than to receive.'"

And when he had thus spoken, he kneeled down, and prayed with them all. And they all wept sore, and fell on Paul's neck, and kissed him, sorrowing most of all for the words which he spake, that they should see his face no more. And they accompanied him unto the ship.

Acts 20:17-38

566 And the LORD spake unto Moses, saying, "Speak unto Aaron and unto his sons, saying, 'On this wise* ye shall bless the children of Israel, saying unto them,

> "The LORD bless thee, and keep thee:
> The LORD make his face shine upon thee, and be gracious
>   unto thee:
> The LORD lift up his countenance upon thee, and
>   give thee peace."'"

Numbers 6:22-26

567 Rejoice in the Lord always: and again I say, Rejoice. Let your moderation be known unto all men. The Lord is at hand. Be careful* for nothing; but in every thing by prayer and supplication with thanksgiving let your requests be made known unto God. And the peace of God, which passeth all understanding, shall keep your hearts and minds through Christ Jesus. Finally, brethren, whatsoever things are true, whatsoever things are honest, whatsoever things are just, whatsoever things are pure, whatsoever things are lovely, whatsoever things are of good report; if there be any virtue, and if there be any praise, think on these things. Those things, which ye have both learned, and received, and heard, and seen in me, do: and the God of peace shall be with you.

Philippians 4:4-9

568 I will both lay me down in peace, and sleep:
      For thou, LORD, only makest me dwell in safety.

Psalm 4:8

Glossary

Astonied dazed or stunned; filled with dismay or consternation

Bowels the seat of pity, tenderness, or courage in a human being (compare "guts")

Careful anxious, worried

Charity love, benevolent goodwill

Cleave stick to; adhere firmly with unwavering loyalty

Cloke alternative spelling of "cloak": a loose-fitting outer garment

Cockatrice a poisonous snake

Convenient suitable, proper

Corn a grain or small hard seed; or a region's most important cereal crop

Creature the created universe; creation

Cubit an ancient measurement of length, about 18-21 inches, probably the distance of a carpenter's forearm from the elbow to the tip of the middle finger

Dam a female parent among domesticated animals

Doctors teachers of the Law

Dreadful instilling awe or dread

Elias alternative spelling of "Elijah," the prophet

Eliseus alternative spelling of "Elisha," the prophet

Ensample example, instance

Ephah an ancient Hebrew unit of dry measure just over a bushel

Esaias alternative spelling of "Isaiah," the prophet

Even evening

Firkin a small cask, capable of holding about one-quarter of a barrel

Froward habitually or perversely disobedient

Gat got

Girdle a garment encircling the body at the waist

Goodman master or manager of a household

Haply by chance

Hardly with difficulty

Holden held, restrained

Holpen helped

Hosen trousers (compare "lederhosen")

Howbeit although; nevertheless

Instant urgently attentive

Jealous zealous

Jeremy, Jeremias alternative renderings of "Jeremiah," the prophet

Jesus alternative rendering of "Joshua," Israel's leader during its takeover of Canaan

Jonas alternative spelling of "Jonah," the prophet.

Kid young goat

Glossary

Lees dregs, sediment after fermentation of wine or liquor

Meat sustaining food of any kind (not merely animal tissue); a meal, especially dinner

Meet altogether fitting, precisely adapted to a particular circumstance or need

Messias alternative spelling of "Messiah": Christ, or the anointed one

Overlaid suffocated or smothered by lying upon

Overlive outlive

Pennyworth value for the money spent; a small amount

Peradventure possibly, perhaps, perchance

Plaister alternative spelling of "plaster"

Precious scarce and esteemed, therefore, for its value

Prevent be ready for; meet or satisfy in advance

Privily privately, in secret

Prove test the validity or genuineness of

Psaltery an ancient stringed instrument, similar to a zither

Quick, quicken alive, to make living

Rahel alternative spelling of "Rachel," the matriarch

Sackbut a medieval musical instrument, akin to a trombone

Selah the transliteration of an obscure Hebrew term appearing in the text of Psalms. Though its meaning remains uncertain, it may have been an ancient musical direction.

Single honest; free from deceit

Sion alternative spelling of "Zion": Israel or the Jewish homeland

Sottish stupid, doltish

Straitly strictly, rigorously

Stripe a wound or blow administered by a rod or lash

Subtil, subtilty cunning, with craftiness

Suffer allow, permit (as in "sufferance")

Tabernacle a tent, hut, or other wilderness sanctuary

Teil an oaklike hardwood tree with a fragrant resin: a terebinth

Touching concerning, pertaining or related to

Try test (as in "to try a case")

Turtle turtledove

Twain two, a couple or pair

Vail veil

Wasted laid waste

Wherefore why

Whiles during the time, while

Wise manner, way

Wist know, knew. *See also* **wot**.

Wit know, see

Wot know. Related to "wit" in the sense of "witting." *See also* **wist**.

Wroth stirred to wrath; irate

Appendices

1. A Timeline

2000 B.C.	1500	1250	1100	1000	900	800	700	600
Patriarchal Period		**Exodus /**		**United**	**Northern Kingdom of Israel**			**Fall of**
Hammurabi		**Wilderness**		**Monarchy**	Kings Jeroboam I, Omri, Ahab, Jehu,			**Samaria,**
					Jeroboam II (among others)			**722 - Exile**
	Egyptian		**Occupation**		Prophets: Elijah, Elisha, Hosea			
	Captivity		**of Canaan /**					
			Period of the					
	Rameses II		**Judges**		**Southern Kingdom of Judah**			**Fall of**
								Jerusalem,
				FIRST JERUSALEM (SOLOMON'S) TEMPLE				**587 - Exile**
					Destroyed by Babylonians, 587			
Abraham and		Moses and	Joshua and	Saul,	Kings Rehoboam, Jehoshaphat,			Nebuchadnezzar
Sarah		Aaron	the	David,	Azariah/Uzziah, Ahaz,			(Babylonian)
			Judges:	Solomon	Hezekiah, Manasseh, Josiah,			
Isaac and			Othniel,		Jehoiakim, Jehoiachin (among others)			
Rebekah			Ehud,					Cyrus II
			Deborah,					(Persian)
Jacob and			Gideon,					
Rachel			Jephtha,					
			Samson		Prophets: Amos, Isaiah, Micah,			2 Isaiah;
Joseph and			(and others)		Jeremiah, Ezekiel (among others)			3 Isaiah
His Brothers								

Ruth	*Amos, Hosea,*	*Deuteronomy*
	Isaiah, Micah	*Joshua, Judges,*
		1, 2 Samuel; 1, 2 Kings
		Jeremiah / Lamentations
		Habakkuk
		Nahum / Obadiah (?)
		Zephaniah / Joel (?)

All Dates Approximate

400	300	200	150	100	50	A.D. 50	100	150
Persian Period			**Hellenistic Period**		**Roman Period**			
	Alexander the Great		Antiochus IV **(Jewish) Maccabean Period**		Herod the Great	Augustus Tiberius Claudius	**Jewish Revolt vs. Rome (66-73)**	
Ezra and Nehemiah						John the Baptist		
						Jesus	John	
						Peter and	of Patmos	
						the Twelve		
						Paul		
			SECOND JERUSALEM TEMPLE (REBUILT)		HERODIAN EXPANSION OF THE TEMPLE		*Second Temple Destroyed by Romans, 70*	

1, 2 Thessalonians

Galatians

1, 2 Corinthians

Romans

Philippians

Philemon

Mark

Colossians

Ephesians

Hebrews

Matthew

400	300	200	150	100	A.D. 50	100
Ezekiel (?)	*1, 2 Chronicles*	*Esther*	*Daniel*		*1 Peter*	*John*
Genesis (?)	*Ezra/Nehemiah*	*Ecclesiastes*			*Luke- Acts*	*1, 2, 3 John*
Exodus (?)	*Leviticus (?)*	*Haggai/Zechariah*				*Revelation*
Numbers (?)	*Psalms (?)*					*1, 2 Timothy/Titus*
Jonah / Job	*Song of Songs (?)*					*James*
Malachi						*Jude*
Proverbs (?)						*2 Peter*

2. The Books of the Bible

The Bible's contents are here listed in the order in which they appear in most Protestant Bibles. Roman Catholic and Eastern Orthodox Bibles contain larger Old Testaments, some of whose books are combined or differently named.

THE OLD TESTAMENT

Genesis	1 Kings	Ecclesiastes	Obadiah
Exodus	2 Kings	Song of Songs	Jonah
Leviticus	1 Chronicles	Isaiah	Micah
Numbers	2 Chronicles	Jeremiah	Nahum
Deuteronomy	Ezra	Lamentations	Habakkuk
Joshua	Nehemiah	Ezekiel	Zephaniah
Judges	Esther	Daniel	Haggai
Ruth	Job	Hosea	Zechariah
1 Samuel	Psalms	Joel	Malachi
2 Samuel	Proverbs	Amos	

THE NEW TESTAMENT

Matthew	2 Corinthians	1 Timothy	2 Peter
Mark	Galatians	2 Timothy	1 John
Luke	Ephesians	Titus	2 John
John	Philippians	Philemon	3 John
Acts	Colossians	Hebrews	Jude
Romans	1 Thessalonians	James	Revelation
1 Corinthians	2 Thessalonians	1 Peter	

Acts of the Apostles, The (Acts) A theological history of events involving the early church, probably written in A.D. 80-90 by the author of **Luke** as that Gospel's continuation (see Acts 1:1-5).

Amos, The Book of The earliest of four prophetic books in the eighth century B.C. (see also **Hosea, Isaiah**, and **Micah**). A native of the southern kingdom of Judah, Amos preaches a relentless message of unmitigated military disaster as God's punishment of Israel's religious pride and social injustice.

1 Chronicles (The First Book of Chronicles) Prefaced by a series of genealogies, 1 Chronicles retells, with a more positive bias, the story of David and his dynasty otherwise known to us from **1** and **2 Samuel**. Probably written in the fourth century B.C., after Israel's Babylonian exile, 1 Chronicles attempts to wed the differing religious viewpoints of the old northern (Israelite) and southern (Judean) kingdoms.

2 Chronicles (The Second Book of Chronicles) A continuation of the story begun in **1 Chronicles**, extending it to Solomon and the building of the first Jerusalem temple. Second Chronicles roughly corresponds to the narrative of **1** and **2 Kings**, from which, with **1** and **2 Samuel**, the Chronicler drew much of his source material.

Colossians, The Epistle to the A letter, purportedly written by the Apostle Paul, addressed to a Gentile Christian congregation fraught by internal controversy in the mid-to-late first century A.D.

1 Corinthians (The First Epistle to the Corinthians) A letter written by the Apostle Paul in the mid-50s A.D. to a predominantly Gentile Christian congregation he had founded in the capital of the Roman province of Achaia (southern Greece). In it Paul addresses various issues raised by him or others in that church.

2 Corinthians (The Second Epistle to the Corinthians) Written by Paul not long after 1 Corinthians and addressed to the same church, 2 Corinthians deals largely with that apostle's relation to that congregation. Its disjointed character suggests that it may be a compilation of portions of several letters of Paul to Corinth.

Daniel, The Book of Like **Revelation** in the New Testament, the Bible's only other book-length apocalypse, Daniel offers a message of consolation and encouragement to persecuted believers. Unlike that of Revelation, Daniel's narrative is set some five centuries earlier than the time of its actual composition: around 167 B.C., when the Syrian king Antiochus IV harassed the Jews (see 11:21-45).

Deuteronomy, The Book of The fifth and climactic book of the Pentateuch (consisting also of **Genesis**, **Exodus**, **Leviticus**, and **Numbers**). Having probably assumed much of its final form in the seventh century B.C., Deuteronomy is a comprehensive articulation of Torah: divinely sanctioned instruction for Israel's continuing life in covenant with God, depicted in Moses' final activities and testaments.

Ecclesiastes, The Book of (also known as **Qoheleth**, *The Preacher*) Associated with but not written by Solomon, a late third-century B.C. compilation of worldly anecdotes and aphorisms that emphasizes with unflinching realism human life's transience, emptiness, and internal contradictions.

Ephesians, The Epistle to the A letter, purportedly written by Paul, addressing issues of religious identity among Gentile Christians in the last third of the first century A.D.

Esther, The Book of A third-century B.C. tale of international intrigue, featuring a canny Jewish heroine who, against the odds, outwits Persian potentates, thereby delivering Diaspora Jews from annihilation.

Exodus, The Book of The second book in the Pentateuch, alongside **Genesis**, **Leviticus**, **Numbers**, and **Deuteronomy**, recounting the Israelites' liberation from Egyptian bondage (c. 1250 B.C.) and their covenant with God at Mount Sinai.

Ezekiel, The Book of A prophet and priest of Judah, the southern kingdom,

Ezekiel, like **Jeremiah**, proclaimed both judgment and hope in the face of Jerusalem's destruction in 587 B.C. by the hand of the Babylonian king Nebuchadnezzar.

Ezra, The Book of Usually coupled with **Nehemiah**, and united as one book (2 Esdras) in the Eastern Orthodox tradition, Ezra offers a fourth-century B.C. sequel to the narrative in **1** and **2 Chronicles**, describing the Jews' rebuilding of the temple and renewal of priestly worship after returning to their homeland from Babylonian exile (539-430 B.C.).

Galatians, The Epistle to the Written by the Apostle Paul to groups of Gentile Christians in the mid-50s A.D., Galatians is a heated letter emphasizing "the truth of the gospel" of Jesus Christ (2:5, 14) over against Gentile attraction to Jewish practices, particularly circumcision.

Genesis, The Book of The first in a major collection of five books (the Pentateuch), which along with **Exodus**, **Leviticus**, **Numbers**, and **Deuteronomy** make up the Torah. Genesis is an artfully interwoven account of Israel's ancient, foundational sagas before and during the so-called patriarchal period of Abraham, Isaac, Jacob, Joseph and his brothers (2000-1300 B.C.).

Habakkuk, The Book of A prophetic book of the late-seventh or early-sixth century B.C., affirming the reliability of God's strength in the face of Judah's invasion by the Chaldeans, or Babylonians.

Haggai, The Book of A sequence of sermons in which the prophet celebrates early stages of the rebuilding and consecration of Jerusalem's second temple, following the Judeans' repatriation from their Babylonian exile (589 B.C.). See also **Zechariah**.

Hebrews, The Epistle to the A sermonic "word of exhortation" (13:22), written between A.D. 60 and 95, for the encouragement of Christians, perhaps some of Jewish origin, in the face of potential religious persecution. Although traditionally attributed to the Apostle Paul, it was neither written by him nor claims to be.

Hosea, The Book of One of four great eighth-century B.C. prophets (see also **Amos**, **Isaiah**, and **Micah**), Hosea announces both harsh judgment and tender mercy for the northern kingdom amidst Israel's political and religious apostasy. Marriage symbolizes Israel's covenant with God; adultery and prostitution, its betrayal.

Isaiah, The Book of A composite volume consisting of prophetic materials from three different eras in Israel's history. The earliest portion, Chapters 1–39, contains oracles associated with Isaiah of Jerusalem, one of four major eighth-century B.C. prophets (see also **Amos**, **Hosea**, and **Micah**), who encouraged Israel's adherence to the Davidic dynasty and repentance from moral decadence. Originating from the nation's Babylonian exile (597-539 B.C.), Isaiah 40–55 (Second Isaiah) is a message of consolation that God remains in control and will restore Israel. Presupposing the Israelites' return to Judah, Isaiah 56–66 (Third Isaiah) announces God's indictment of economic oppression and religious infidelity, with promises of Israel's deliverance.

James, The Epistle of Traditionally associated with the brother of Jesus, a letter of uncertain origin that emphasizes practical morals and loyalty to Jesus' teachings.

Jeremiah, The Book of A prophetic book of the sixth century B.C., containing poetic oracles, sermons, and narratives. Straddling the turbulent period before and during Judah's conquest and exile by the Babylonian empire (597-539 B.C.), Jeremiah offers oracles of both judgment and hope, the latter directed especially to despairing Israelites who could remain in Jerusalem and begin rebuilding their lives.

Job, The Book of Evidently based on a brief folktale that frames the book (1:1–2:13 + 42:7-17), Job captures in a series of poetic arguments Israel's internal debate over perennial questions of undeserved suffering, the possibility among humans of disinterested virtue, and God's justice and sovereignty. The book probably dates from the fifth century B.C.

Joel, The Book of A prophetic book of uncertain date, depicting God's righteous punishment of Israel's crimes in "the day of the LORD" and likening the nation's invasion by a foreign power to an infestation of ravenous locusts.

John, The Gospel According to An anonymous narrative of Jesus' life and teachings, very different in some respects from those of the New Testament's other Gospels (see **Luke, Mark, Matthew**), probably written near the end of the first century A.D. to encourage faith (20:31) at a time when Jewish Christians experienced hostile excommunication from their own synagogues (9:22; 12:42; 16:2).

1 John (The First Epistle of John) A homiletic essay, probably written near the end of the first century A.D., which addresses schism within an early Christian congregation (2:18-27; 4:1-3). First John may or may not have been written by the author of **The Gospel According to John**.

2 John (The Second Epistle of John) A letter, briefer than 1 John and perhaps written by its author (identified here as "the elder": verse 1), urging a congregation to maintain truthful Christian faith and to extend hospitality to Christian travelers.

3 John (The Third Epistle of John) Like 2 John, a short letter written by "the elder" (verse 1). Addressed to a congregational leader named Gaius, it praises his hospitality and admonishes faithful discipline within a local church.

Jonah, The Book of A satirical short story of the sixth or fifth century B.C., whose "anti-hero" is a dedicated though stubborn prophet. Jonah poses questions about undeserved suffering, unmerited forgiveness, and the relation of Israel's God to the rest of the world's nations.

Joshua, The Book of A sequel to **Deuteronomy** and an early volume of the seventh-century Deuteronomistic History continued in **Judges, 1** and **2 Samuel**, and **1** and **2 Kings**. Joshua offers a stylized account of Canaan's occupation by Israel's twelve tribes, fulfilling the divine promise made to the patriarchs in Genesis 12–50. Joshua emphasizes God's gracious enablement of

Israel's military and the imperative of the people to live in unswerving fidelity to the LORD who gave that land to them.

Jude, The Epistle of Traditionally associated with the brother of Jesus (verse 1), a letter of uncertain time and place that warns early Christians away from false teachers who would divorce faith in the Christian gospel from moral obedience to Christ.

Judges, The Book of The continuation of the Deuteronomistic History, roughly begun in **Joshua** and followed by **The Books of Samuel** and **Kings**. Covering the period 1200-1000 B.C., Judges describes the tumultuous, pre-dynastic era in which Israel's tribes were ruled by a series of governors ("judges"), capable or incompetent, with happy or catastrophic consequences for the Israelite people.

1 Kings (The First Book of Kings) With **2 Kings**, the closing chapter of the seventh-century Deuteronomistic History begun in **Joshua**. Spanning the era from the end of David's reign, through the succession of his son Solomon, to the division of monarchy in the north (Israel) and the south (Judah), 1 Kings describes the benefits accrued for Israel's faithfulness to the Sinai Covenant (**Deuteronomy**) and the price paid for its royals' allegiance to pagan gods. In the Eastern Orthodox Bible, **1** and **2 Kings** are referred to as 3 and 4 Kingdoms, following alternative names for **1** and **2 Samuel**.

2 Kings (The Second Book of Kings) The final section of the Deuteronomistic History (see **Joshua**), roughly covering the time from the Judean kings Jehoshaphat (about 873-849 B.C.) and Ahaziah (843 B.C.), through the Assyrian conquest of Israel's capital, Samaria (722 B.C.), to the Babylonians' sack of Jerusalem and deportation of Judean Jews (587 B.C.). Consistent with **Deuteronomy**'s theology, all historical events are interpreted as the outcome of Israel's adherence to, or abandonment of, the Sinai covenant with its LORD.

Lamentations, The Book of A series of five poetic laments, mourning the devastation of Jerusalem and deportation of its citizens by the Babylonian king Nebuchadnezzar in 587 B.C.

Leviticus, The Book of Within the Pentateuch or Torah (alongside **Genesis**, **Exodus**, **Numbers**, and **Deuteronomy**) Leviticus is a priestly manual of indeterminate date, detailing the cultic and moral preservation of Israel's holiness, or separation, from the rest of the world's nations.

Luke, The Gospel According to An anonymous narrative of Jesus' life and teachings, probably written in the latter decades of the first century A.D., that portrays Jesus as an extension of Israel's heritage for the benefit of an increasingly Gentile church. Its author evidently intended this Gospel as a companion volume for **The Acts of the Apostles**.

Malachi, The Book of A fifth-century prophetic work, which condemns corruption among the priesthood of Jerusalem's newly rebuilt temple (see **Haggai** and **Zechariah**), honors genuine worship, and heralds Israel's coming purification in the "great and terrible day of the LORD" (4:5).

Mark, The Gospel According to An anonymous narrative of Jesus' life and teachings, probably written in the 60s or early 70s A.D., for a church of unspecified location that may have been undergoing religious persecutions (see 13:9-13). Many consider Mark to be the earliest of the Gospels, and one of the sources used by the authors of **Matthew** and **Luke** in the composition of those books.

Matthew, The Gospel According to An anonymous narrative of Jesus' life and teachings, likely written in the late first century A.D., that depicts Jesus as the fulfillment and amplification of Israel's heritage. It appears to have been written for Jewish Christians who were growing apart from that era's Pharisaic Judaism.

Micah, The Book of Like **Amos** and **Isaiah** (also in the southern kingdom of Judah), and **Hosea** (in Israel, the northern kingdom), Micah was one of the great prophets of the eighth century B.C. The book condemns social injustice and religious hypocrisy, anticipates a collapse for Jerusalem (in the south) like that of Samaria (in the north: 722 B.C.), and extends a promise of hope in God's ultimate forgiveness.

Nahum, The Book of A sixth-century B.C. prophetical oracle, announcing doom for the Assyrian city of Nineveh and salvation for faithful Israelites in Judah.

Nehemiah, The Book of The continuation of the post-exilic narrative begun in **Ezra**, recounting the Jewish people's restoration to their homeland under Persian oversight. Nehemiah concentrates on the rebuilding of Jerusalem, the renewal of the Mosaic covenant, and the purging from Israel of foreign influences.

Numbers, The Book of The continuation of the narrative in **Exodus**, Numbers tells of Israel's forty-year wandering in the Sinai wilderness, its near destruction owing to religious apostasy, and its renewal for occupation of Canaan, "the promised land." Numbers is the fourth book of the Torah, or Pentateuch (see also **Genesis**, **Exodus**, **Leviticus**, and **Deuteronomy**).

Obadiah, The Book of In this shortest of the Old Testament's books, the prophet attacks the nations, especially Edom, for ill treatment of Judah, while promising the southern kingdom's vindication.

1 Peter (The First Epistle of Peter) A letter, purportedly written by the Apostle Peter, to Christians in five Roman provinces of Asia Minor (modern-day Turkey). Dated anywhere from the mid- to late-first century A.D., 1 Peter encourages allegiance to the gospel of Christ amid social tensions and political persecution.

2 Peter (The Second Epistle of Peter) A testament in the form of a letter, purportedly written by the Apostle Peter, exhorting Christians' faith, moral discipline, and continued expectation of Christ's return in glory. Evidently dependent on **Jude** and probably written in the early decades of the second century A.D., 2 Peter appears to be the latest of the New Testament's writings.

Philemon, The Epistle to A brief letter, written in the mid-50s A.D. by Paul while imprisoned, to a Christian in Colossae, Asia Minor (modern Turkey), requesting lenience for Onesimus: a slave, converted by the apostle to Christian faith, who is returning to his master, Philemon.

Philippians, The Epistle to the Like **Philemon**, another "captivity letter" written by Paul in the mid-50s A.D. Addressed to Christians in Philippi, a Roman colony in the province of Macedonia (northern Greece), the apostle writes to a church he has founded, expressing concern for their well-being along with remarkable joy in spite of his circumstances.

Proverbs, The Book of A collection of sayings, structured as poetic couplets and likely compiled during Israel's post-exilic period (sixth century B.C. and later), most of which express conventional or worldly wisdom that accents humanity's proper reverence of God ("the fear of the LORD") and the dependable effect of either reward or punishment from the corresponding cause of justice or unrighteousness.

Psalms, The Book of Israel's hymnal, largely anonymous in origin despite its association with David, who nevertheless could have composed some of its contents. Arranged as a collection of five books, created and compiled across many centuries, the Psalms crystallize and convey most of the Old Testament's theological claims in different generic forms: laments, thanksgivings, hymns of praise, and royal canticles.

Revelation to John, The Written by a certain John of Patmos (1:1, 4, 9; 22:8) to seven churches in the Roman province of Asia, probably near the end of the first century A.D. Like **Daniel**, the only other book-length apocalypse in the Bible, Revelation is an extravagantly visionary encouragement to those suffering persecution for their religious faith.

Romans, The Epistle to the One of the latest of Paul's letters (around A.D. 57), written to a congregation he had not founded, while *en route* to Jerusalem and thence to Spain (15:22-23; 16:22). Romans is the longest, most penetrating expression available to us of the apostle's understanding of the gospel.

Ruth, The Book of A lovely, idyllic short story, written sometime between 950 and 700 B.C., that highlights the preservation and continuity of family within the context of committed faithfulness.

1 Samuel (The First Book of Samuel) The continuation of the seventh-century Deuteronomistic History, begun with **Joshua** and **Judges**. First Samuel describes Israel's transition, in the figure of Samuel, from a confederacy of tribal governors ("judges") to a more unified monarchy, emerging in the late eleventh century B.C. and personified in the figures of Saul and David. In the Eastern Orthodox tradition, **1** and **2 Samuel** are referred to as 1 and 2 Kingdoms.

2 Samuel (The Second Book of Samuel) The Deuteronomistic History continues (see **Joshua**, **Judges**, and **1 Samuel**), as Israel's fortunes under David's reign wax and wane in proportion to his fidelity to the Sinai Covenant and abuse of royal power.

Song of Songs, The (*or* The Song of Solomon) An anonymous love poem of uncertain date, celebrating human sexuality and sensuality.

1 Thessalonians (The First Epistle to the Thessalonians) The earliest of Paul's extant letters (about A.D. 51), thus the oldest book in the New Testament. Addressed to a Christian congregation founded by the Apostle in the capital of the Roman province of Macedonia, 1 Thessalonians is affectionately pastoral in tenor, illuminating the inner life of a young church adjusting itself to Greek society.

2 Thessalonians (The Second Epistle to the Thessalonians) Purportedly though not indisputably by Paul, this letter attempts to cool down over-heated expectations for an imminent return of Jesus in glory. If by Paul, it was written soon after **1 Thessalonians**. If not, then its date could be any time in the late first or early second century A.D.

1 Timothy (The First Epistle to Timothy) Purportedly though almost certainly not written by Paul, 1 Timothy is concerned with church discipline and pastoral oversight in local congregations of the late first century A.D. With **2 Timothy** and **Titus**, it is characterized as one of "The Pastoral Epistles."

2 Timothy (The Second Epistle to Timothy) Like **2 Peter**, a letter in the form of an apostolic testament, intended to bolster a second generation of Christians for endurance in the face of suffering. See also **1 Timothy**.

Titus, The Epistle to Like the other Pastoral Epistles (see **1 Timothy**), a letter intending to interpret the Apostle Paul's tradition for a later Christian generation by offering structure to the local church and its leadership.

Zechariah, The Book of A composite prophetic work (see also **Isaiah**). Like **Haggai**, Zechariah 1–8 celebrates the rebuilding of Jerusalem's temple after the Judeans' release from their Babylonia captivity (539 B.C.). Zechariah 9–14, by contrast, adopts a more jaundiced view of restoration under priestly leadership and yearns instead for deliverance in "the day of the LORD" (12:1–14:21).

Zephaniah, The Book of A late-seventh-century B.C. prophetic oracle, coupling promises of judgment and restoration for Judah in "the day of the LORD."

3. The Narrative of Creation in Genesis 1:1–2:3

Every religious tradition declares assumptions about, and frequently some account of, the origin of things. Among the indigenous peoples of North America, the White River Sioux tell of a playful, good-hearted rabbit that chanced upon a blood-clot that, after much kicking, assumed a human form called *We-Ote-Wichasha:* Much-Blood Boy, or Rabbit Boy. From places and times roughly contemporaneous with The Book of Genesis come different tales. One Mesopotamian epic describes creation as the outcome of a cosmic battle between Marduk, a cagey warrior-prince, and the goddess Tiamat, whose belly Marduk ripped open with a well-placed arrow.

Since the nineteenth century of our era, biblical scholars have recognized not one but two stories of creation in Genesis. The older of the two, the tale of Adam and Eve, appears a bit later in that book (Genesis 2:4–3:24; see above, **217, 219, 221, 223, 225, 227**). The younger, appearing first in the Bible (Genesis 1:1–2:3), is the equally familiar myth of origins in seven days, which serves as the present volume's preface (pp. 3-6). This stately narrative may have been committed to writing sometime in the sixth or fifth century B.C., during or just after the Babylonians' conquest and deportation of the Israelites. In those circumstances many of the ancient Hebrews were in exile from their homeland, suffering all the trauma of a displaced and captive people, desperately trying to retain their distinctive identity and beliefs and practices in a strange and often hostile environment. That context sheds light on one of the ways in which Jewish and Christian forebears made sense of the world "in the beginning."

The first thing to notice in this creation myth is that one and only one God is the creative agent, responsible for everything that comes into being. About how that God came to be there is neither story nor speculation. God's existence is a given in both of Genesis's creation narratives. While simple on its surface, this was in fact a formidable theological assertion in an age when almost every other culture assumed the existence of "many gods and many lords" (1 Corinthians 8:5). One God — monotheism — remains a distinguishing characteristic of all the so-called Abrahamic religions that continue to this day: Judaism, Christianity, and Islam. "Before me no god was formed,/... and besides me there is no savior" (Isaiah 43:10-11). This single God is, moreover, capable and desirous of effortless creation independent of any external force. In Genesis, God is *inherently* creative. On the other hand, God's creation is inherently *relational:* The Creator consults with what appears to be a heavenly council, inviting their cooperation with the creative enterprise (see 1:26).

A second thing to observe: God creates by speaking. "And God said, 'Let there be'": as it was spoken, so it came to be. This theme of divine, purposive speech runs as a scarlet thread throughout the Christian Bible: from an anonymous prophet in the Book of Isaiah (40:8; 55:11) to the Evangelist of the Fourth Gospel, which opens by associating Jesus Christ with "the Word" who in the beginning was with God and was what God was (John 1:1).

Another noteworthy aspect: This is an orderly God, who proceeds deliberately and methodically, day by day, to wrest being and form out of a vast, dark chaos. "The face of the waters," bestirred by God's creative Spirit, captures the human fear of a watery abyss, as well as the typical threat that Israel experienced from many maritime invasions of its land. Creation unfolds in a rhythmic, meaningful progression, just as God wills it. For a displaced people lacking control over their own fortunes, assailed by understandable fears that life was bereft of meaning, the claim that God was and remains ultimately in charge over the disposition of all things in heaven and on earth was a remarkable testimony of faith.

All of God's creation is just that: creaturely. The creature's existence depends on but is in no way equal to the God who calls it into being. Israel's one God is without competition, near and yet distant. Even the heavenly bodies, the sun and moon and stars, are creatures: lamps, as it were, suspended by a homemaker God to illuminate the world in helpful ways. Over this God the astral bodies exert no power of their own — a challenge to alternative religious beliefs, to which reference is made in the much later Letter to the Colossians (2:8, 20), as well as to modern astrology's preoccupation with the zodiac.

Each thing created by God has its proper place and purpose. Once divided, both light and darkness have their roles to play, as rulers over day and night; there is no contest or ensuing combat between them. This, too, is a subtle yet decisive challenge to any worldview, ancient or modern, that sees things "in black and white," assuming the one good and the other evil. God reigns over all that God has created. At the same time, God invites his creatures to collaborate with him in creation's perpetuation. The earth is called upon to bring forth vegetation (1:11); human beings, to multiply and exercise derivative dominion over their fellow creatures (1:26-28). When all things cooperate as intended by their Creator, they are repeatedly regarded as fundamentally good (Genesis 1:4a, 10b, 12b, 18b, 21b, 25b) or, as one might translate the climactic comment in 1:31a, "absolutely perfect" or "just right." In this sense, contrary to ancient Greek or modern philosophical thought, God is a moved mover: God's creation moves its Creator to responsive delight.

3. The Narrative of Creation in Genesis 1:1–2:3

This narrative in Genesis presents a protective God. The firmament — a transparent bowl through which earthly creatures can observe their heavenly counterparts — is inserted between the waters of the earth (oceans and rivers) and the heavenly waters (rain and snow). Only once and with good reason, later in Genesis (6:1–8:5), does God throw open the firmament's windows (7:11) for a devastating flood, after which comes the promise that such should never again happen on a scale so colossal (9:8-17; see above, **145, 148, 154, 156, 158**). Again, however, nothing occurs by accident. All decisions finally reside with the one Sovereign who, with discretionary authority, disposes of all that he has created. In Genesis 1–2, that disposition is ecologically balanced and harmonious.

God rejoices in life and can't get enough of it. God blesses all living creatures with life, encouraging their fruitfulness and multiplication: whales, fish, birds, animals, creepy crawlers, and human beings (Genesis 1:22, 28). Life is the Creator's blessed gift, which God wants creatures to keep on giving. Life, derived from God, is intended to be a perpetual feedback loop of reflected blessedness and continued blessing. Indeed, in this narrative, the words "death" and "curse" are never mentioned.

According to this account, God's creation reaches its climax in humanity, "in our image, after our likeness." Again note the twofold aspect of nearness and remoteness. *Both* male *and* female reflect God's image and likeness; sexuality is neither feared nor deified. Since, in Hebrew thought, God could not and should not be depicted (Exodus 20:4), this story itself provides the clue for how this image and likeness should be understood and realized. The "dominion" that God awards human beings is precisely that which the Creator has demonstrated throughout creation's progress: careful and inviting stewardship over the rest of all living things. Here is no mandate for reckless pillage of the earth. The God who provides every living creature with appropriate sustenance for life invites and expects those creatures, within their allotted powers, to perpetuate that provision for life. In this account no animal is carnivorous: humanity's "meat" is vegetable and fruit, just as the food for all other creatures is herbal (Genesis 1:29-30). All creatures partake of God's life-giving property; human beings are the Creator's appointed trustees for the rest of the created order.

Not even humanity, however, constitutes God's crowning glory. After regarding everything made and deeming it all "very good," God rests. The seventh day of creation is sanctified — set apart — from all others by virtue of its quiescence, thereby putting all work, however virtuous, in a restorative perspective. Throughout history the maintenance of a Sabbath, a day every week for all labor's cessation, was a defining feature of Jewish culture, in Babylon and beyond. We have our work to do, but in God's hands creation is sustained without us, thank you. Modern workaholism finds no justification in this tale of origins.

A final comment: The creation story in Genesis 1:1–2:3, like those of others past and present, is typically referred to as a myth. That term, lamentably, has in many contexts become synonymous with "a falsity." By their very nature, however, myths are neither true nor false. It is more accurate to say that myths live or die as meaningful accounts of basic things that by their nature defy total comprehension. Every culture lives by such stories, whether one is speaking of religious groups or of the creation myths of nations and other human societies. Even scientists operate with myths — in their parlance "theories" or "models" — that are foundational for their ongoing research. The Bible's creation myths are poetic expressions of faith in a particular Deity, how that God operates, and how God's creatures should live. Jews and Christians continue to discover in stories like Genesis 1:1–2:3 deep explanatory power that help them make theological sense of the world.

4. For Further Reading

The beginner who wishes to learn more about the Bible will find most useful three kinds of works: an annotated Bible, introductions to the Old and New Testaments, and one-volume commentaries in which each biblical book receives careful interpretation.

The HarperCollins Study Bible: New Revised Standard Version, Revised Edition (New York: Harper Collins, 2006), edited by Harold W. Attridge, offers reliable introductory articles and annotations to all the biblical books, maps of the biblical world, and other helps. Its contributing authors are all members of The Society of Biblical Literature, a professional society over a century old, whose members include thousands of Jewish, Roman Catholic, Orthodox, and Protestant scholars from around the globe.

There are many one-volume introductions to the Old and New Testaments. Two may be recommended for their readable overviews and extensive engagement with the primary texts: *Understanding the Old Testament,* 5th edition, by Bernhard W. Anderson, with Steven Bishop and Judith H. Newman (Upper Saddle, NJ: Pearson Prentice Hall, 2007), and *Anatomy of the New Testament,* 6th edition, by Robert A. Spivey, D. Moody Smith, and C. Clifton Black (Upper Saddle, NJ: Pearson Prentice Hall, 2007).

One-volume commentaries lead the thoughtful reader even more deeply into each of the Bible's books. Two such works, both excellent, are

The HarperCollins Bible Commentary, revised edition, edited by James Luther Mays (San Francisco: Harper San Francisco, 2000), and *Eerdmans Commentary on the Bible,* edited by James D. G. Dunn and John W. Rogerson (Grand Rapids and Cambridge: Eerdmans, 2003).

Topical Index

Page numbers in regular typeface are usually followed by parenthetical numbers in **boldface**, which refer to the sequential numerals assigned to biblical segments throughout this book.

(**103**), 66-67 (**104**), 84 (**133**), 88
(**140**), 90, 92 (**145**), 93 (**148**), 94-95
(**150**), 112 (**179**), 140 (**228**), 146
(**239**), 148-49 (**243**), 154-55 (**254**),
155-56 (**256**), 160-61 (**264**), 164
(**270**), 168 (**280**), 172-73 (**289**), 188-
89 (**308**), 189-90 (**309**), 194-95
(**317**), 196 (**319**), 196-97 (**320**), 217-
18 (**354**), 234 (**381**), 238-39 (**389**),
239 (**390**), 259-60 (**427**), 266-67
(**432**), 271 (**440**), 281 (**460**), 282
(**462**), 290-91 (**479**), 291-92 (**480**),
293 (**482**), 300 (**494**), 309 (**508**),
311-12 (**512**), 313 (**514**), 317-18 (**523**),
318-19 (**525**), 357, 358 *(bis)*, 365. *See
also* Astral Phenomena; Day of the
Lord; God, Wrath of; Revelation

Just, Justice, Justification. *See* Righteous, Righteousness

Kill. *See* Murder

Kindness. *See* Mercy

King, Kingship, 13 (**11**), 60 (**91**), 86-87
(**138**), 88 (**140**), 94-95 (**150**), 107-8
(**172**), 108-9 (**174**), 110-11 (**176**), 111-
12 (**178**), 113 (**180**), 126 (**206**), 156-
57 (**257**), 162 (**266**), 163 (**268**), 185-
86 (**305**), 192 (**313**), 194-95 (**317**),
196 (**319**), 202 (**329**), 232 (**378**), 235
(**382**), 238-39 (**389**), 290-91 (**479**),
295 (**487**), 296 (**489**), 310 (**510**),
352, 360 *(bis)*, 364 *(bis)*. *See also*
Pastor; Shepherd

Kingdom of God. *See* God, Kingdom
of

Kingdom of Heaven. *See* God, Kingdom of

Knowledge, 62-63 (**95**), 91 (**144**), 113
(**180**), 122 (**197**), 134 (**217**), 135
(**219**), 137 (**223**), 142 (**231**), 226
(**366**). *See also* God, Knowledge of

Kosher Food, 166 (**277**), 167 (**278**),
167 (**279**), 168 (**280**), 168-69 (**281**)

Labor. *See* Birth, Birthing; Work

Lamb. *See* God, Lamb of

Lament, 22-23 (**26**), 24 (**29**), 37 (**55**),
37 (**56**), 55-57 (**86**), 57 (**87**), 58 (**88**),
58-59 (**89**), 75 (**119**), 80 (**127**), 95
(**151**), 96-97 (**153**), 98-99 (**157**), 110-
11 (**176**), 120 (**193**), 124 (**201**), 139-
40 (**227**), 152-53 (**250**), 153 (**251**),
153-54 (**252**), 157 (**259**), 180 (**298**),
184 (**303**), 205-6 (**335**), 206 (**336**),
208 (**339**), 213-14 (**348**), 215 (**350**),
218 (**356**), 224 (**363**), 225 (**365**), 230
(**374**), 240 (**391**), 283 (**463**), 284-85
(**467**), 288-89 (**475**), 291-92 (**480**),
293-94 (**483**), 315 (**519**), 315-16
(**520**), 319-20 (**526**), 360, 363

Land, 24 (**29**), 25-26 (**31**), 59 (**90**), 68-
69 (**109**), 76-77 (**122**), 101 (**162**),
117-18 (**188**), 122-23 (**198**), 127-28
(**208**), 133-34 (**216**), 146 (**239**), 166
(**275**), 193-94 (**315**), 203-4 (**332**),
212-13 (**347**), 218 (**356**), 242-43
(**395**), 268 (**434**), 299 (**493**), 306

Season(s), 28-29 (**38**), 158-59 (**262**), 176, 177 (**290**), 177 (**292**), 178 (**293**), 180-81 (**299**), 210 (**341**), 211 (**344**), 217-18 (**354**), 218 (**355**), 219 (**358**). *See also* Time

Secrecy, Secret, 33 (**46**), 39 (**61**), 43 (**69**), 64 (**99**), 68 (**108**), 73 (**115**), 76 (**121**), 81 (**129**), 137-38 (**224**), 182-83 (**301**), 184 (**302**), 199 (**324**), 201 (**328**), 207 (**337**), 266-67 (**432**), 290-91 (**479**), 317-18 (**523**). *See also* Mystery

Security, 67 (**105**), 86 (**137**), 193-94 (**315**). *See also* God, Sustenance of; Protection; Salvation, Savior, Saving

Seed, 25-26 (**31**), 59 (**90**), 72 (**114**), 88 (**142**), 93 (**148**), 99 (**158**), 117-18 (**188**), 119 (**192**), 132, 133 (**214**), 139-40 (**227**), 145-46 (**238**), 154-55 (**254**), 155-56 (**256**), 162 (**267**), 172 (**288**), 189-90 (**309**), 216-17 (**352**), 246 (**402**), 252 (**413**), 253-54 (**416**), 265 (**429**), 319-20 (**526**)

Seek, Seeking. *See* Search, Searching

Seraphims. *See* Angel(s)

Sermon. *See* Preach, Preaching

Servant, Service, 11-12 (**8**), 20 (**22**), 27-28 (**36**), 28-29 (**38**), 35 (**50**), 55-57 (**86**), 62 (**94**), 68 (**107**), 76 (**121**), 77-78 (**123**), 82-83 (**131**), 84 (**133**), 102 (**164**), 107-8 (**172**), 109-10 (**175**), 122-23 (**198**), 123 (**199**), 124-25 (**203**), 127-28 (**208**), 129 (**210**), 141 (**230**), 149-50 (**244**), 152-53 (**250**), 153-54 (**252**), 154-55 (**254**), 158-59 (**262**), 169-70 (**283**), 172 (**288**), 184 (**302**), 192-93 (**314**), 196-97 (**320**), 207-8 (**338**), 209 (**340**), 217-18 (**354**), 237-38 (**387**), 244-45 (**400**), 253-54 (**416**), 256-57 (**422**), 257-58 (**423**), 258 (**424**), 258-59 (**425**), 265-66 (**430**), 266-67 (**432**), 267-68 (**433**), 278 (**454**), 292-93 (**481**), 293-94 (**483**), 309 (**507**), 316-17 (**522**), 319-20 (**526**), 320 (**528**), 362

Setting apart. *See* Holiness, Holy

Sex, 19-20 (**21**), 115 (**183**), 118 (**190**), 119 (**192**), 127-28 (**208**), 136-37 (**222**), 151-52 (**248**), 152-53 (**250**), 170-71 (**285**), 182-83 (**301**), 199 (**324**), 238 (**388**), 264, 265 (**429**), 273 (**444**), 274 (**445**), 275 (**447**), 275 (**448**), 275-76 (**449**), 286-87 (**471**), 287-88 (**473**), 293-94 (**483**), 364, 368, 369

Shame, 118 (**189**), 136 (**221**), 137 (**223**), 186-87 (**306**), 254 (**417**), 270 (**438**), 305-6 (**499**), 320 (**527**)

Shepherd, 68-69 (**109**), 94-95 (**150**), 114 (**181**), 115 (**183**), 195-96 (**318**), 248 (**406**), 249 (**407**), 271 (**440**), 278 (**454**), 279-80 (**457**), 281 (**460**), 282 (**461**), 282 (**462**), 285 (**468**), 286 (**469**), 294 (**484**). *See also* King; Pastor

Sight. *See* Vision

Sign, 40 (**63**), 44-45 (**72**), 46 (**74**), 65-66 (**102**), 101 (**162**), 144-45 (**236**), 154 (**253**), 177 (**290**), 180-81 (**299**),

Index of Scriptural Personages

Page numbers in regular typeface are usually followed by parenthetical numbers in **boldface**, which refer to the sequential numerals assigned to biblical segments throughout this book.

(**154**), 98 (**156**), 99 (**158**), 100 (**159**),
100-101 (**161**)

Obed, father of Jesse and grandfather
of King David, 171-72 (**287**)

Paul the Apostle, 40 (**64**), 81 (**128**), 82
(**130**), 83-84 (**132**), 109-10 (**175**), 111
(**177**), 161 (**265**), 233 (**379**), 274
(**445**), 343-44 (**565**), 353, 355 *(tris)*,
356, 357 *(bis)*, 362, 363, 364 *(tris)*

Peter the Apostle, 60 (**91**), 61 (**93**), 73
(**115**), 108 (**173**), 144-45 (**236**), 147
(**241**), 167 (**279**), 168-69 (**281**), 257-
58 (**423**), 268-69 (**435**), 283 (**463**),
286 (**469**), 317-18 (**523**), 335-36
(**553**), 353, 362 *(bis)*

Pharaoh, king of Egypt, 68-69 (**109**),
102 (**164**), 205 (**334**), 207 (**337**), 209
(**340**), 319-20 (**526**)

Philip the Apostle, 60 (**91**)

Pilate, Pontius, Roman prefect of
Judea (A.D. 26-36), 124 (**202**), 125
(**204**)

Potiphar, Egyptian officer and pur-
chaser of Joseph from the Ishmael-
ites, 203-4 (**332**), 207-8 (**338**)

Queen of Sheba, consultant of fellow
sovereign Solomon, 237-38 (**387**),
239 (**390**)

Rachel (Rahel), younger daughter of
Laban and Jacob's second wife, 62

(**94**), 115 (**183**), 205-6 (**335**), 206
(**336**), 352

Rahab the Harlot, protector of Joshua
before the Israelites' conquest of
Jericho, 255 (**419**), 255-56 (**420**)

Rebekah, wife of Isaac, 52-53 (**81**), 55-
57 (**86**), 115 (**183**), 315-16 (**520**), 352

Reuben, firstborn son of Jacob, 202-3
(**330**), 203-4 (**332**)

Ruth, Moabite wife of Boaz, 169-70
(**283**), 170-71 (**285**), 171-72 (**287**)

Samson, Israelite judge, 274 (**446**), 275
(**448**), 276 (**450**), 277 (**452**), 352

Samuel, eleventh-century B.C.
prophet, son of Elkanah and
Hannah, 82-83 (**131**), 84 (**133**), 186-
87 (**306**), 191 (**311**), 364

Sarah (Sarai), wife of Abraham, 118
(**190**), 119 (**192**), 315-16 (**520**), 352

Saul of Tarsus. *See* Paul the Apostle

Saul, son of Kish and Israel's first king,
278 (**454**), 290-91 (**479**), 321-22
(**530**), 364

Shadrach, Meshach, and Abednego,
companions of Daniel, 106 (**170**),
107-8 (**172**)

Silas (Silvanus), apostolic associate of
Paul and Peter, 33 (**45**), 109-10
(**175**), 111 (**177**),

Simeon, righteous Jerusalemite at the
time of Jesus' birth, 196-97 (**320**)

Simon (Peter). *See* Peter the Apostle

411